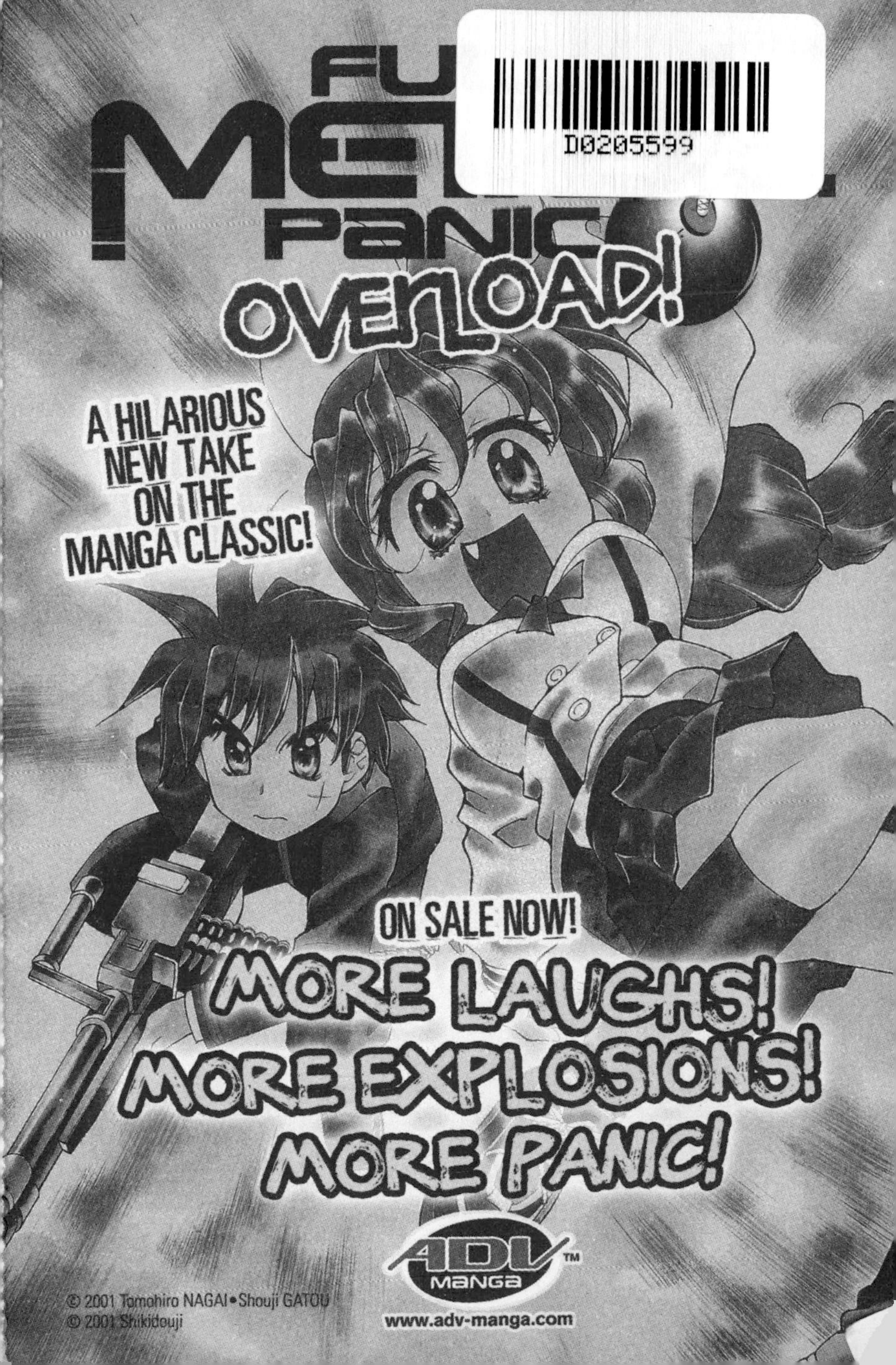
FU
ME
Panic
OVERLOAD!
A HILARIOUS NEW TAKE ON THE MANGA CLASSIC!
ON SALE NOW!
MORE LAUGHS!
MORE EXPLOSIONS!
MORE PANIC!
ADV Manga ™
© 2001 Tomohiro NAGAI • Shouji GATOU
© 2001 Shikidouji
www.adv-manga.com

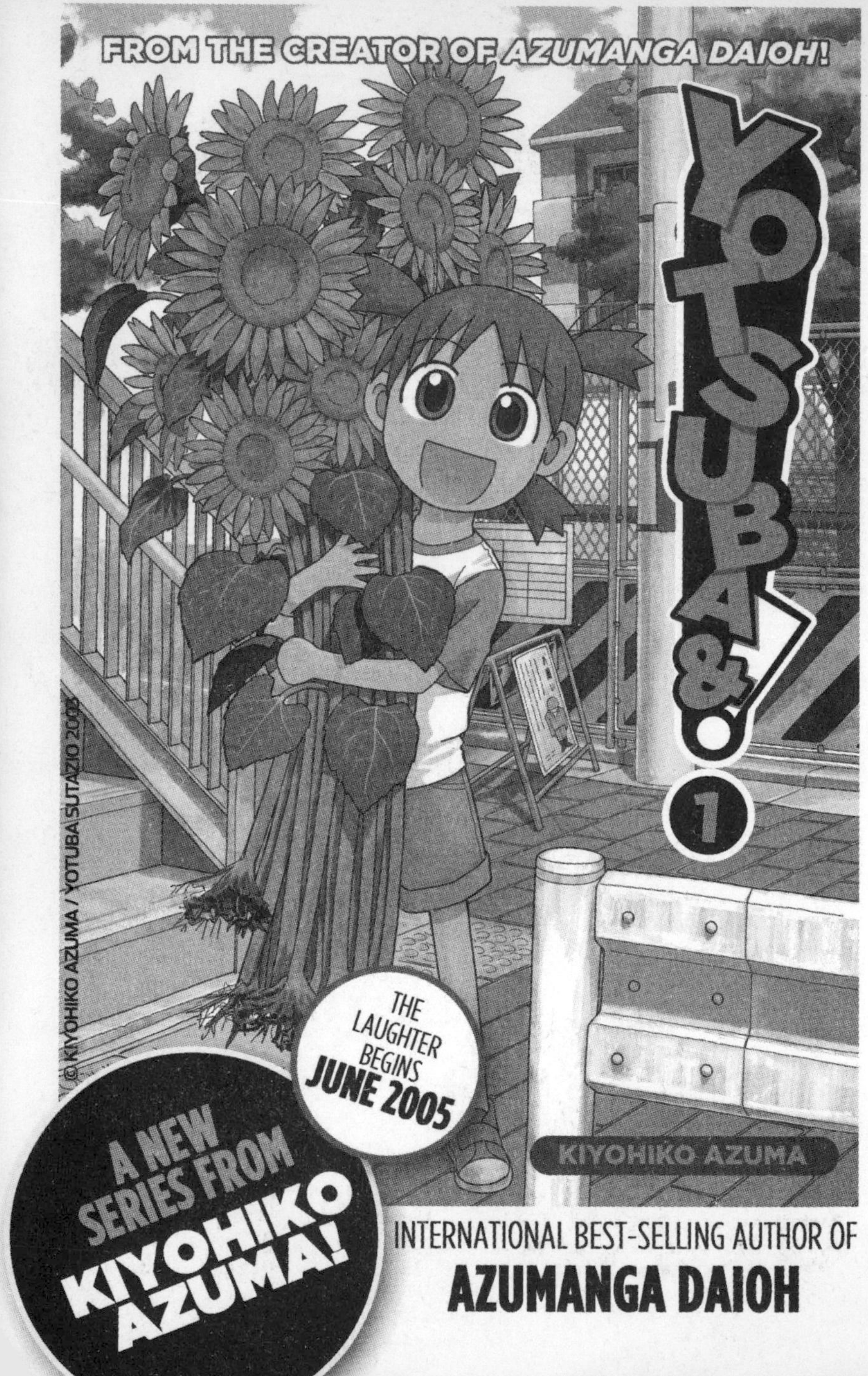
FROM THE CREATOR OF AZUMANGA DAIOH!
YOTSUBA&!
1
KIYOHIKO AZUMA
THE LAUGHTER BEGINS JUNE 2005
A NEW SERIES FROM KIYOHIKO AZUMA!
INTERNATIONAL BEST-SELLING AUTHOR OF
AZUMANGA DAIOH
© KIYOHIKO AZUMA / YOTUBA SUTAZIO 2003

Orphen is now the target of both bow-wielding assassins and venom-spitting snakemen,

but his battle with the black arts will soon be interrupted by a very deadly— and very attractive—adversary.

This saucy sniper is after more than his blood!

Love might be in the air, but evil is all around as Orphen's romantic interlude will lead him into the face of madness in

⊕RPHEN

Vol.3

Orphen Volume Two

© 1999 Yoshinobu Akita/Hajime Sawada
© 1999 Yuuya Kusaka
Originally published in Japan in 1999 by
KADOKAWA SHOTEN PUBLISHING CO., LTD., Tokyo.
English translation rights arranged with
KADOKAWA SHOTEN PUBLISHING CO., LTD., Tokyo.

Translator BRENDAN FRAYNE
Translation Staff KAY BERTRAND & AMY FORSYTH
Editor JAVIER LOPEZ
Assistant Editor SHERIDAN JACOBS
Graphic Artists HEATHER GARY & NATALIA REYNOLDS
Intern MARK MEZA

Editorial Director GARY STEINMAN
Creative Director JASON BABLER
Sales and Marketing CHRIS OARR
Print Production Manager BRIDGETT JANOTA
Pre-press Manager KLYS REEDYK

International Coordinators TORU IWAKAMI, ATSUSHI KANBAYASHI,
KYOKO DRUMHELLER & AI TAKAI

President, CEO & Publisher JOHN LEDFORD

Email: editor@adv-manga.com
www.adv-manga.com
www.advfilms.com

For sales and distribution inquiries please call 1.800.282.7202

 is a division of A.D. Vision, Inc.
10114 W. Sam Houston Parkway, Suite 200, Houston, Texas 77099

ISBN: 1-4139-0267-7
First printing, June 2005
10 9 8 7 6 5 4 3 2 1
Printed in Canada

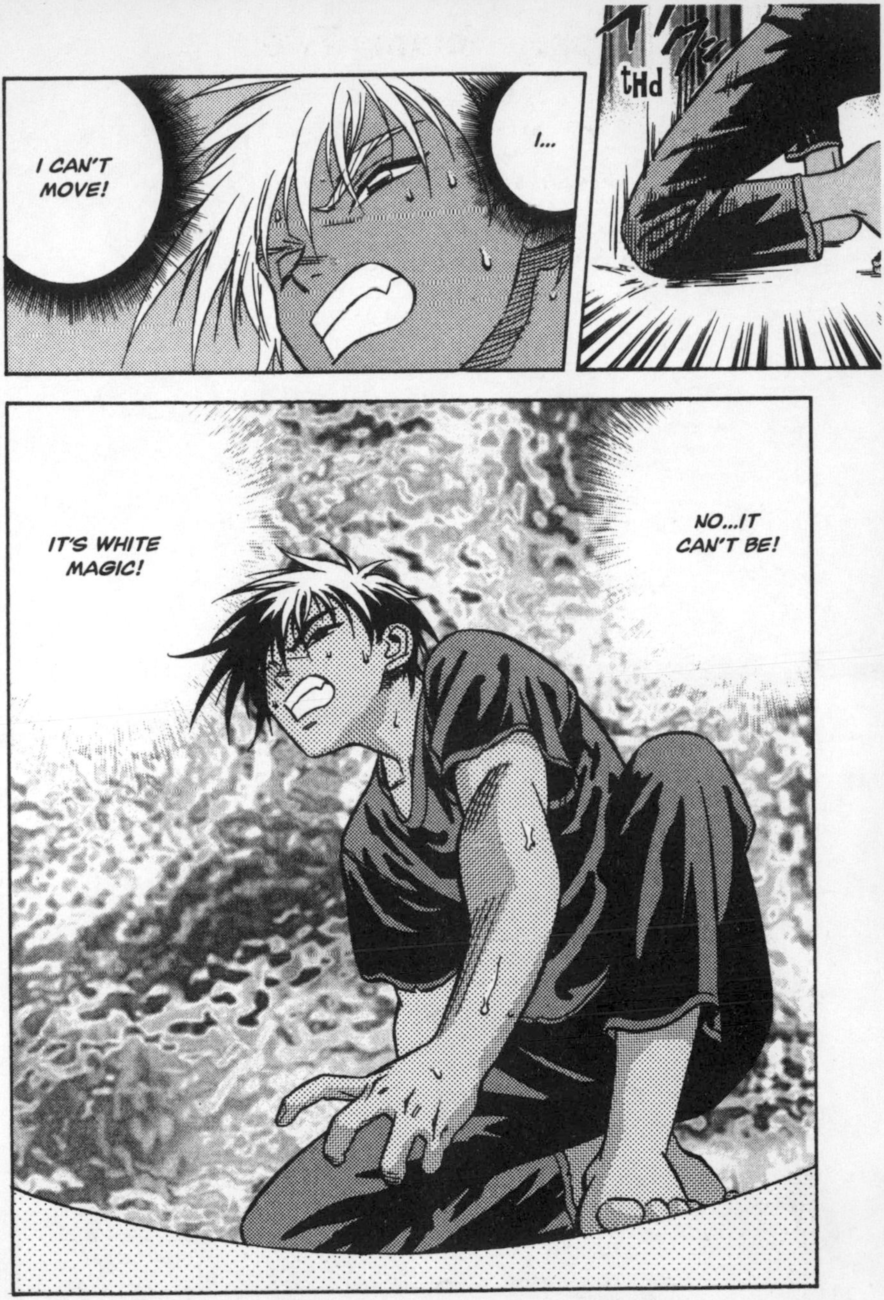
tHd
I...
I CAN'T MOVE!
NO...IT CAN'T BE!
IT'S WHITE MAGIC!

To be continued in Volume 3...

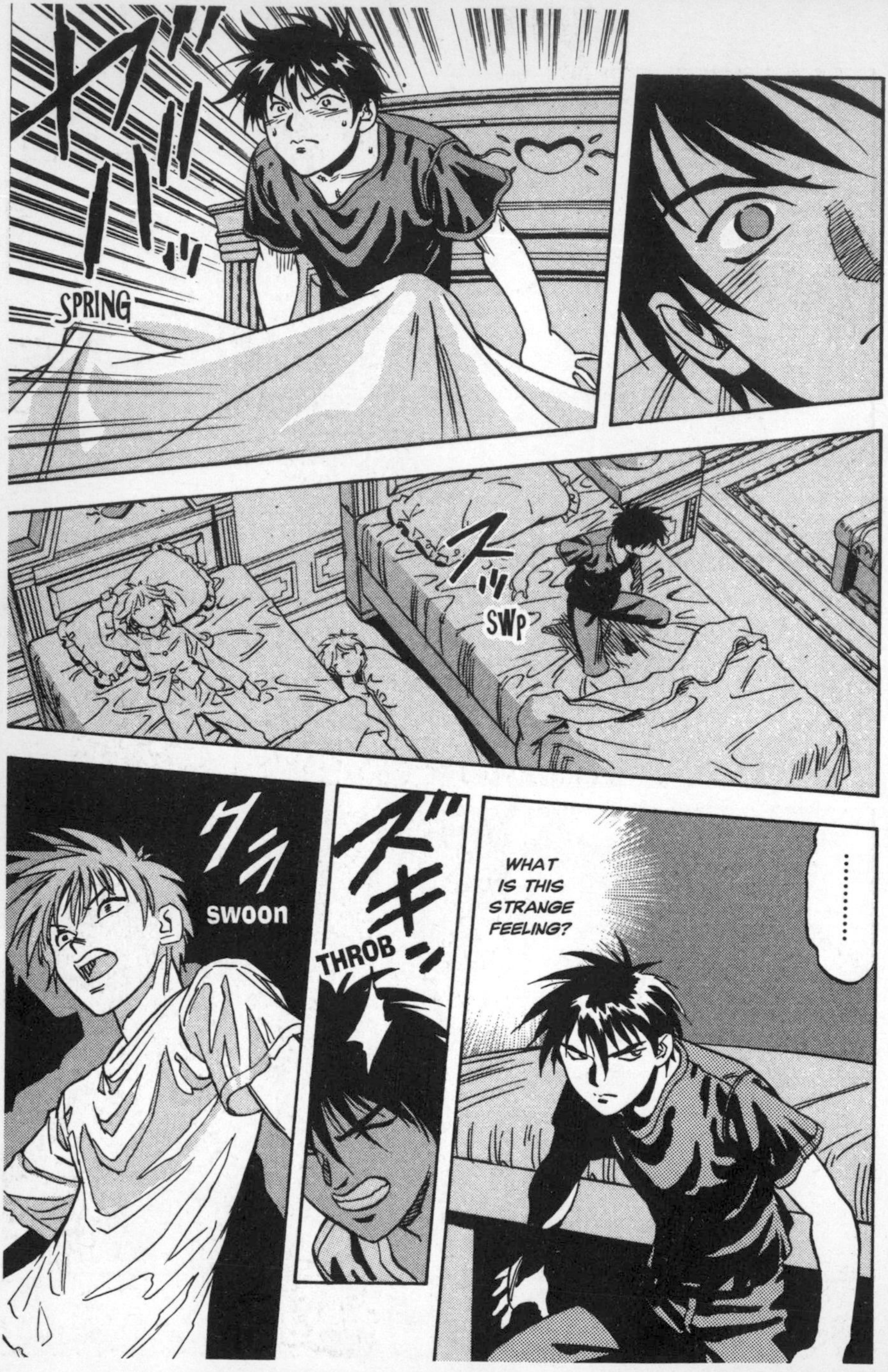

SPRING
SWP
....
WHAT IS THIS STRANGE FEELING?
THROB
swoon

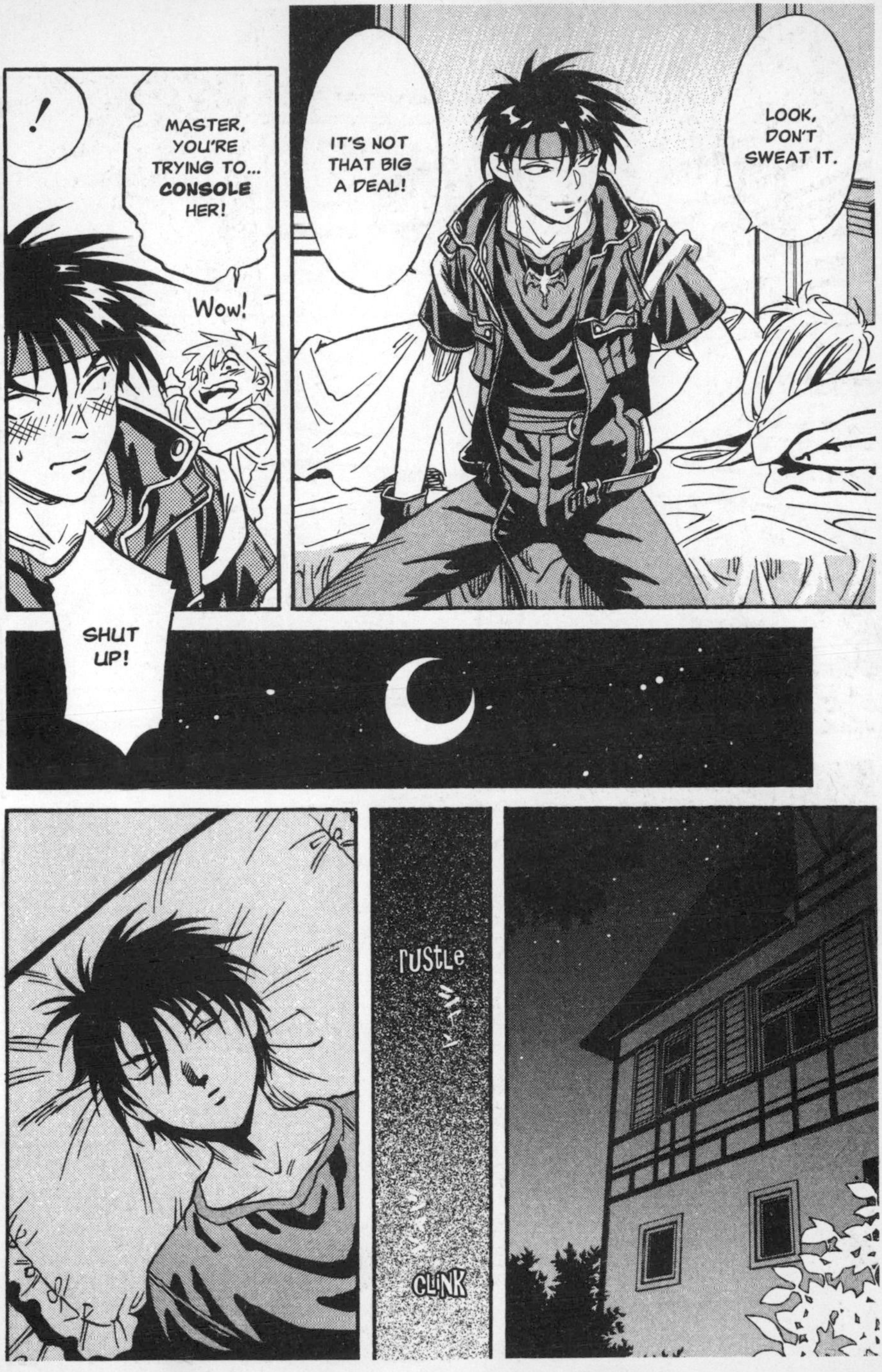
LOOK, DON'T SWEAT IT.
IT'S NOT THAT BIG A DEAL!
!
MASTER, YOU'RE TRYING TO... **CONSOLE** HER!
Wow!
SHUT UP!
rustle
CLINK

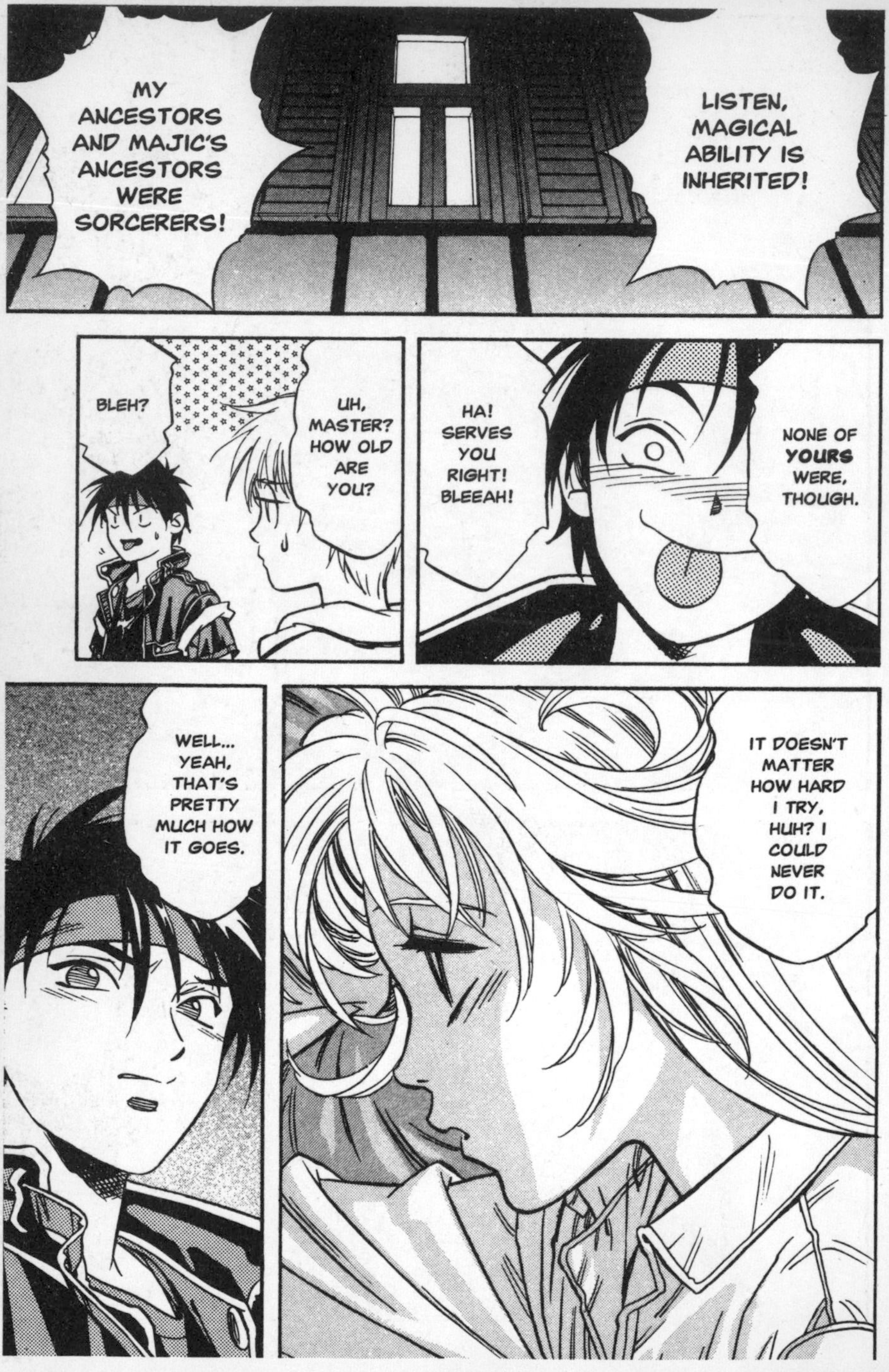

LISTEN, MAGICAL ABILITY IS INHERITED!
MY ANCESTORS AND MAJIC'S ANCESTORS WERE SORCERERS!
NONE OF YOURS WERE, THOUGH.
HA! SERVES YOU RIGHT! BLEEAH!
UH, MASTER? HOW OLD ARE YOU?
BLEH?
IT DOESN'T MATTER HOW HARD I TRY, HUH? I COULD NEVER DO IT.
WELL... YEAH, THAT'S PRETTY MUCH HOW IT GOES.

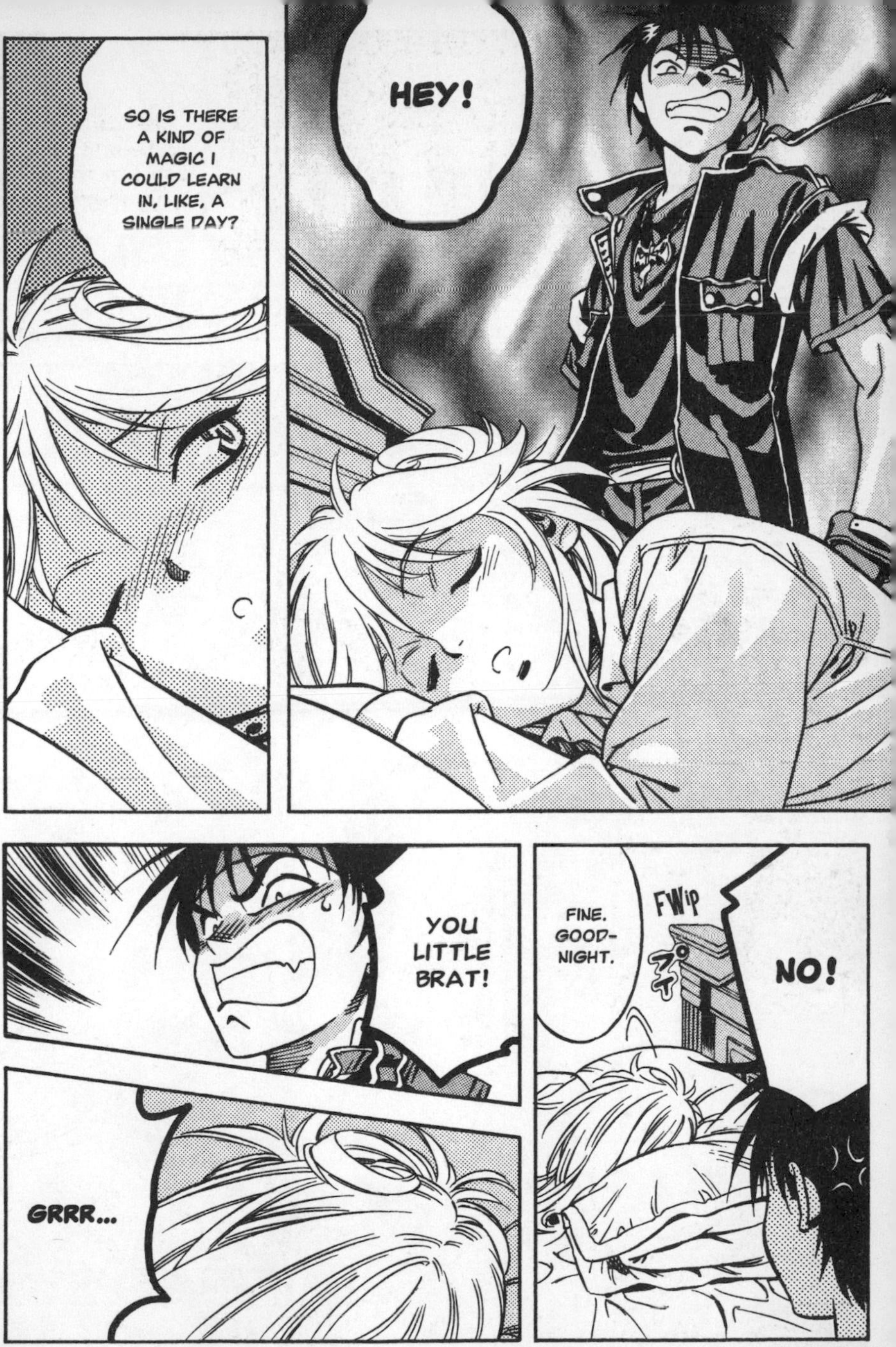
HEY!
SO IS THERE A KIND OF MAGIC I COULD LEARN IN, LIKE, A SINGLE DAY?
NO!
FWip
FINE. GOOD-NIGHT.
YOU LITTLE BRAT!
GRRR...

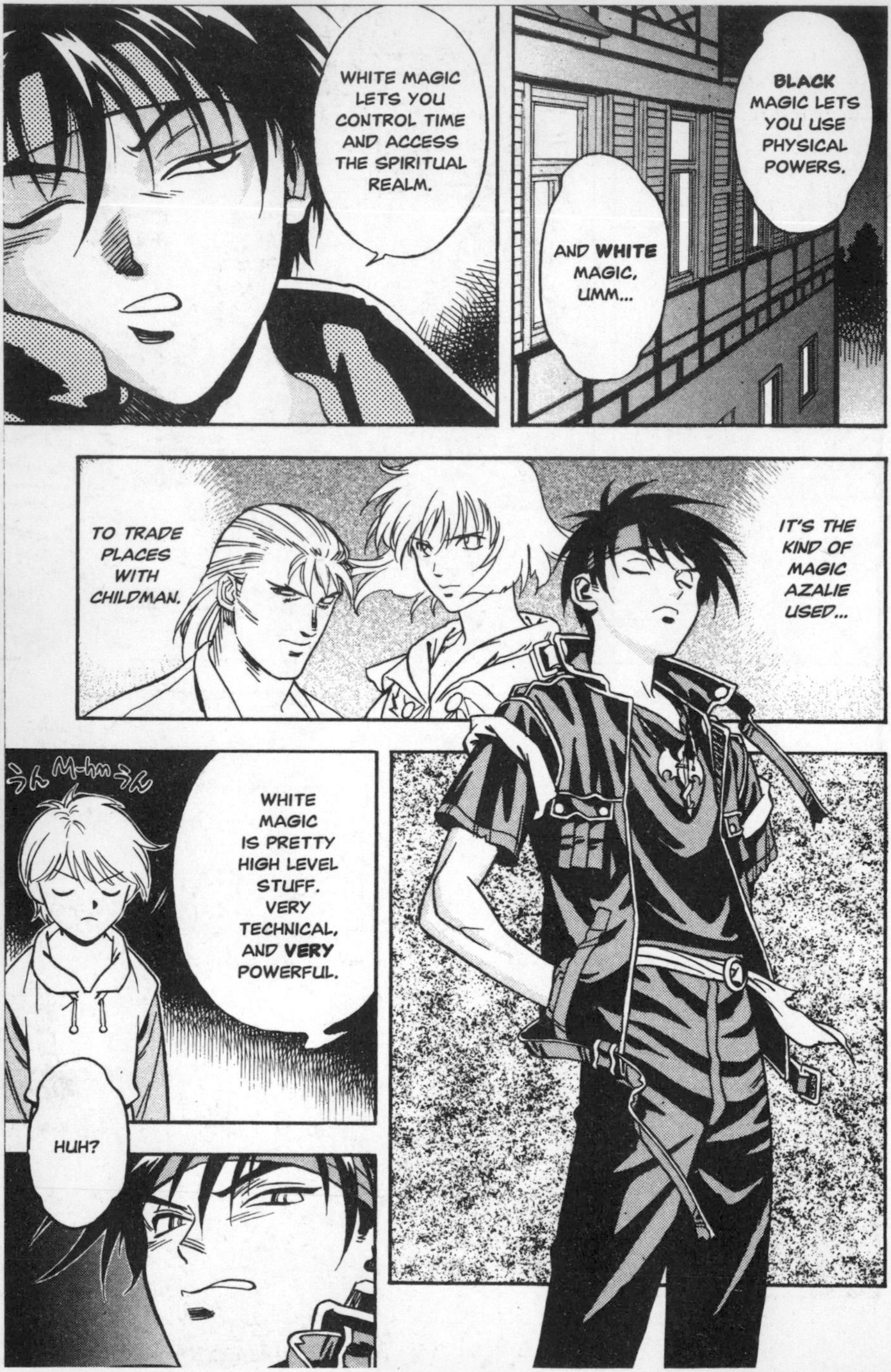
BLACK MAGIC LETS YOU USE PHYSICAL POWERS.
AND WHITE MAGIC, UMM...
WHITE MAGIC LETS YOU CONTROL TIME AND ACCESS THE SPIRITUAL REALM.
IT'S THE KIND OF MAGIC AZALIE USED...
TO TRADE PLACES WITH CHILDMAN.
WHITE MAGIC IS PRETTY HIGH LEVEL STUFF. VERY TECHNICAL, AND VERY POWERFUL.
うん M-hm うん
HUH?

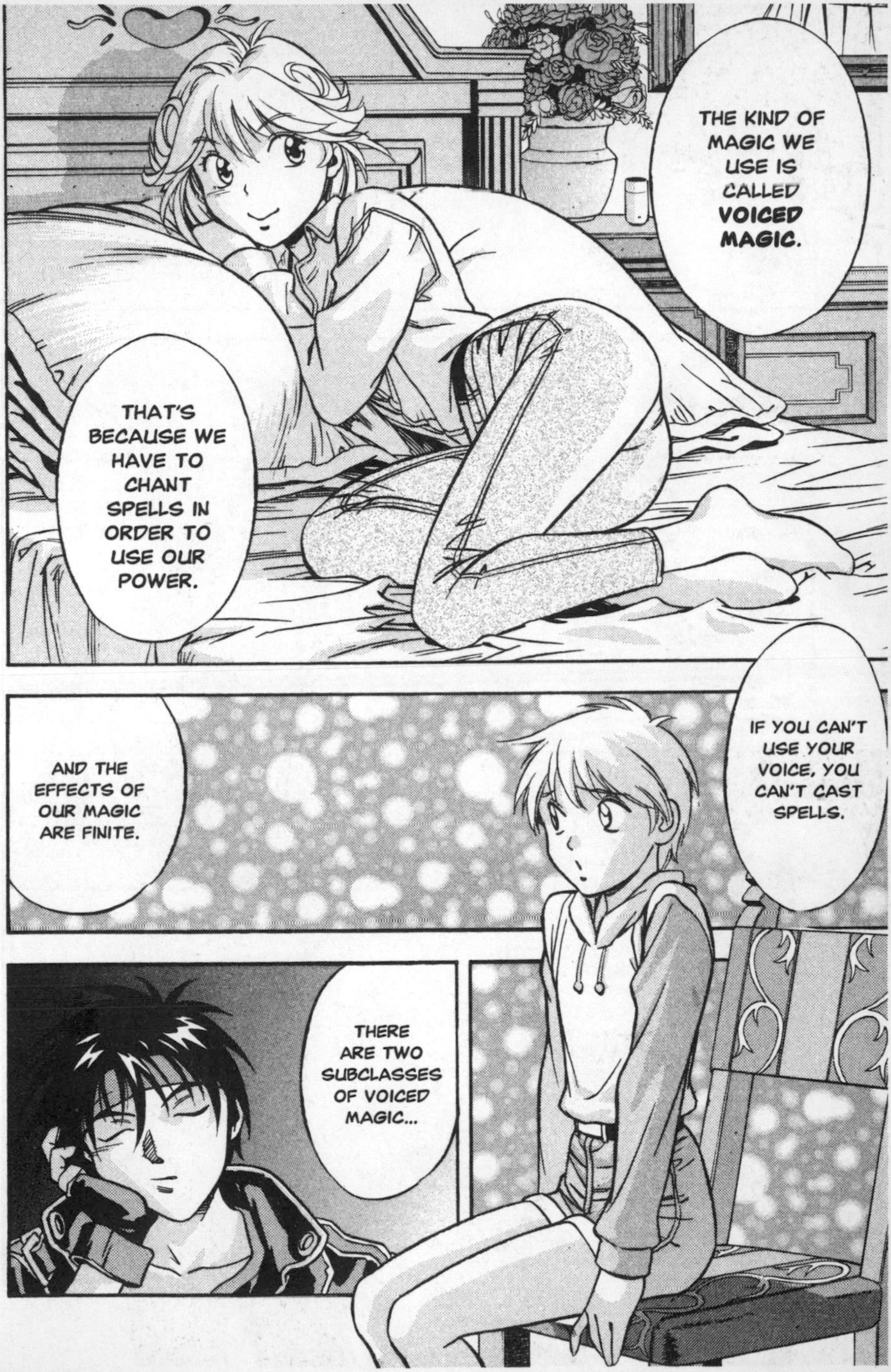
THE KIND OF MAGIC WE USE IS CALLED **VOICED MAGIC.**
THAT'S BECAUSE WE HAVE TO CHANT SPELLS IN ORDER TO USE OUR POWER.
IF YOU CAN'T USE YOUR VOICE, YOU CAN'T CAST SPELLS.
AND THE EFFECTS OF OUR MAGIC ARE FINITE.
THERE ARE TWO SUBCLASSES OF VOICED MAGIC...

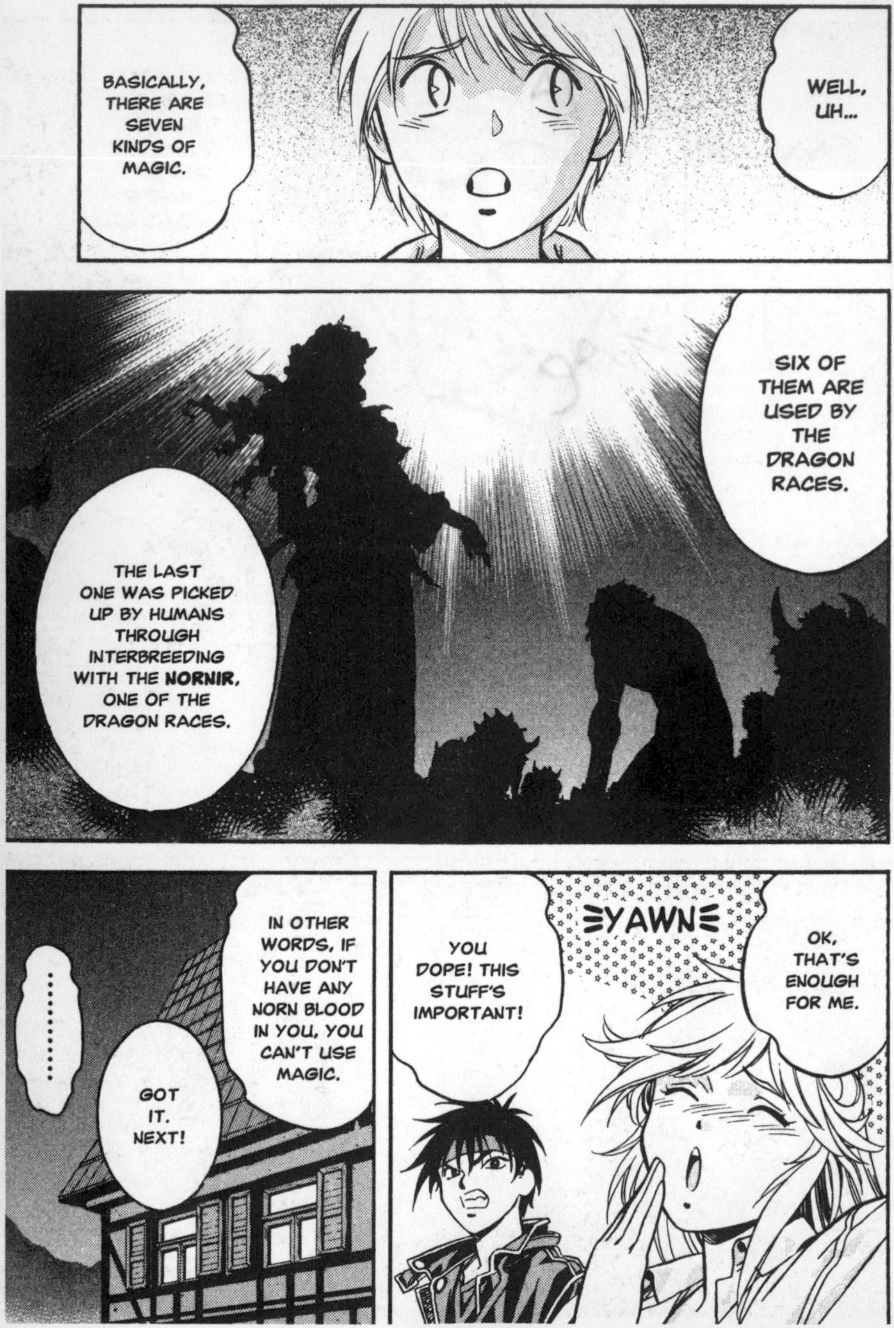

BASICALLY, THERE ARE SEVEN KINDS OF MAGIC.
WELL, UH...
SIX OF THEM ARE USED BY THE DRAGON RACES.
THE LAST ONE WAS PICKED UP BY HUMANS THROUGH INTERBREEDING WITH THE **NORNIR**, ONE OF THE DRAGON RACES.
IN OTHER WORDS, IF YOU DON'T HAVE ANY NORN BLOOD IN YOU, YOU CAN'T USE MAGIC.
GOT IT. NEXT!
....
YOU DOPE! THIS STUFF'S IMPORTANT!
YAWN
OK, THAT'S ENOUGH FOR ME.

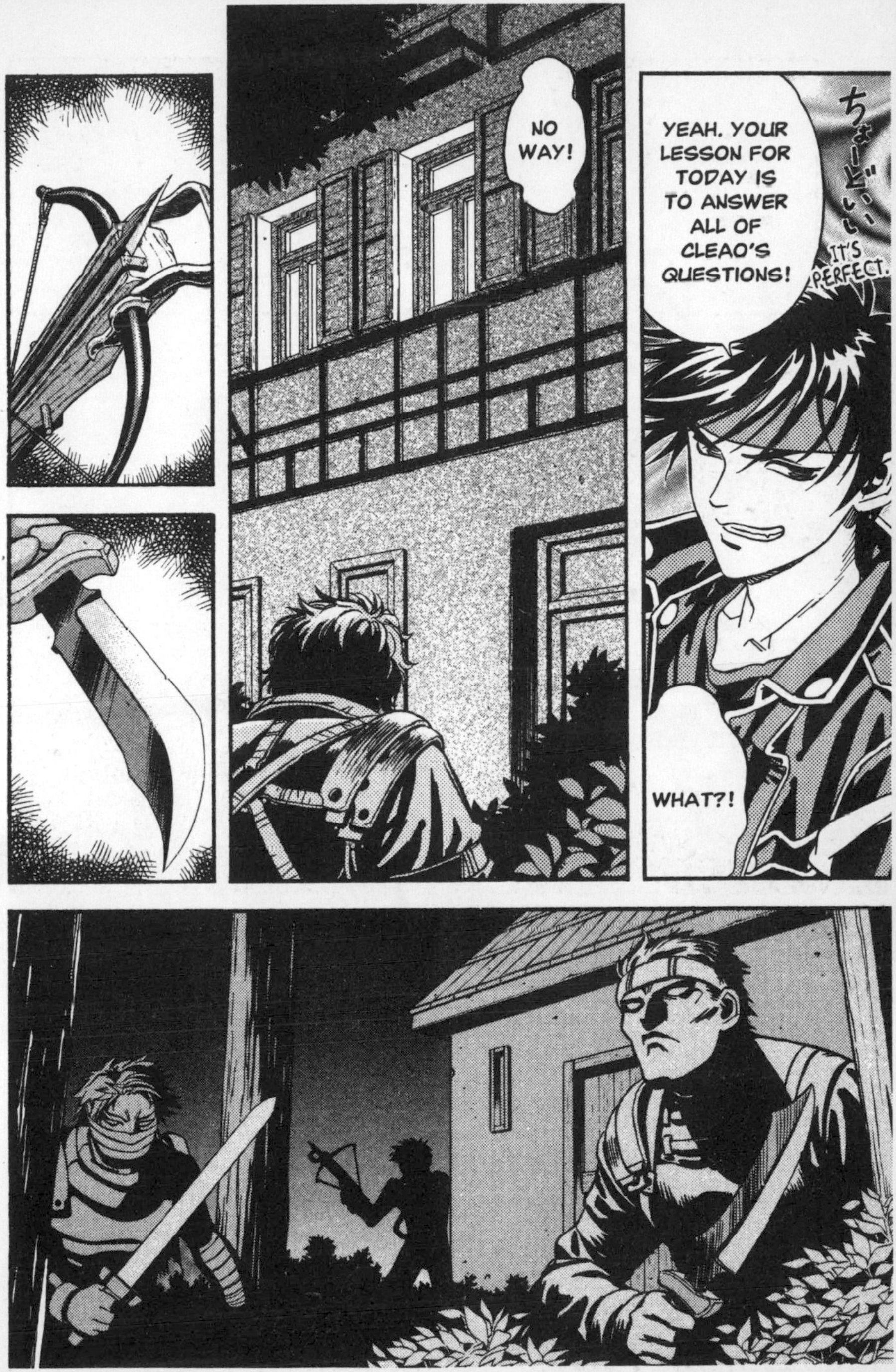
ちょーどいい
IT'S PERFECT.
YEAH. YOUR LESSON FOR TODAY IS TO ANSWER ALL OF CLEAO'S QUESTIONS!
WHAT?!
NO WAY!

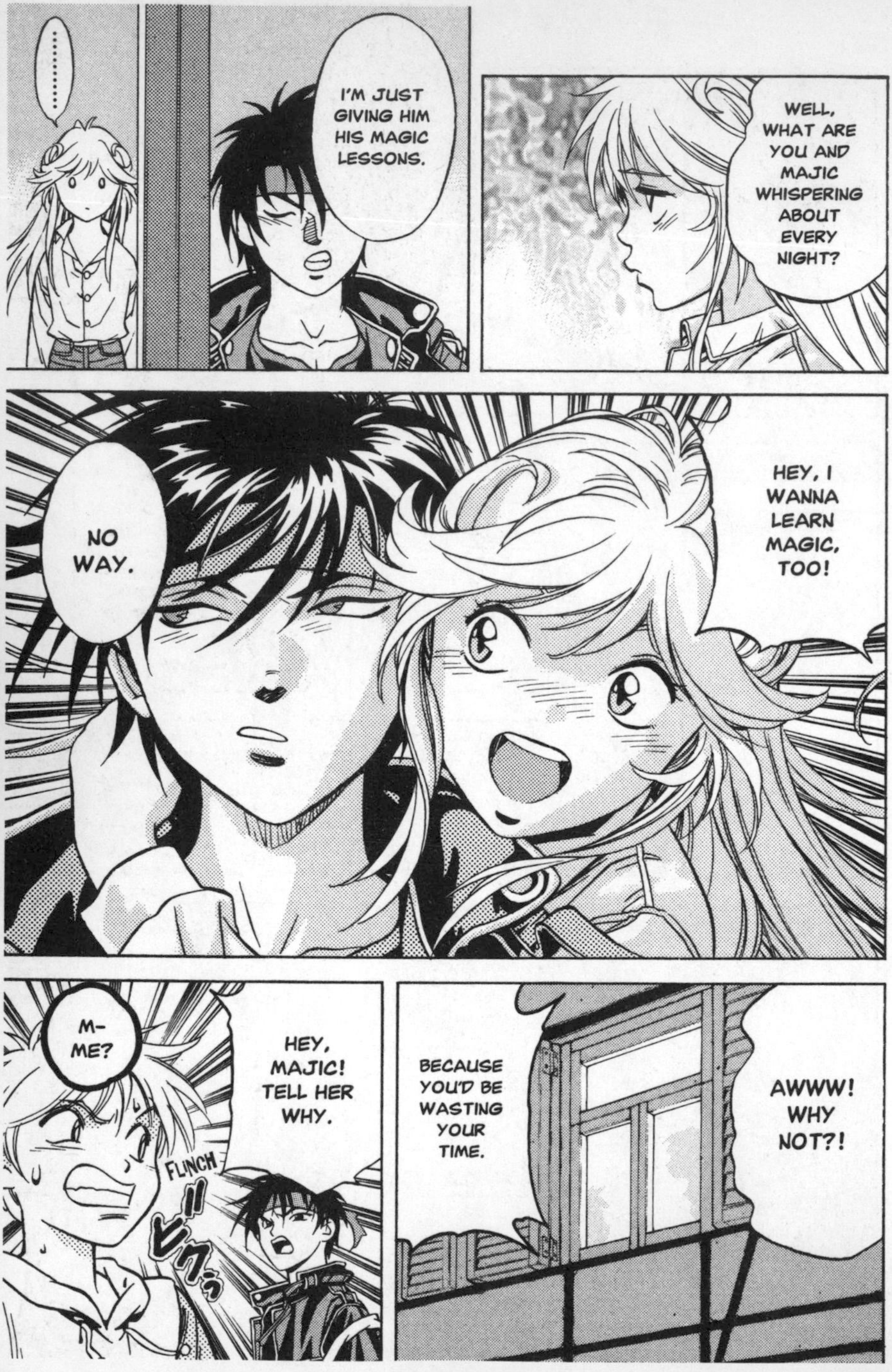
WELL, WHAT ARE YOU AND MAJIC WHISPERING ABOUT EVERY NIGHT?
I'M JUST GIVING HIM HIS MAGIC LESSONS.
…………
HEY, I WANNA LEARN MAGIC, TOO!
NO WAY.
AWWW! WHY NOT?!
BECAUSE YOU'D BE WASTING YOUR TIME.
HEY, MAJIC! TELL HER WHY.
FLINCH
M-ME?

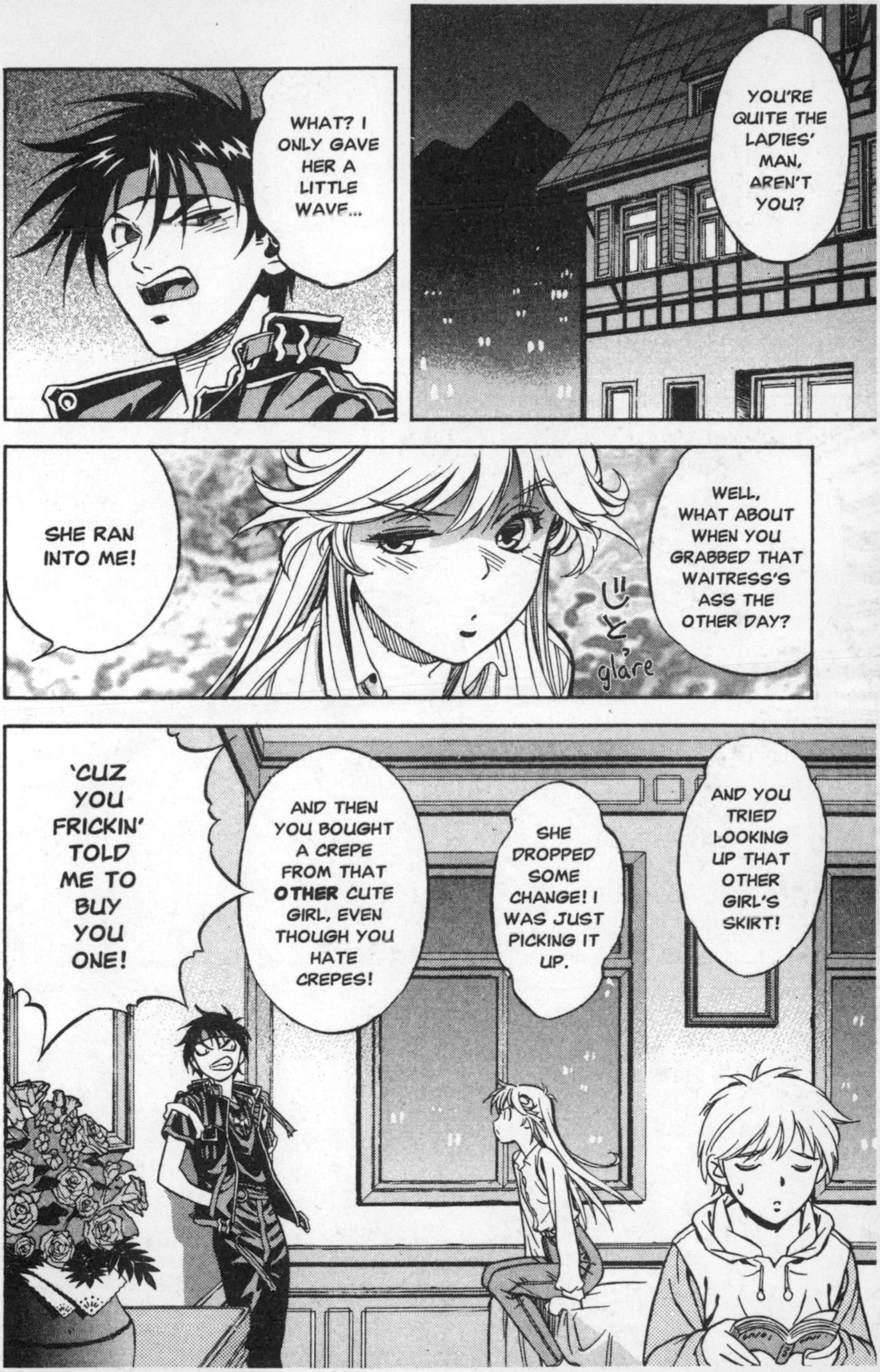
YOU'RE QUITE THE LADIES' MAN, AREN'T YOU?
WHAT? I ONLY GAVE HER A LITTLE WAVE...
WELL, WHAT ABOUT WHEN YOU GRABBED THAT WAITRESS'S ASS THE OTHER DAY?
じと
glare
SHE RAN INTO ME!
AND YOU TRIED LOOKING UP THAT OTHER GIRL'S SKIRT!
SHE DROPPED SOME CHANGE! I WAS JUST PICKING IT UP.
AND THEN YOU BOUGHT A CREPE FROM THAT **OTHER** CUTE GIRL, EVEN THOUGH YOU HATE CREPES!
'CUZ YOU FRICKIN' TOLD ME TO BUY YOU ONE!

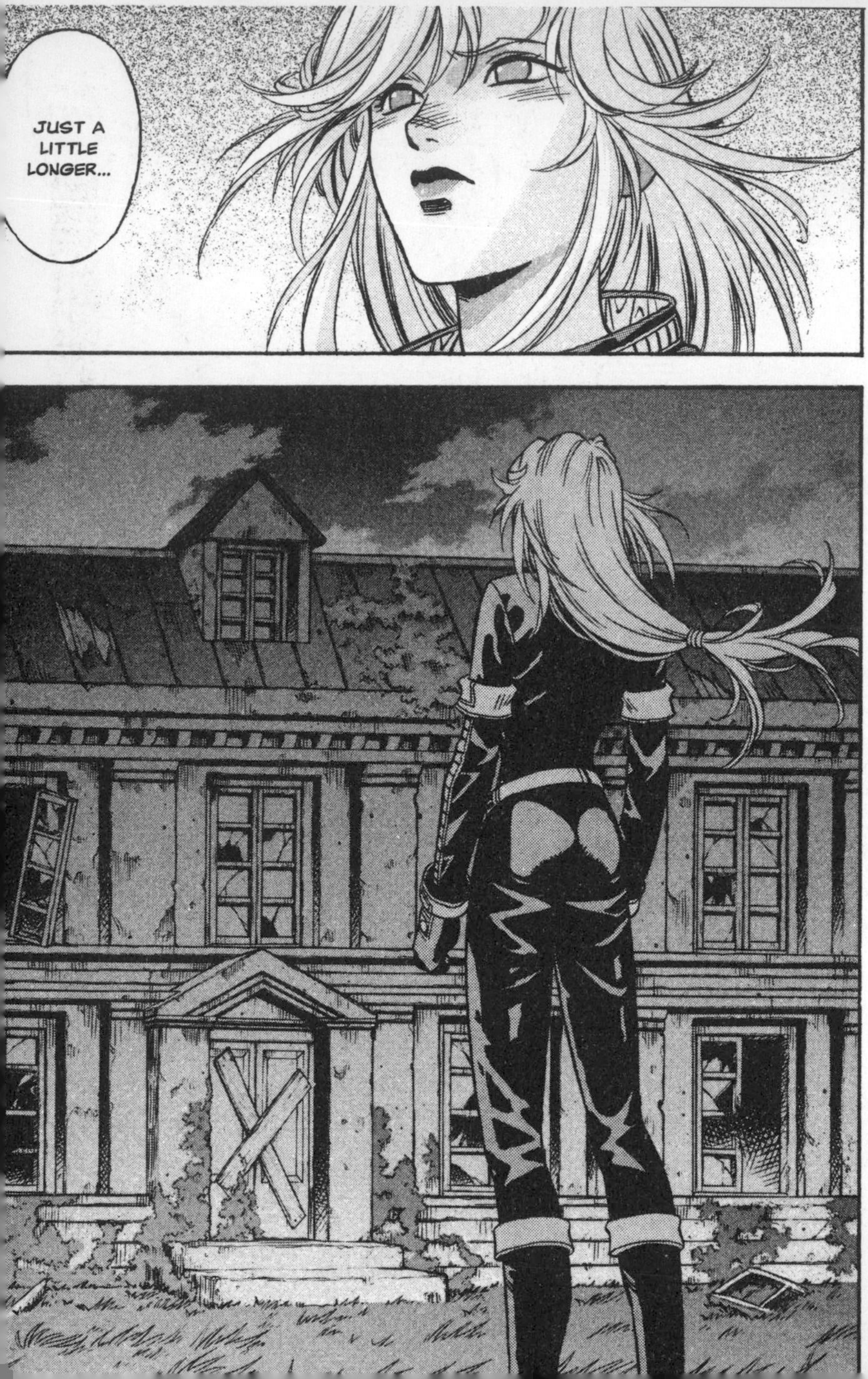
JUST A LITTLE LONGER...

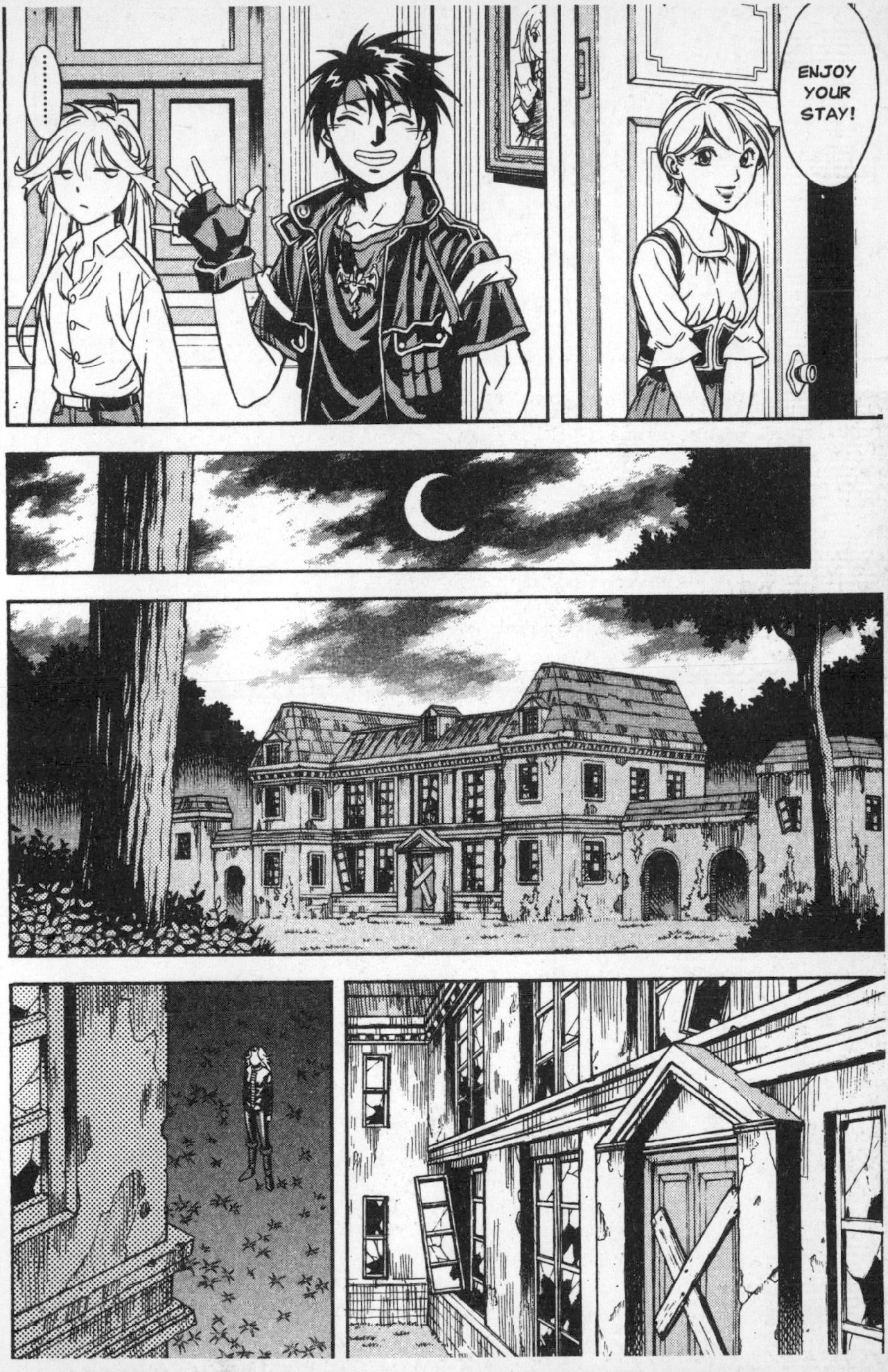
......
ENJOY YOUR STAY!

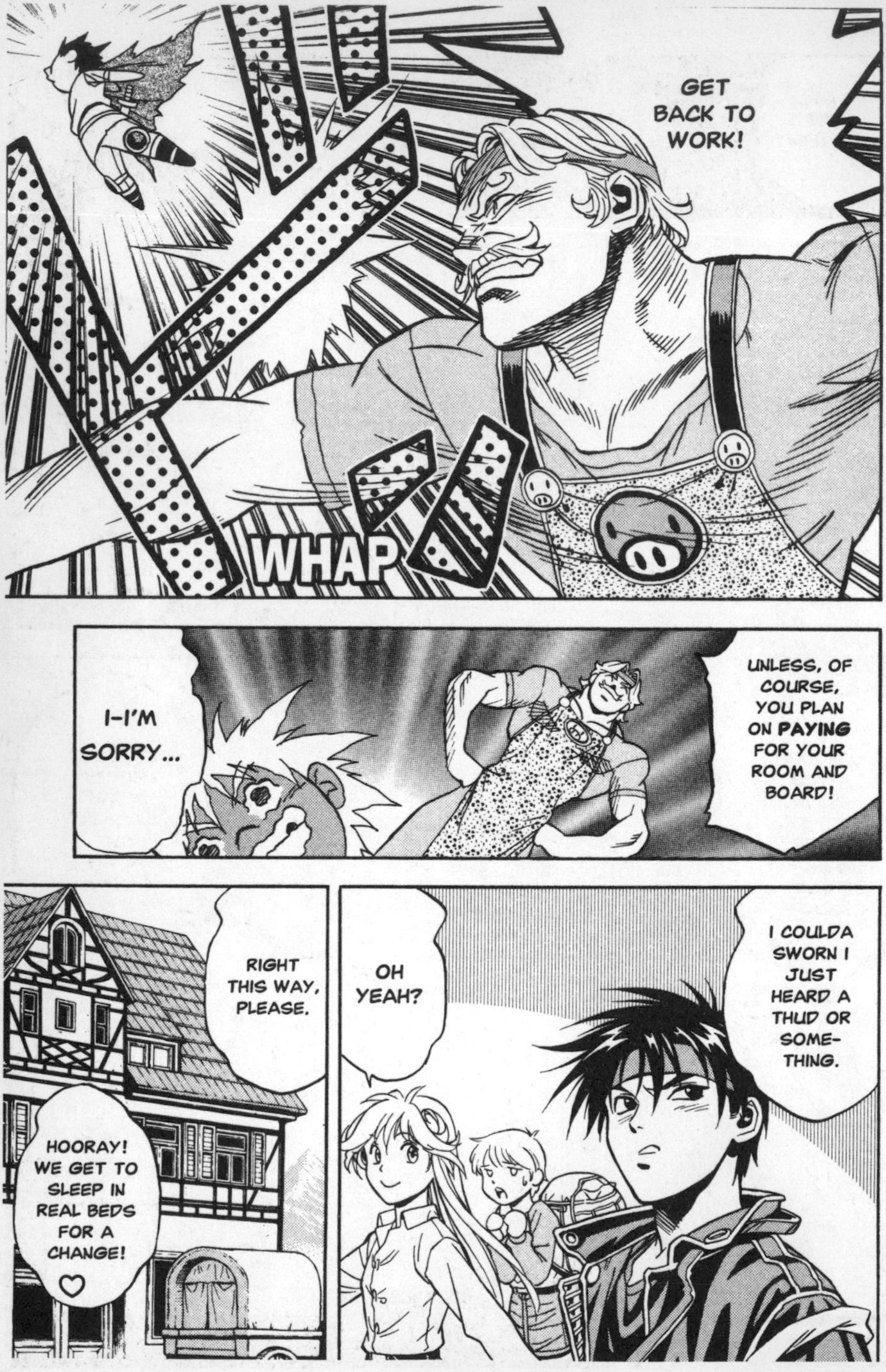
GET BACK TO WORK!
WHAP
I-I'M SORRY...
UNLESS, OF COURSE, YOU PLAN ON PAYING FOR YOUR ROOM AND BOARD!
RIGHT THIS WAY, PLEASE.
HOORAY! WE GET TO SLEEP IN REAL BEDS FOR A CHANGE! ♡
I COULDA SWORN I JUST HEARD A THUD OR SOME-THING.
OH YEAH?

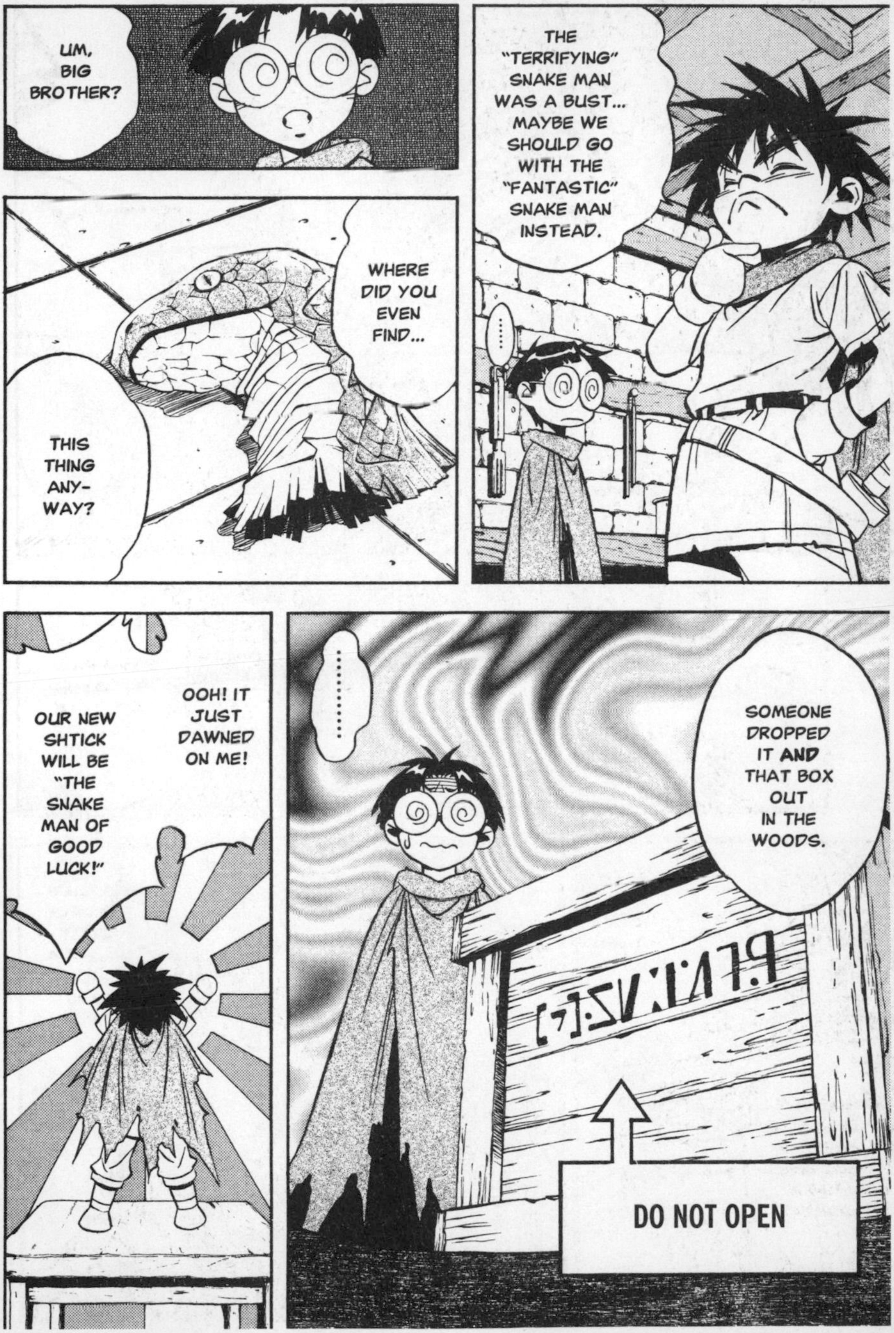

THE "TERRIFYING" SNAKE MAN WAS A BUST... MAYBE WE SHOULD GO WITH THE "FANTASTIC" SNAKE MAN INSTEAD.
......
UM, BIG BROTHER?
WHERE DID YOU EVEN FIND...
THIS THING ANY-WAY?
....
SOMEONE DROPPED IT AND THAT BOX OUT IN THE WOODS.
DO NOT OPEN
OOH! IT JUST DAWNED ON ME!
OUR NEW SHTICK WILL BE "THE SNAKE MAN OF GOOD LUCK!"

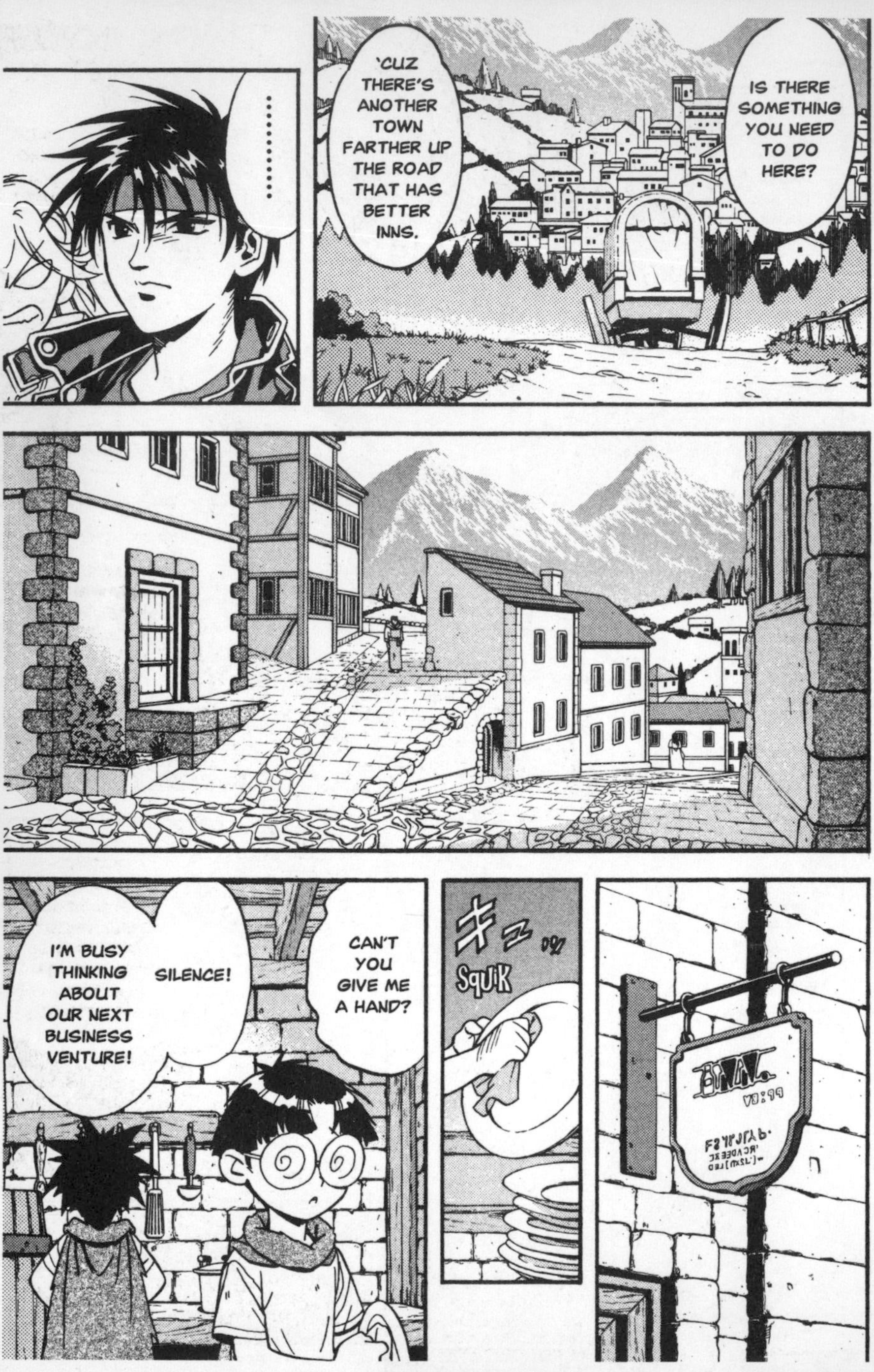
IS THERE SOMETHING YOU NEED TO DO HERE?
'CUZ THERE'S ANOTHER TOWN FARTHER UP THE ROAD THAT HAS BETTER INNS.
......
SQUIK
CAN'T YOU GIVE ME A HAND?
SILENCE!
I'M BUSY THINKING ABOUT OUR NEXT BUSINESS VENTURE!

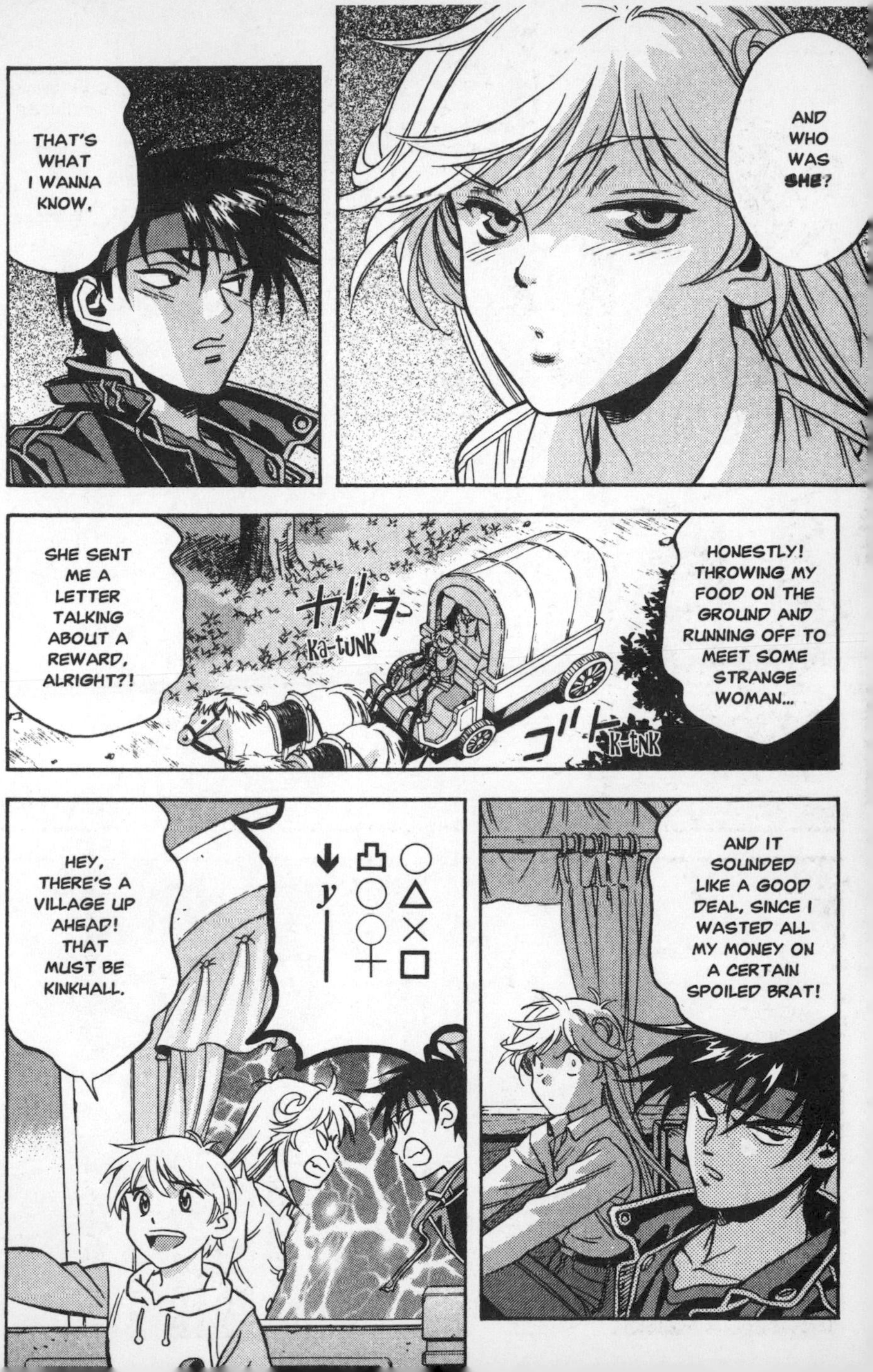
AND WHO WAS SHE?
THAT'S WHAT I WANNA KNOW.
HONESTLY! THROWING MY FOOD ON THE GROUND AND RUNNING OFF TO MEET SOME STRANGE WOMAN...
SHE SENT ME A LETTER TALKING ABOUT A REWARD, ALRIGHT?!
Ka-tUNK
K-tNK
AND IT SOUNDED LIKE A GOOD DEAL, SINCE I WASTED ALL MY MONEY ON A CERTAIN SPOILED BRAT!
HEY, THERE'S A VILLAGE UP AHEAD! THAT MUST BE KINKHALL.

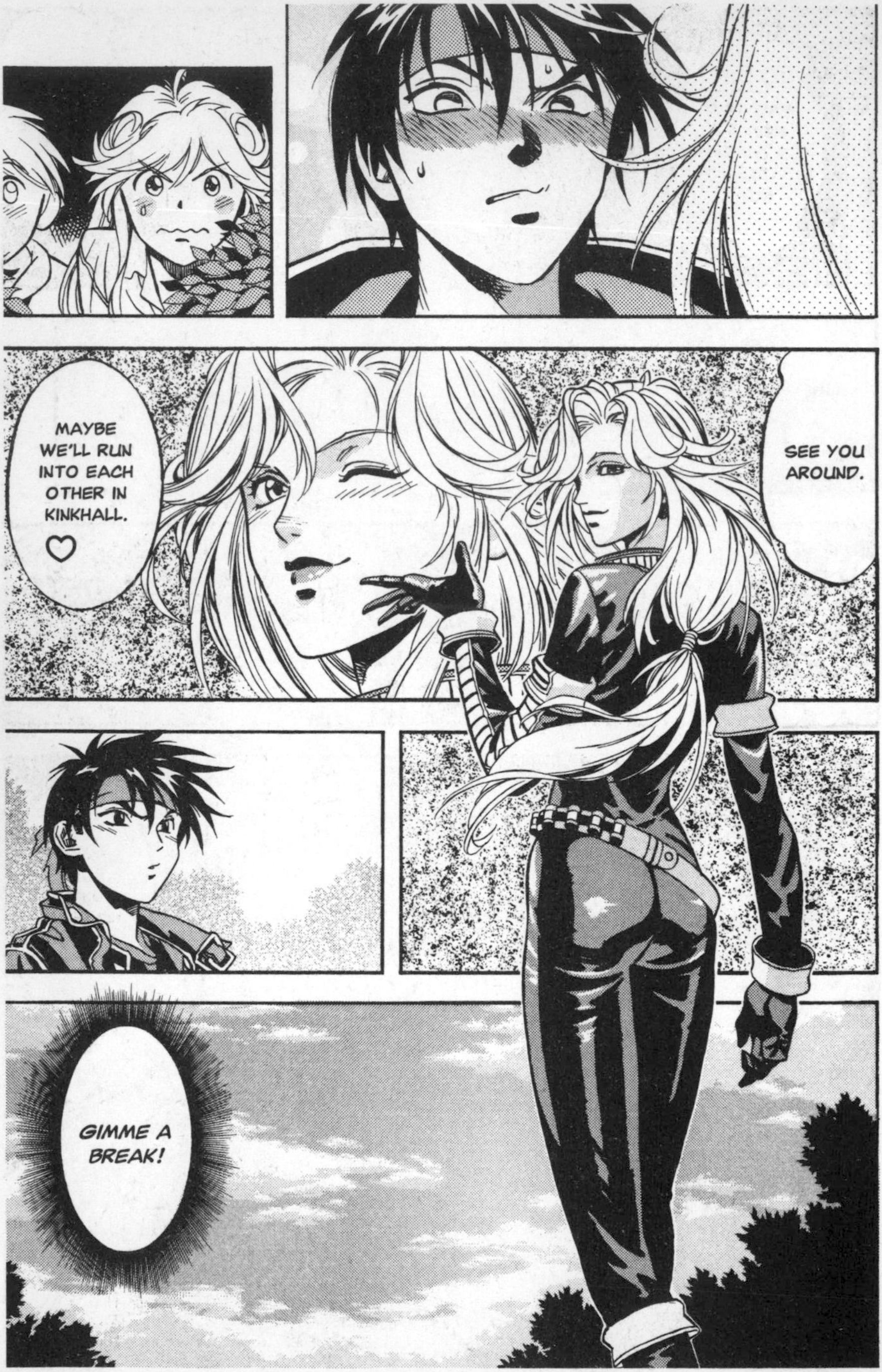
SEE YOU AROUND.
MAYBE WE'LL RUN INTO EACH OTHER IN KINKHALL. ♡
GIMME A BREAK!

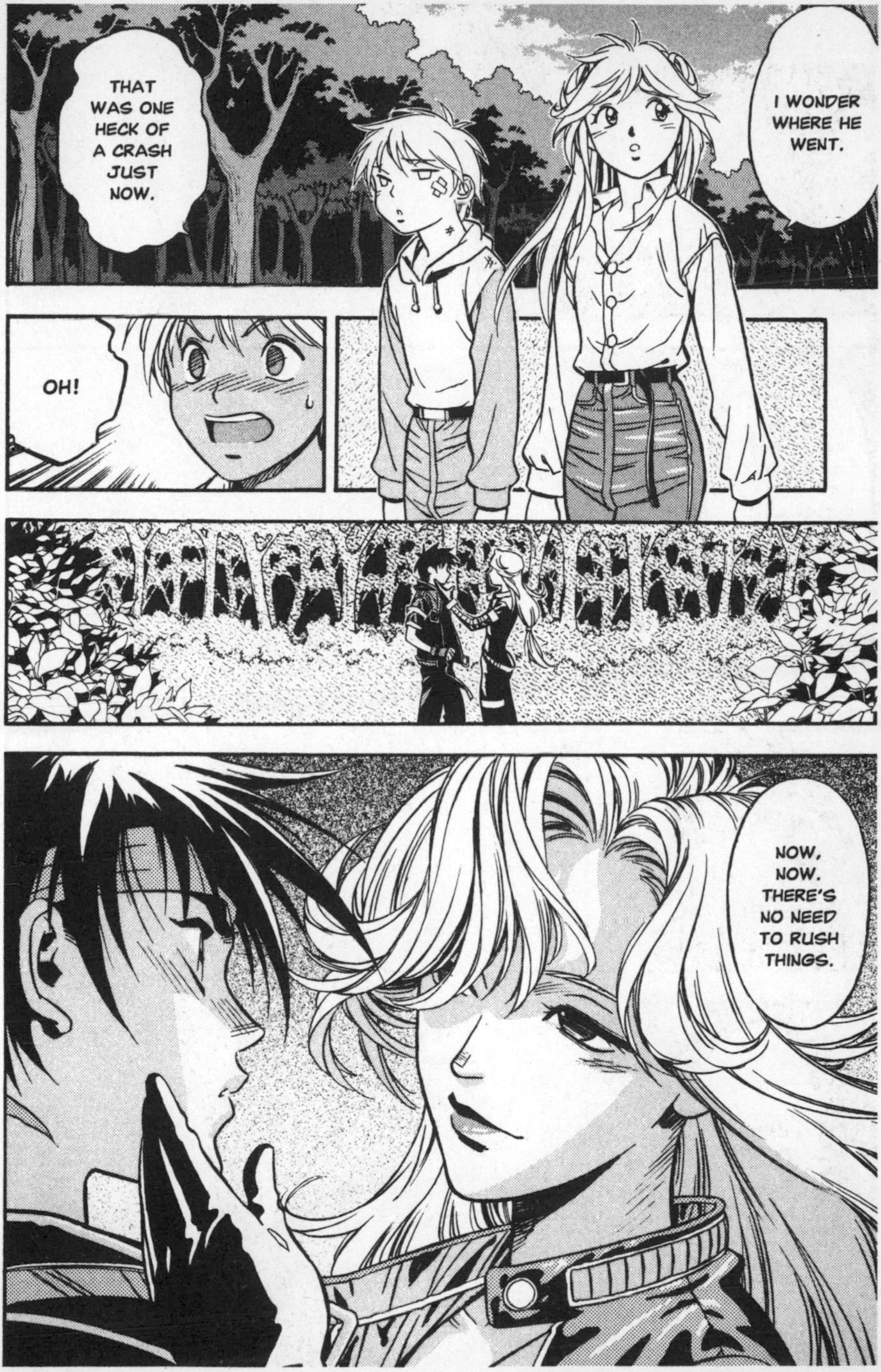
I WONDER WHERE HE WENT.
THAT WAS ONE HECK OF A CRASH JUST NOW.
OH!
NOW, NOW. THERE'S NO NEED TO RUSH THINGS.

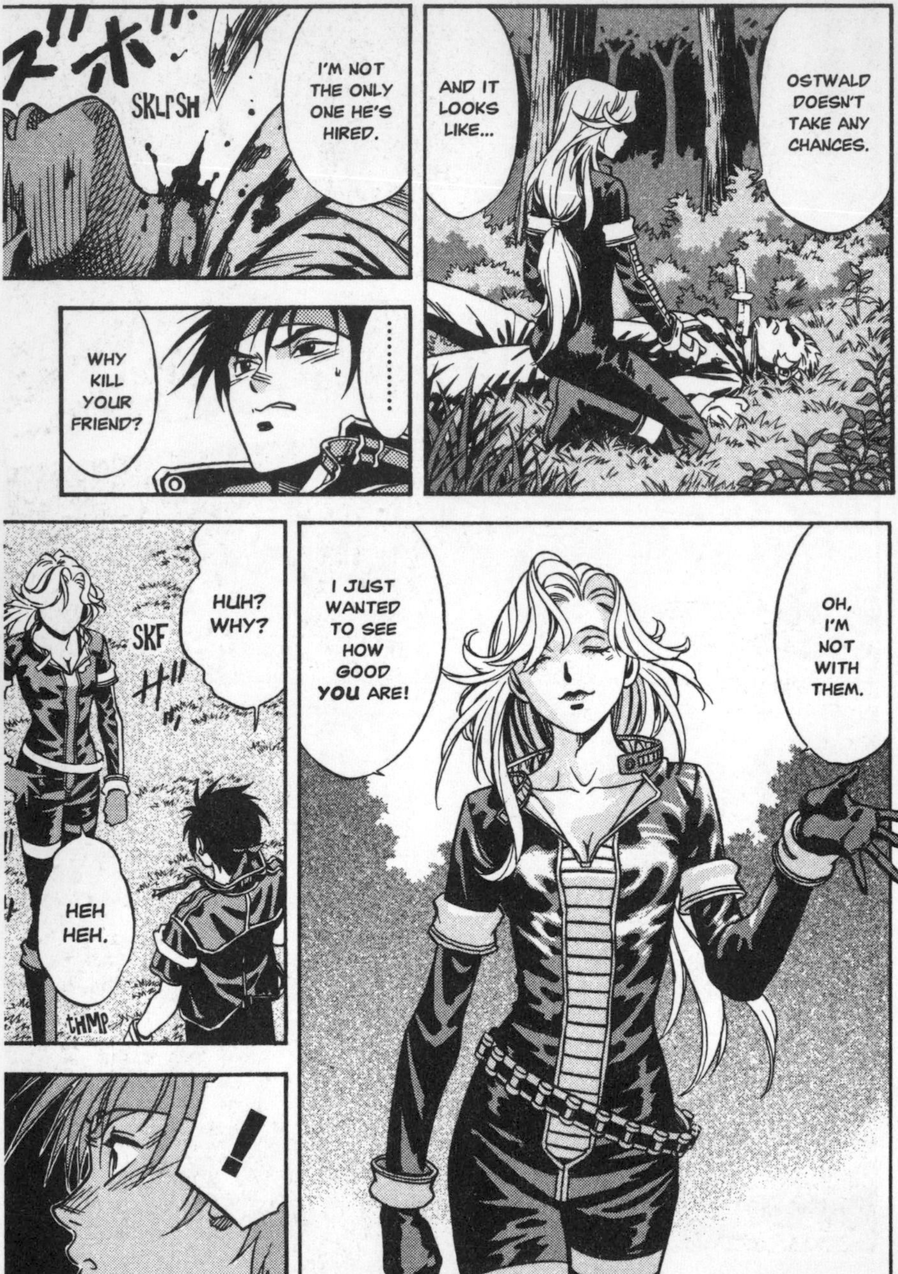
OSTWALD DOESN'T TAKE ANY CHANCES.
AND IT LOOKS LIKE...
I'M NOT THE ONLY ONE HE'S HIRED.
SKLRSH
......
WHY KILL YOUR FRIEND?
OH, I'M NOT WITH THEM.
I JUST WANTED TO SEE HOW GOOD YOU ARE!
HUH? WHY?
SKF
HEH HEH.
THMP
!

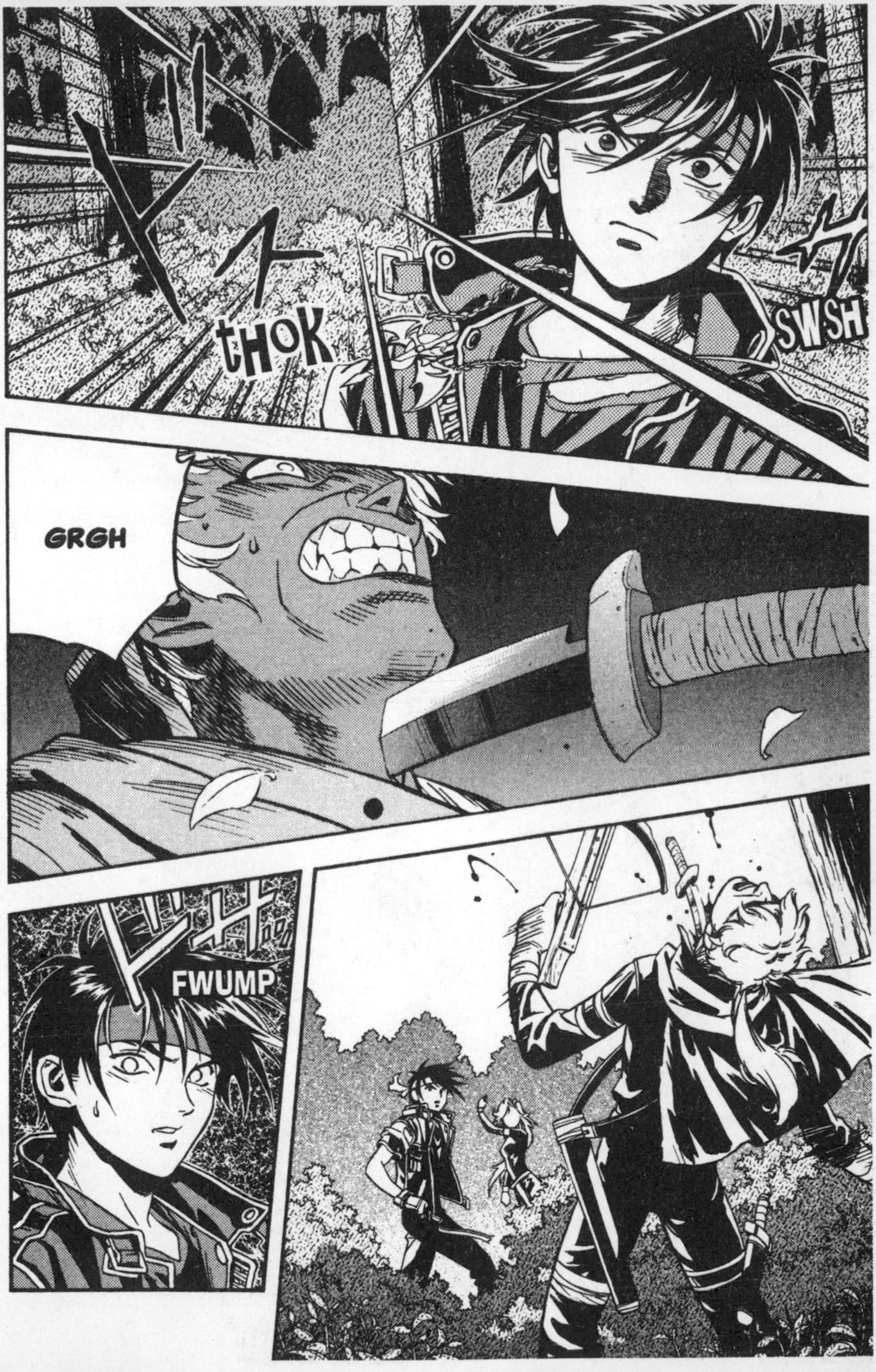
SWSH
THOK
GRGH
FWUMP

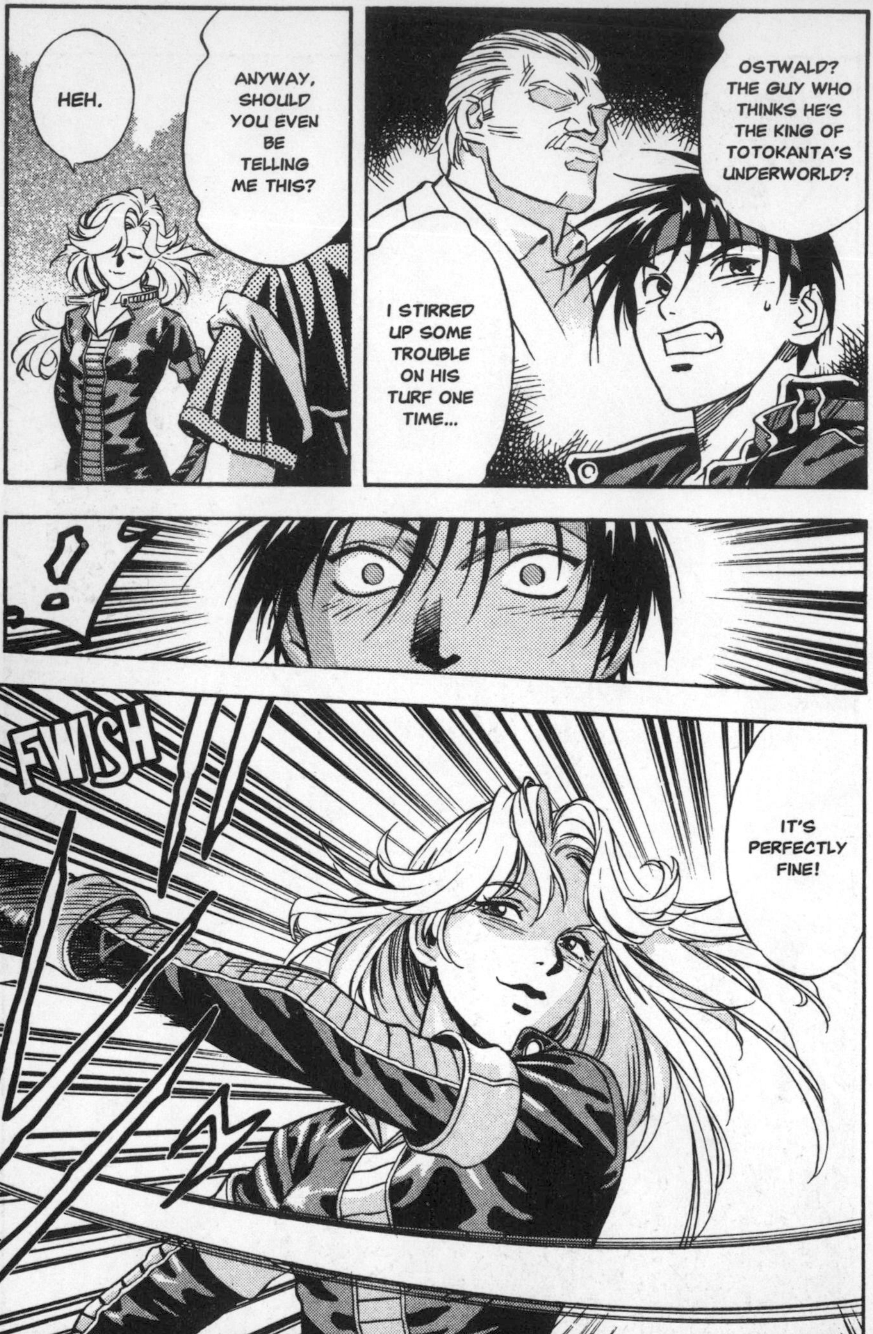
OSTWALD? THE GUY WHO THINKS HE'S THE KING OF TOTOKANTA'S UNDERWORLD?
I STIRRED UP SOME TROUBLE ON HIS TURF ONE TIME...
HEH.
ANYWAY, SHOULD YOU EVEN BE TELLING ME THIS?
!
FWISH
IT'S PERFECTLY FINE!

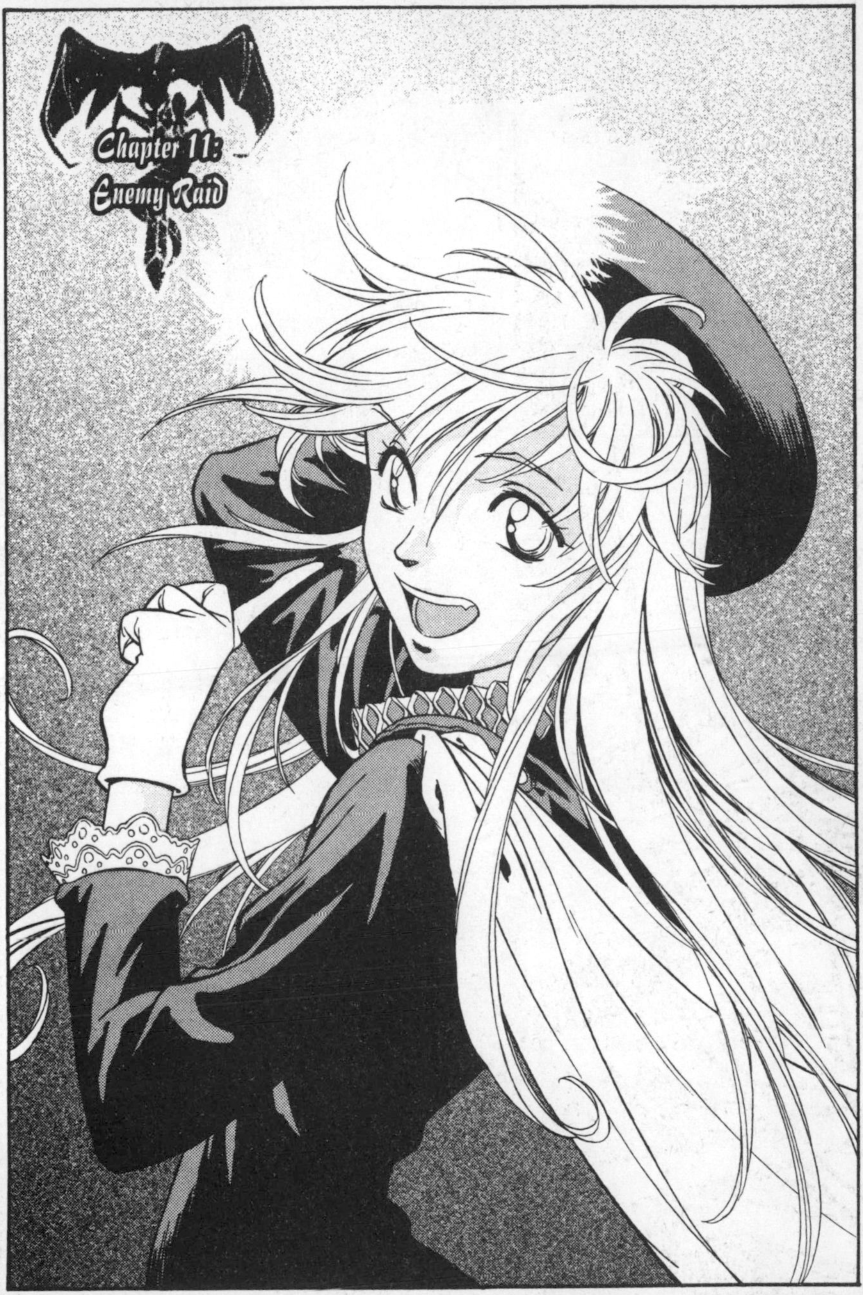
Chapter 11:
Enemy Raid

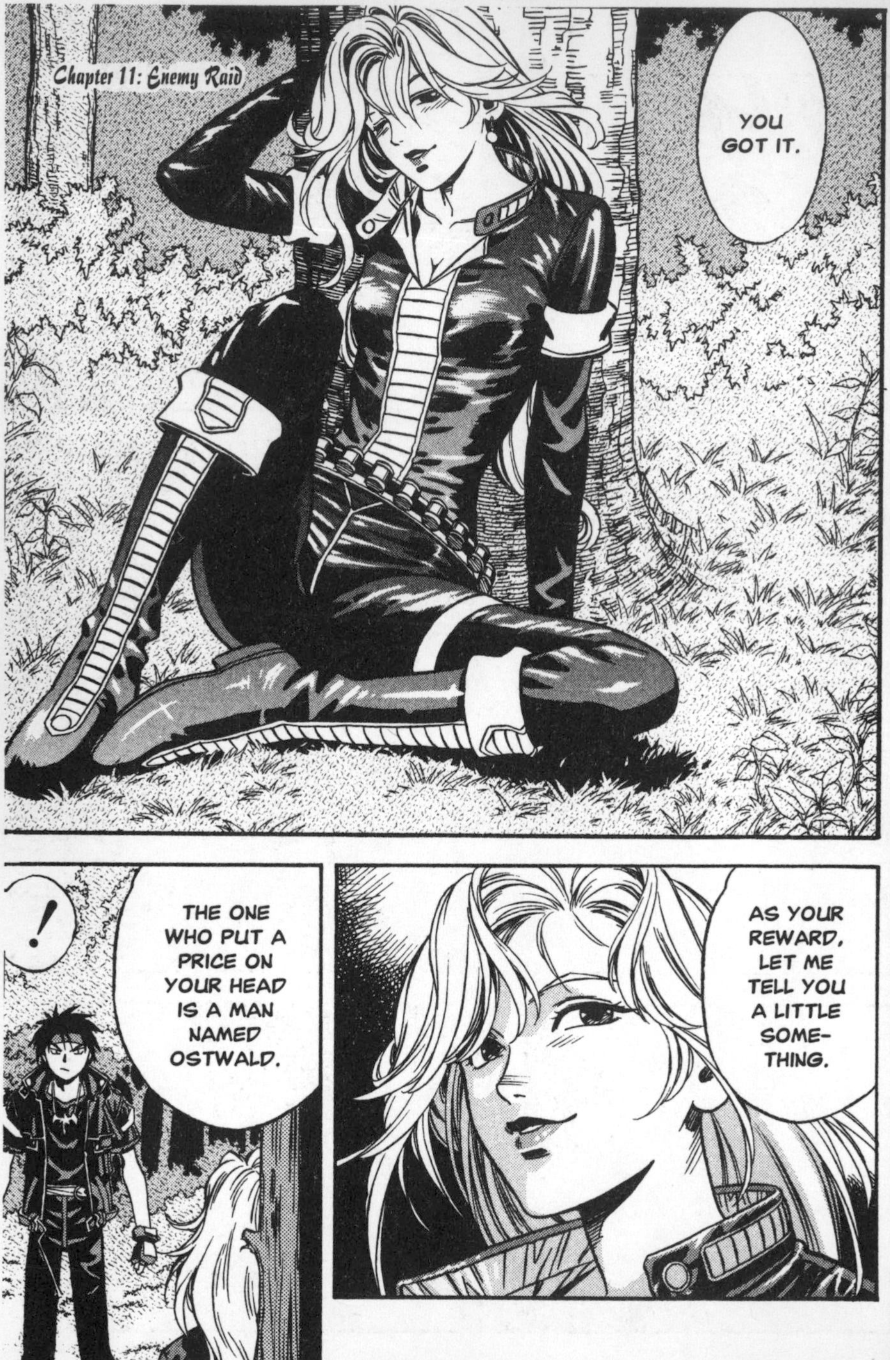
Chapter 11: Enemy Raid
YOU GOT IT.
AS YOUR REWARD, LET ME TELL YOU A LITTLE SOME-THING.
THE ONE WHO PUT A PRICE ON YOUR HEAD IS A MAN NAMED OSTWALD.
!

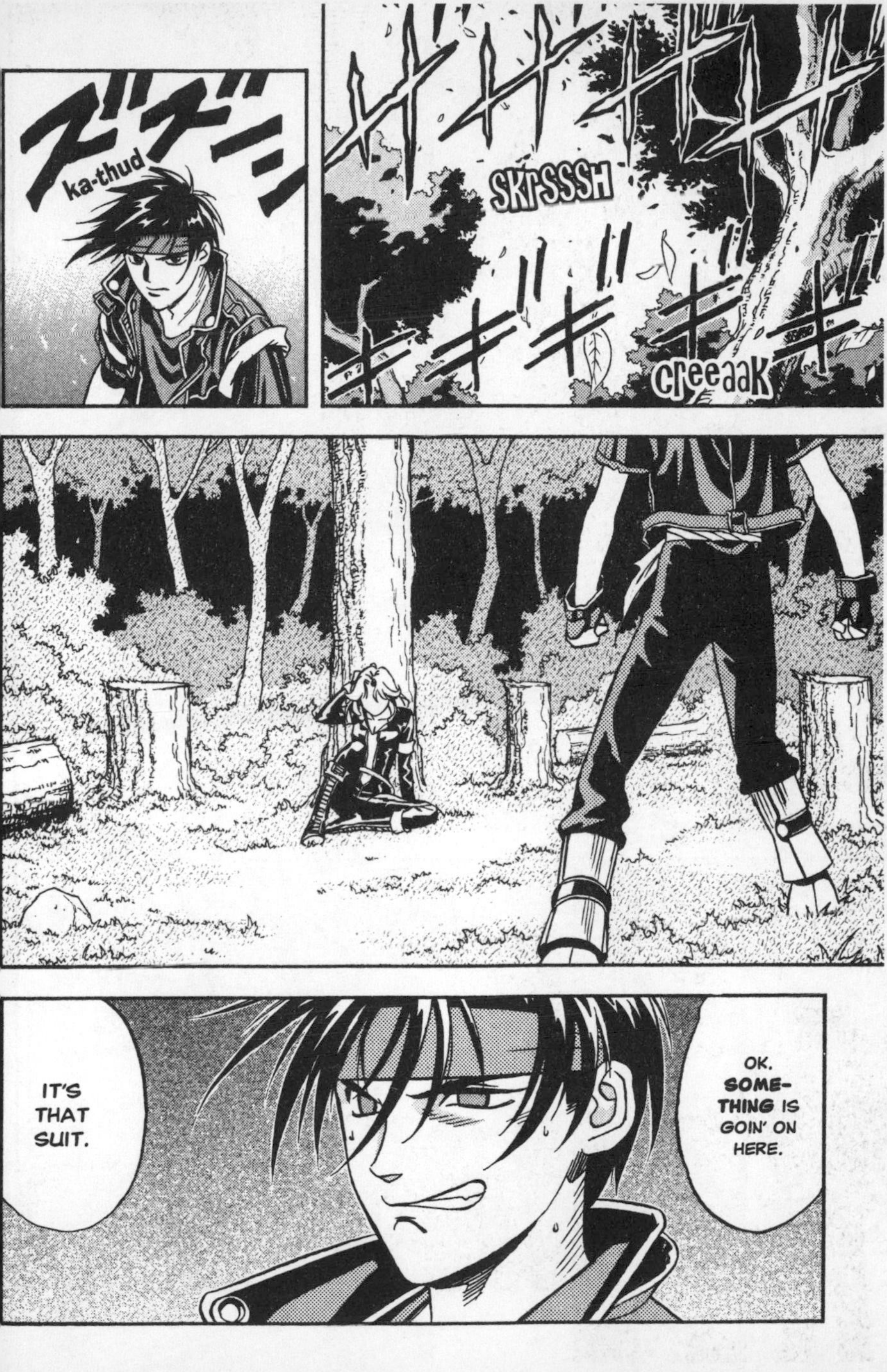
SKRSSSH
creeaak
ka-thud
OK. SOMETHING IS GOIN' ON HERE.
IT'S THAT SUIT.

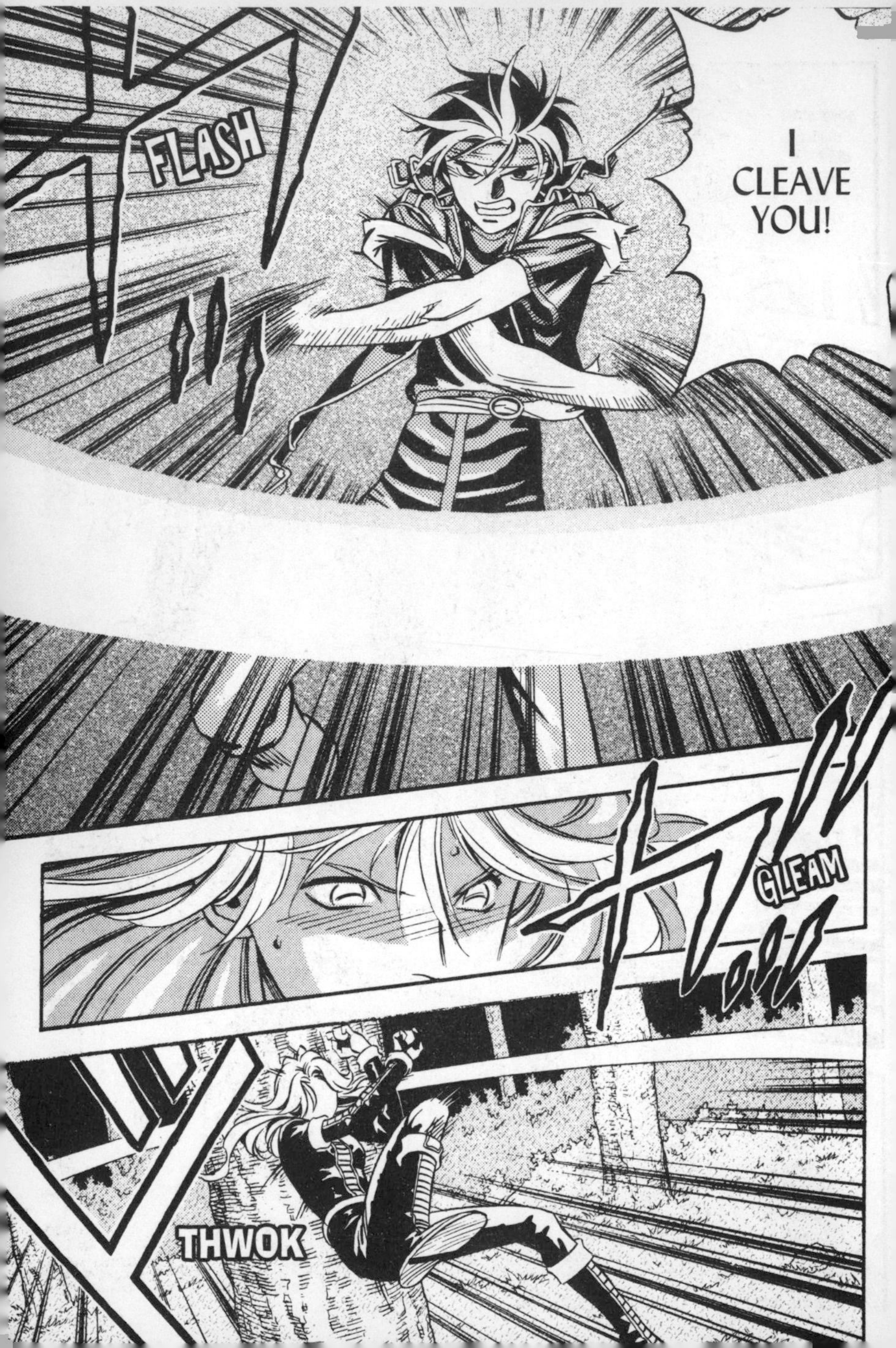
I CLEAVE YOU!
FLASH
GLEAM
THWOK

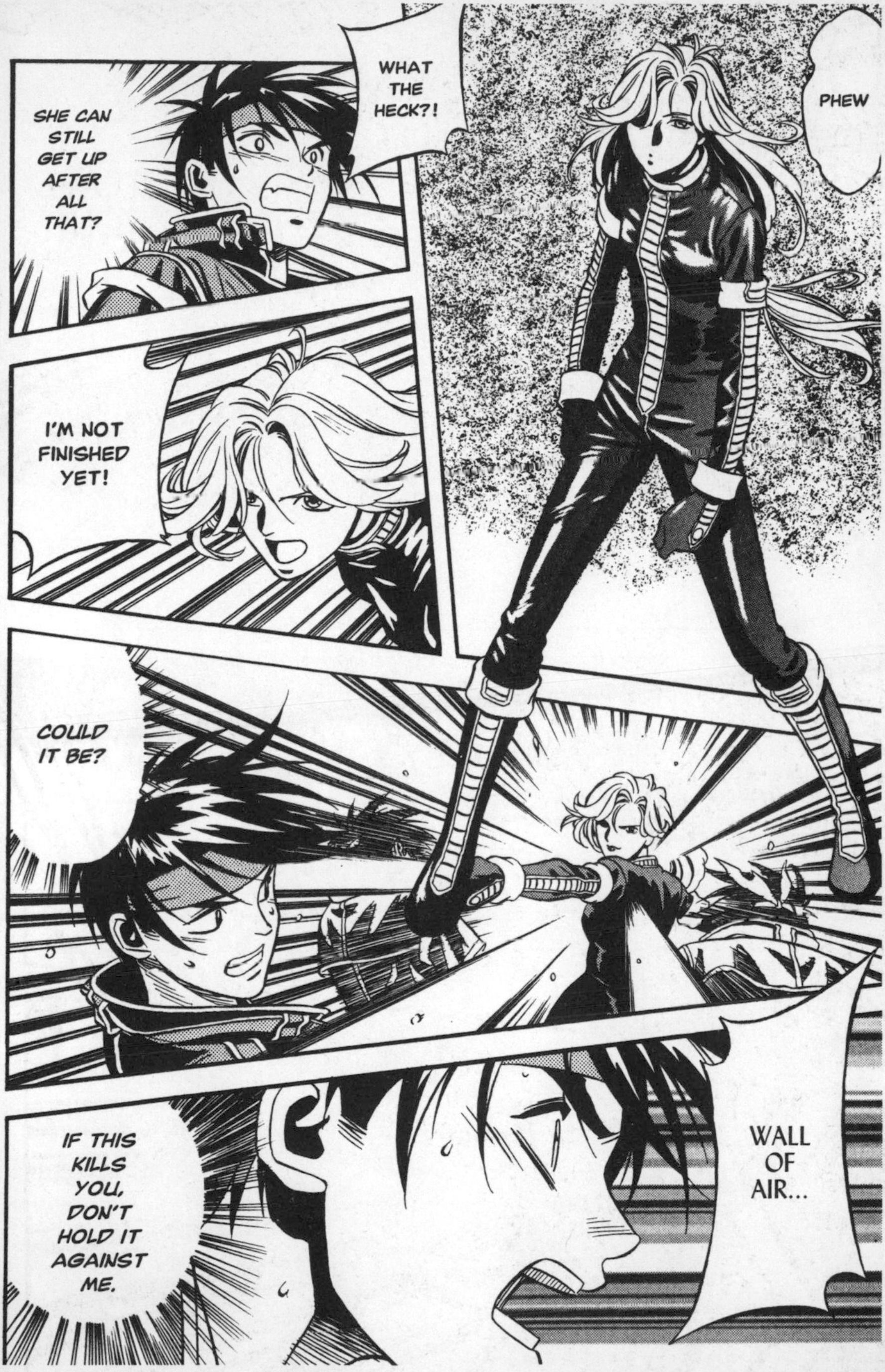
PHEW
WHAT THE HECK?!
SHE CAN STILL GET UP AFTER ALL THAT?
I'M NOT FINISHED YET!
COULD IT BE?
WALL OF AIR...
IF THIS KILLS YOU, DON'T HOLD IT AGAINST ME.

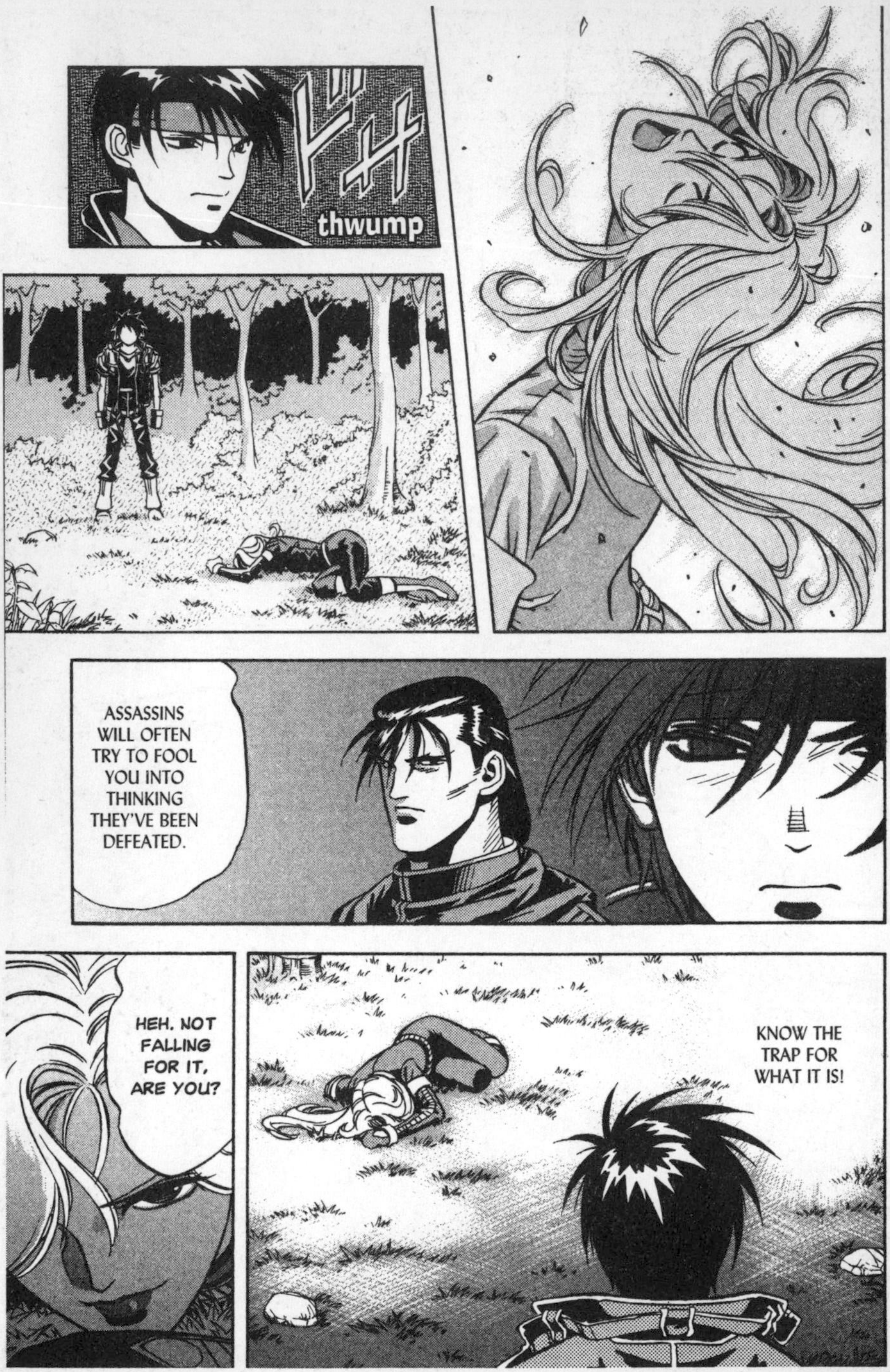
ドサッ
thwump
ASSASSINS WILL OFTEN TRY TO FOOL YOU INTO THINKING THEY'VE BEEN DEFEATED.
KNOW THE TRAP FOR WHAT IT IS!
HEH. NOT FALLING FOR IT, ARE YOU?

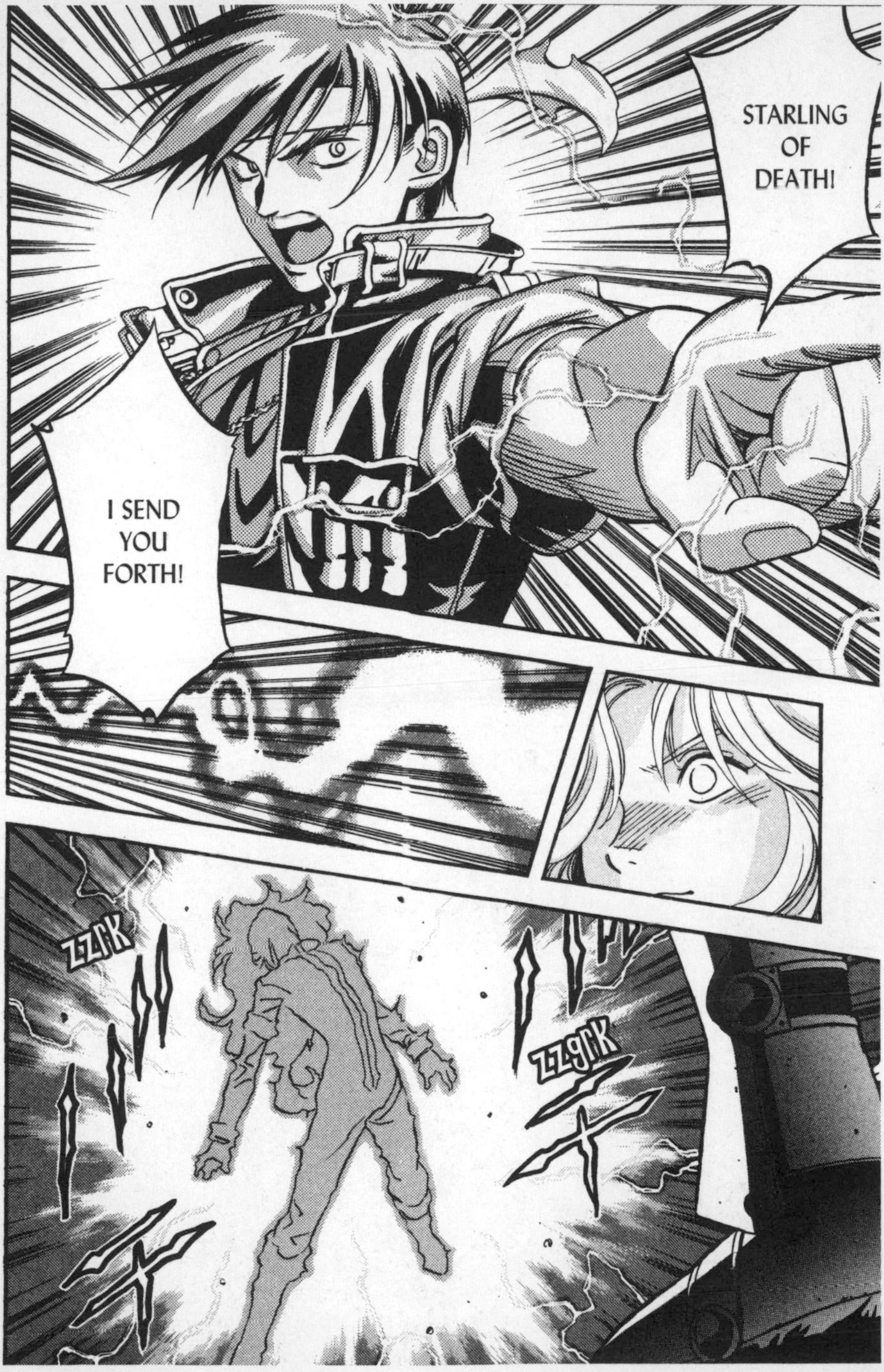
STARLING OF DEATH!
I SEND YOU FORTH!
ZZAK
ZZGAK

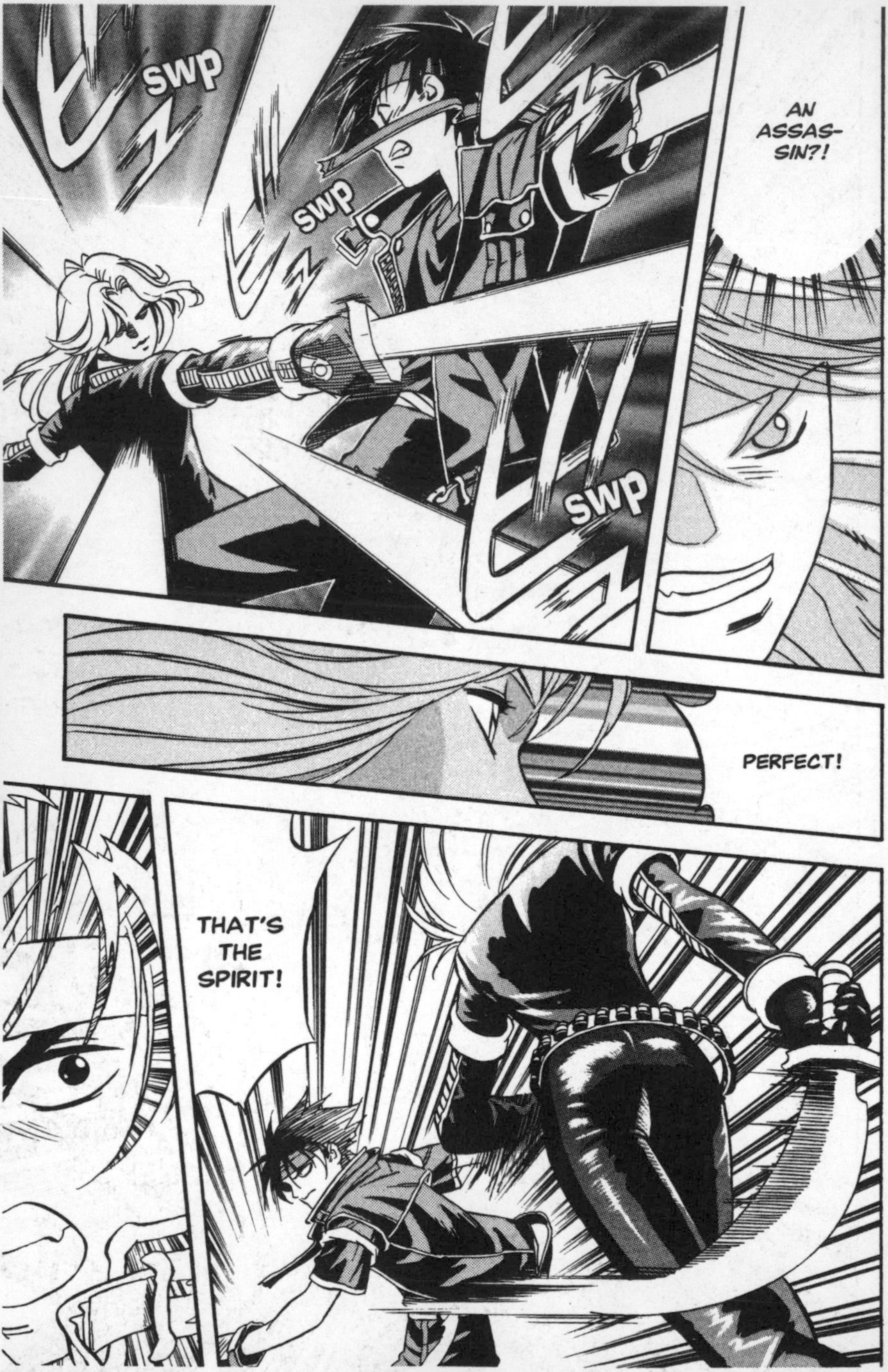
AN ASSAS-
SIN?!
SWP
SWP
SWP
PERFECT!
THAT'S THE SPIRIT!

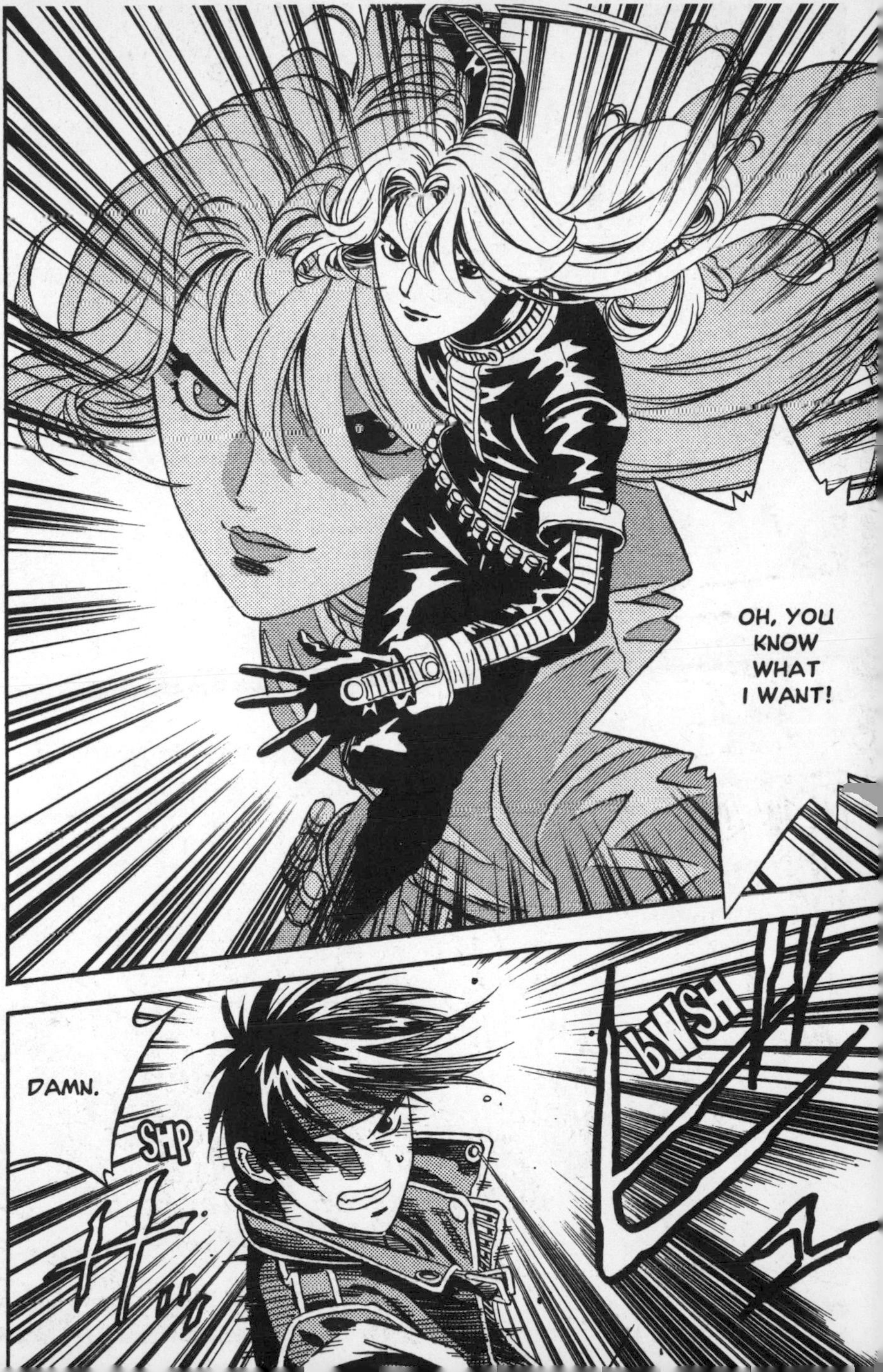

OH, YOU KNOW WHAT I WANT!
BWSH
DAMN.
SHP

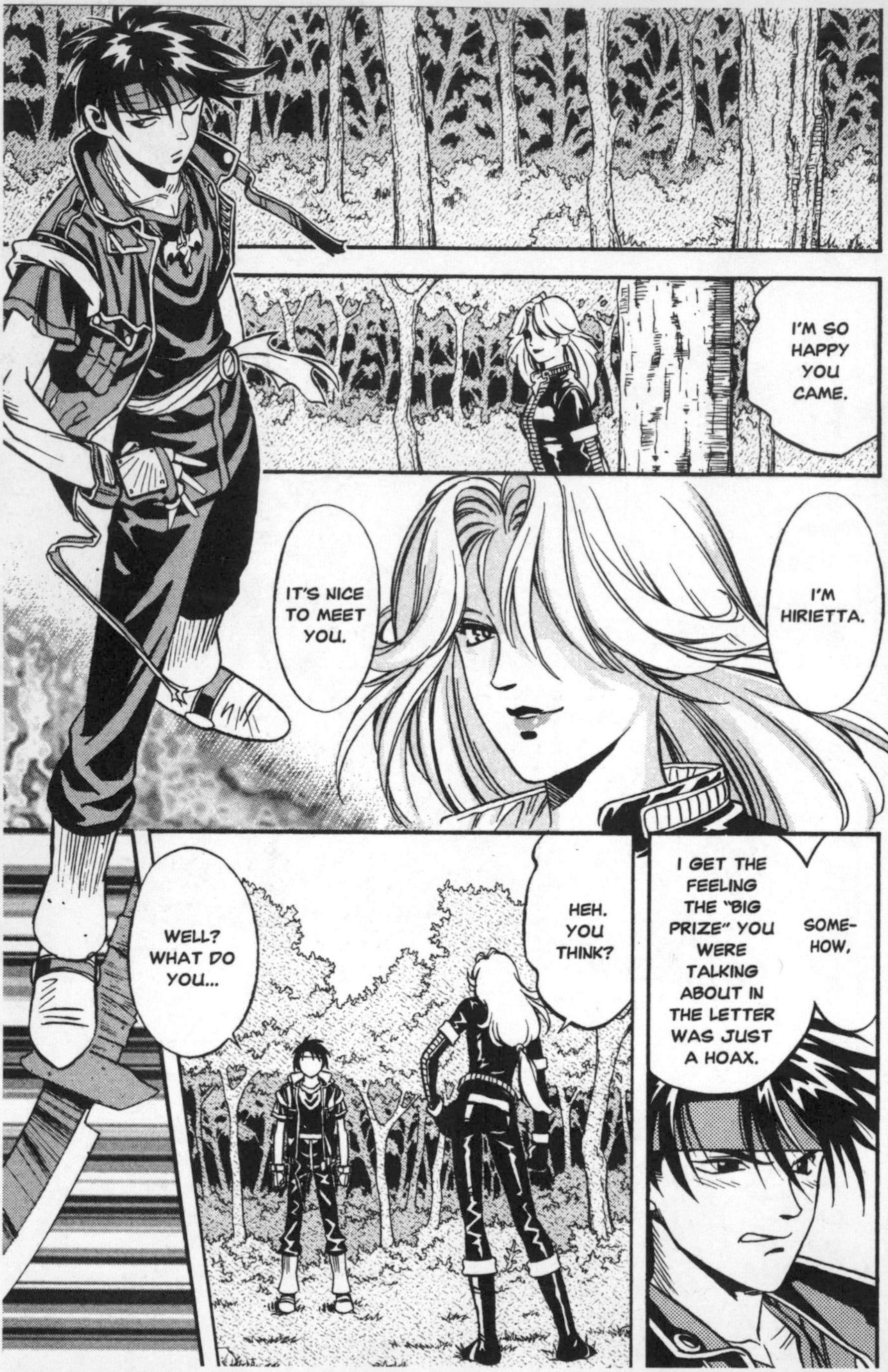
I'M SO HAPPY YOU CAME.
I'M HIRIETTA.
IT'S NICE TO MEET YOU.
SOME-HOW,
I GET THE FEELING THE "BIG PRIZE" YOU WERE TALKING ABOUT IN THE LETTER WAS JUST A HOAX.
HEH. YOU THINK?
WELL? WHAT DO YOU...

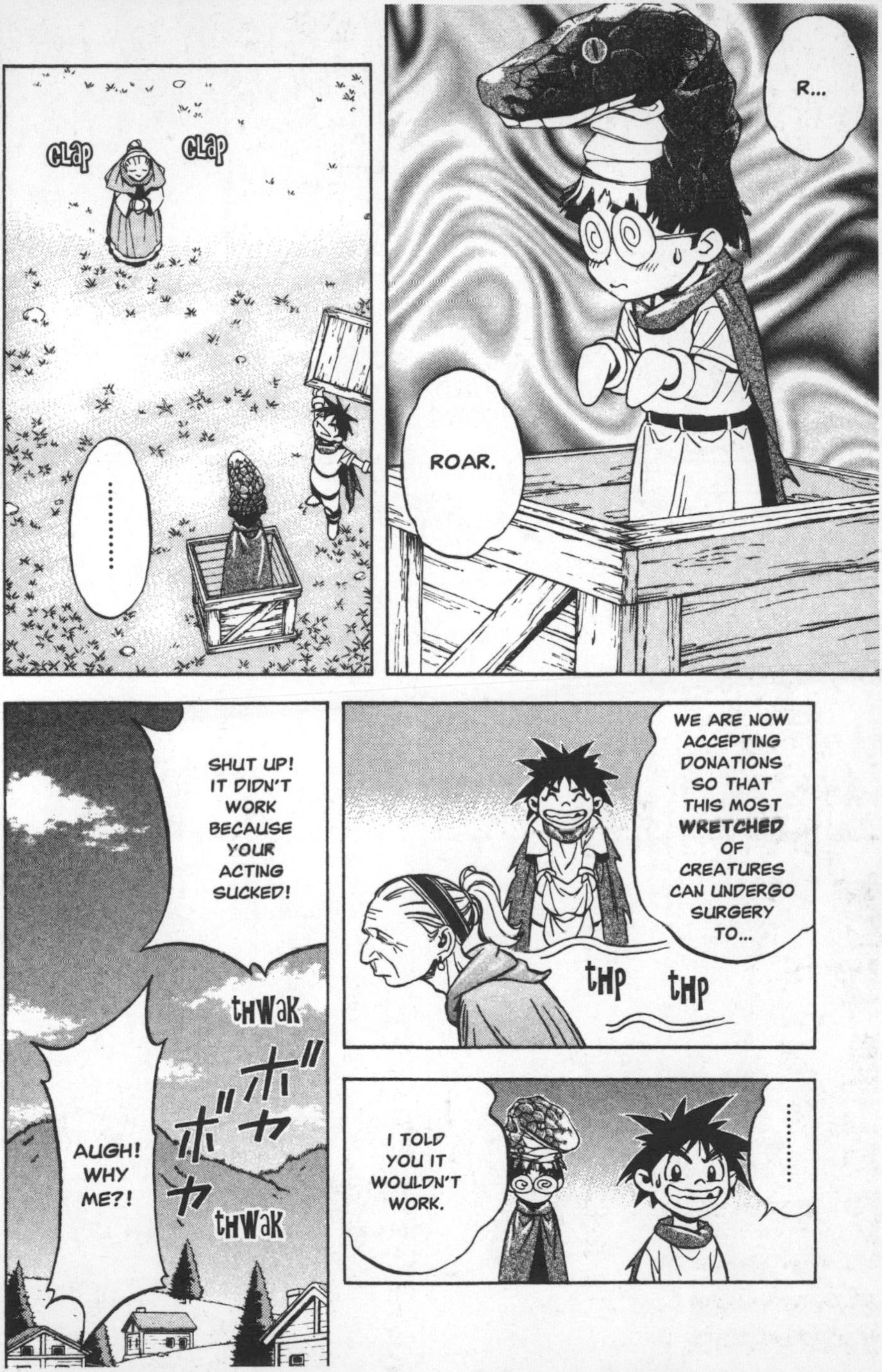
R...
ROAR.
CLAP
CLAP
......
WE ARE NOW ACCEPTING DONATIONS SO THAT THIS MOST WRETCHED OF CREATURES CAN UNDERGO SURGERY TO...
THP
THP
......
I TOLD YOU IT WOULDN'T WORK.
SHUT UP! IT DIDN'T WORK BECAUSE YOUR ACTING SUCKED!
THWAK
ボカ
ボカ
THWAK
AUGH! WHY ME?!

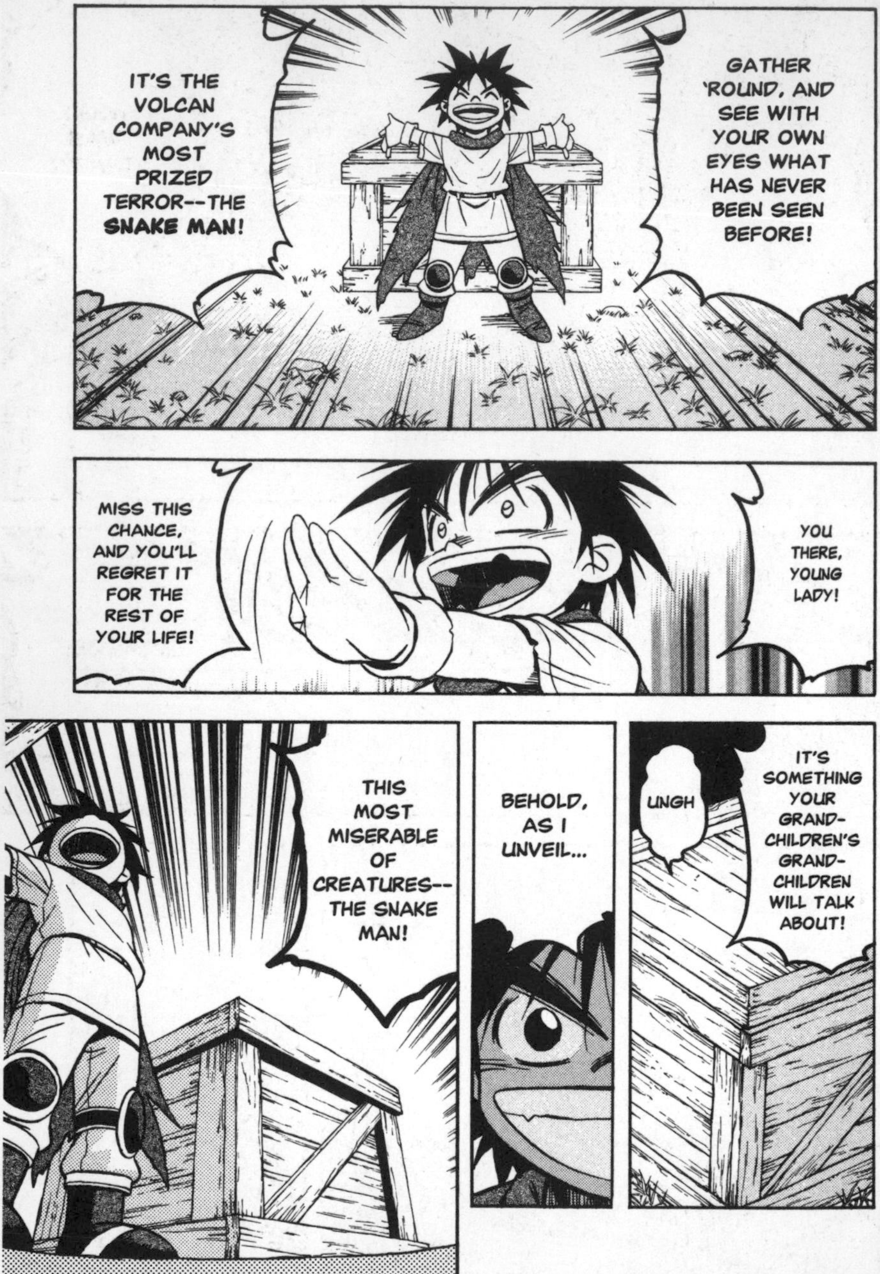
GATHER 'ROUND, AND SEE WITH YOUR OWN EYES WHAT HAS NEVER BEEN SEEN BEFORE!
IT'S THE VOLCAN COMPANY'S MOST PRIZED TERROR--THE SNAKE MAN!
YOU THERE, YOUNG LADY!
MISS THIS CHANCE, AND YOU'LL REGRET IT FOR THE REST OF YOUR LIFE!
IT'S SOMETHING YOUR GRAND-CHILDREN'S GRAND-CHILDREN WILL TALK ABOUT!
UNGH
BEHOLD, AS I UNVEIL...
THIS MOST MISERABLE OF CREATURES--THE SNAKE MAN!

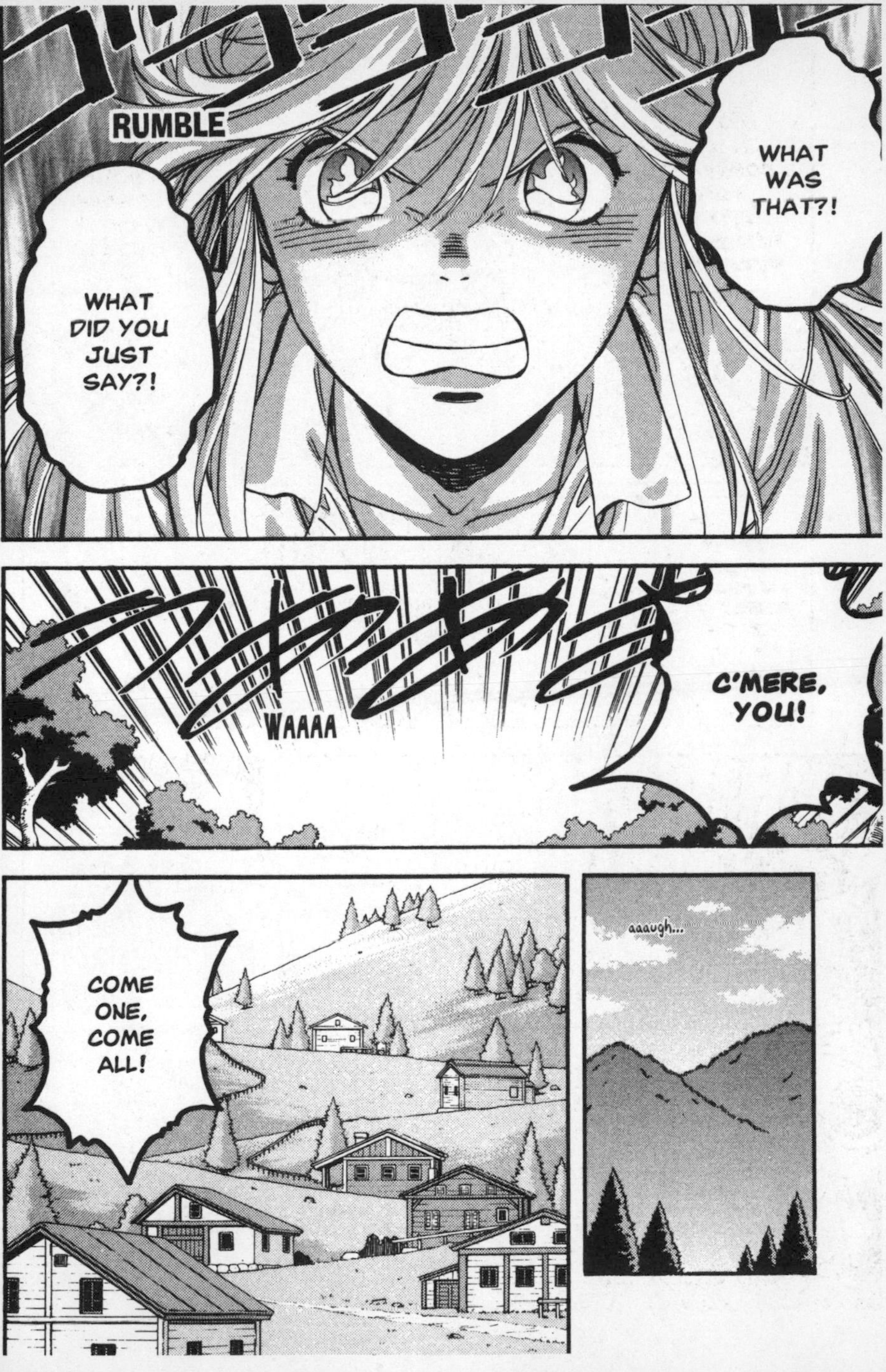
RUMBLE
WHAT WAS THAT?!
WHAT DID YOU JUST SAY?!
C'MERE, YOU!
WAAAA
aaaugh...
COME ONE, COME ALL!

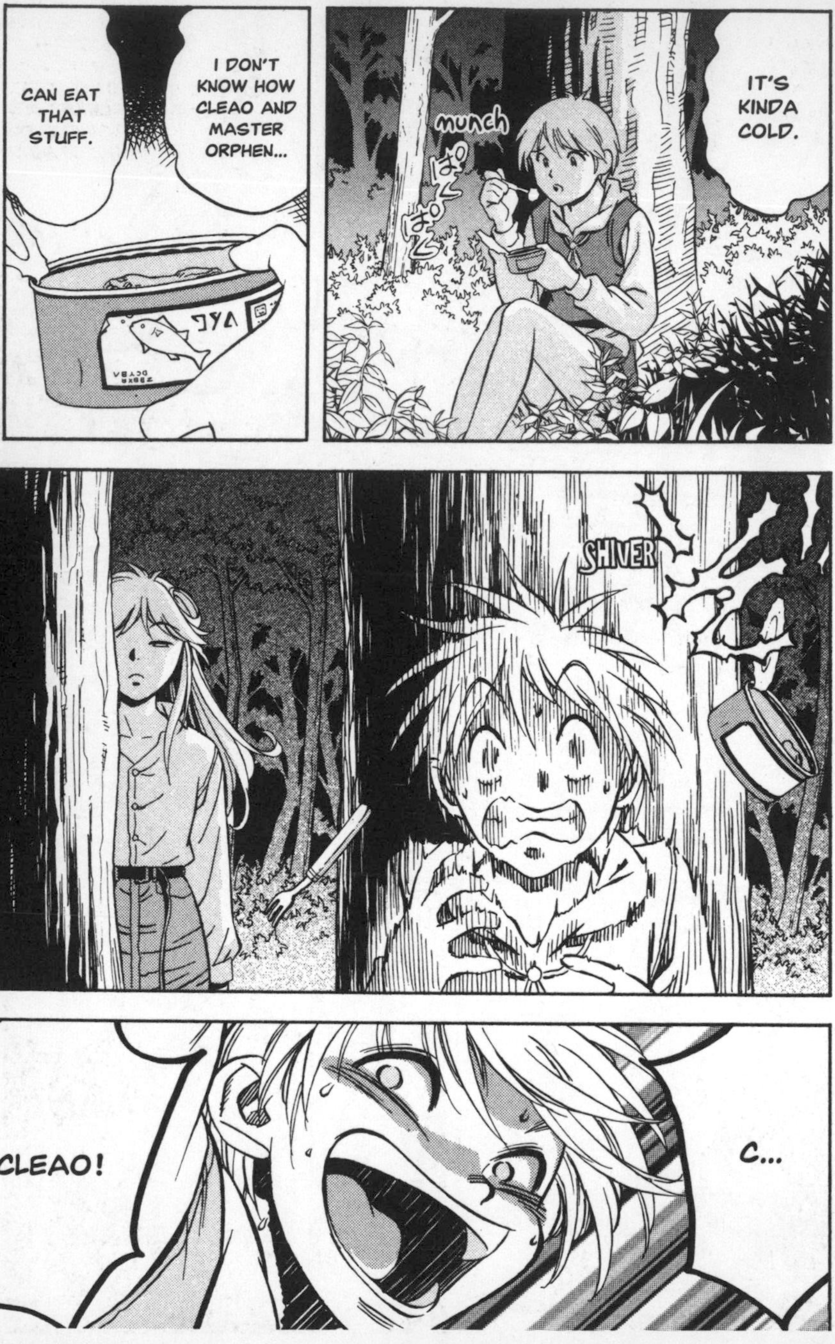
IT'S KINDA COLD.
munch
ぱくぱく
I DON'T KNOW HOW CLEAO AND MASTER ORPHEN...
CAN EAT THAT STUFF.
SHIVER
C...
CLEAO!

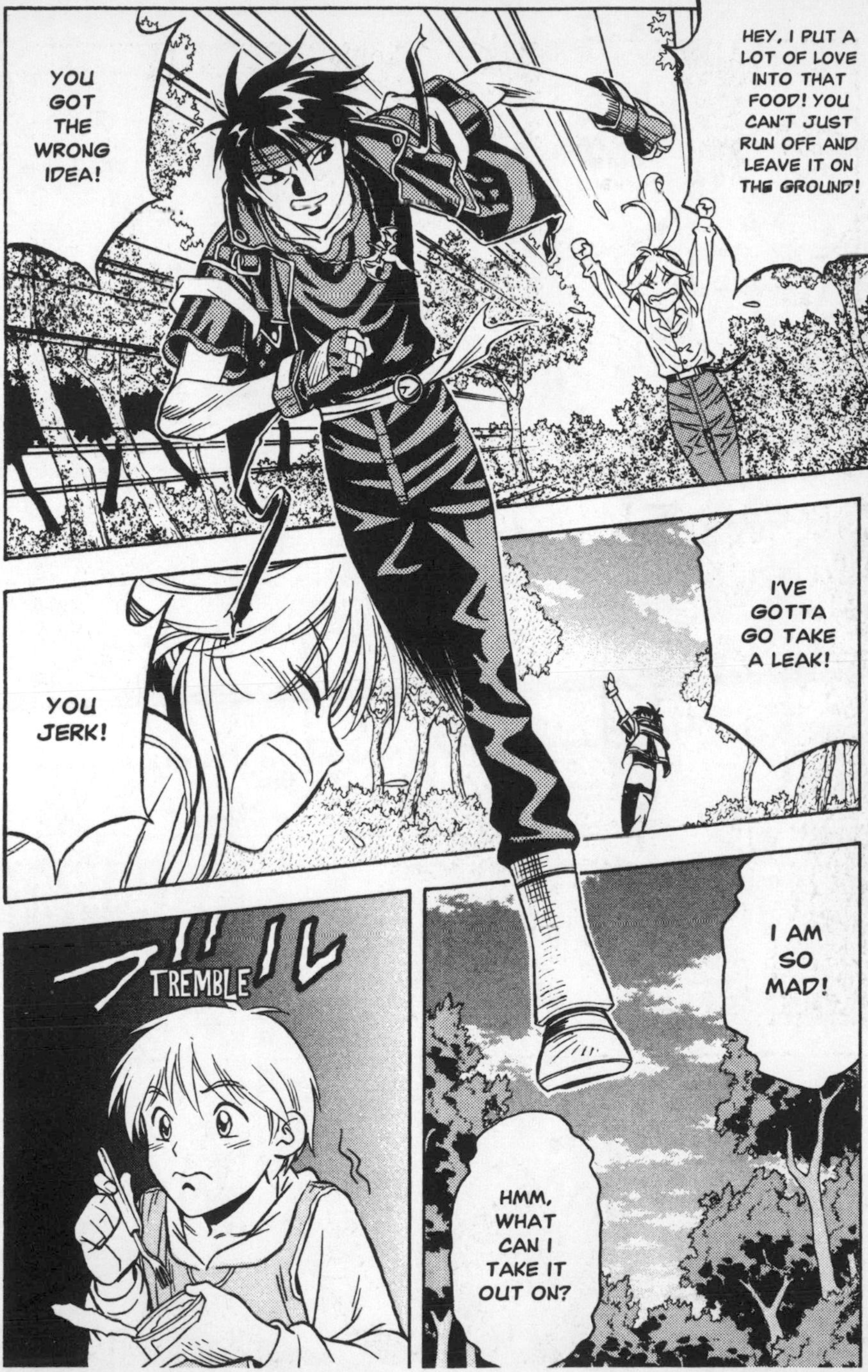
HEY, I PUT A LOT OF LOVE INTO THAT FOOD! YOU CAN'T JUST RUN OFF AND LEAVE IT ON THE GROUND!
YOU GOT THE WRONG IDEA!
I'VE GOTTA GO TAKE A LEAK!
YOU JERK!
TREMBLE
I AM SO MAD!
HMM, WHAT CAN I TAKE IT OUT ON?

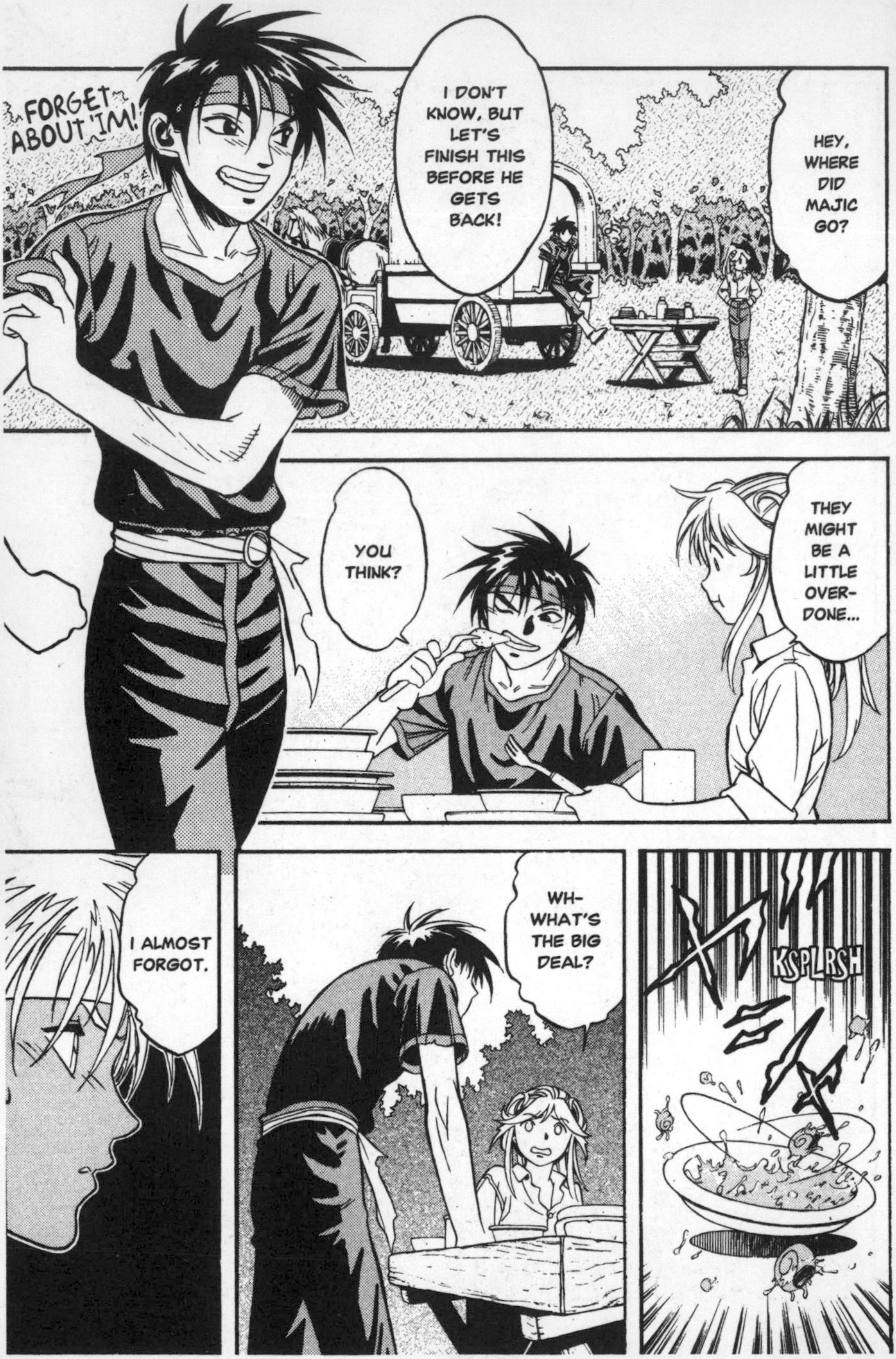
HEY, WHERE DID MAJIC GO?
I DON'T KNOW, BUT LET'S FINISH THIS BEFORE HE GETS BACK!
FORGET ABOUT 'IM!
THEY MIGHT BE A LITTLE OVER-DONE...
YOU THINK?
KSPLRSH
WH-WHAT'S THE BIG DEAL?
I ALMOST FORGOT.

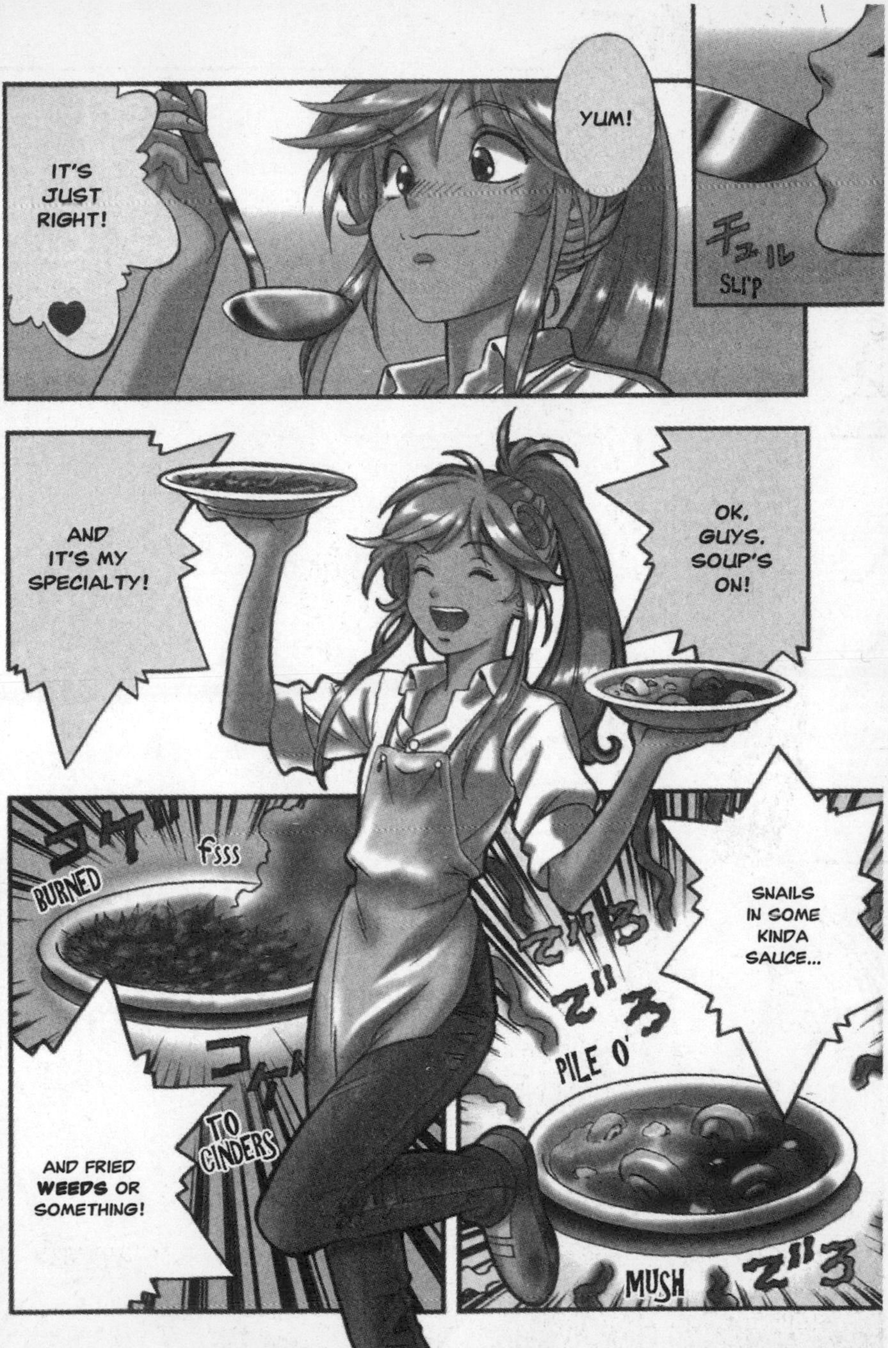
チュル
SLI'P
YUM!
IT'S JUST RIGHT!
OK, GUYS. SOUP'S ON!
AND IT'S MY SPECIALTY!
SNAILS IN SOME KINDA SAUCE...
PILE O'
MUSH
fsss
BURNED
TO CINDERS
AND FRIED WEEDS OR SOMETHING!

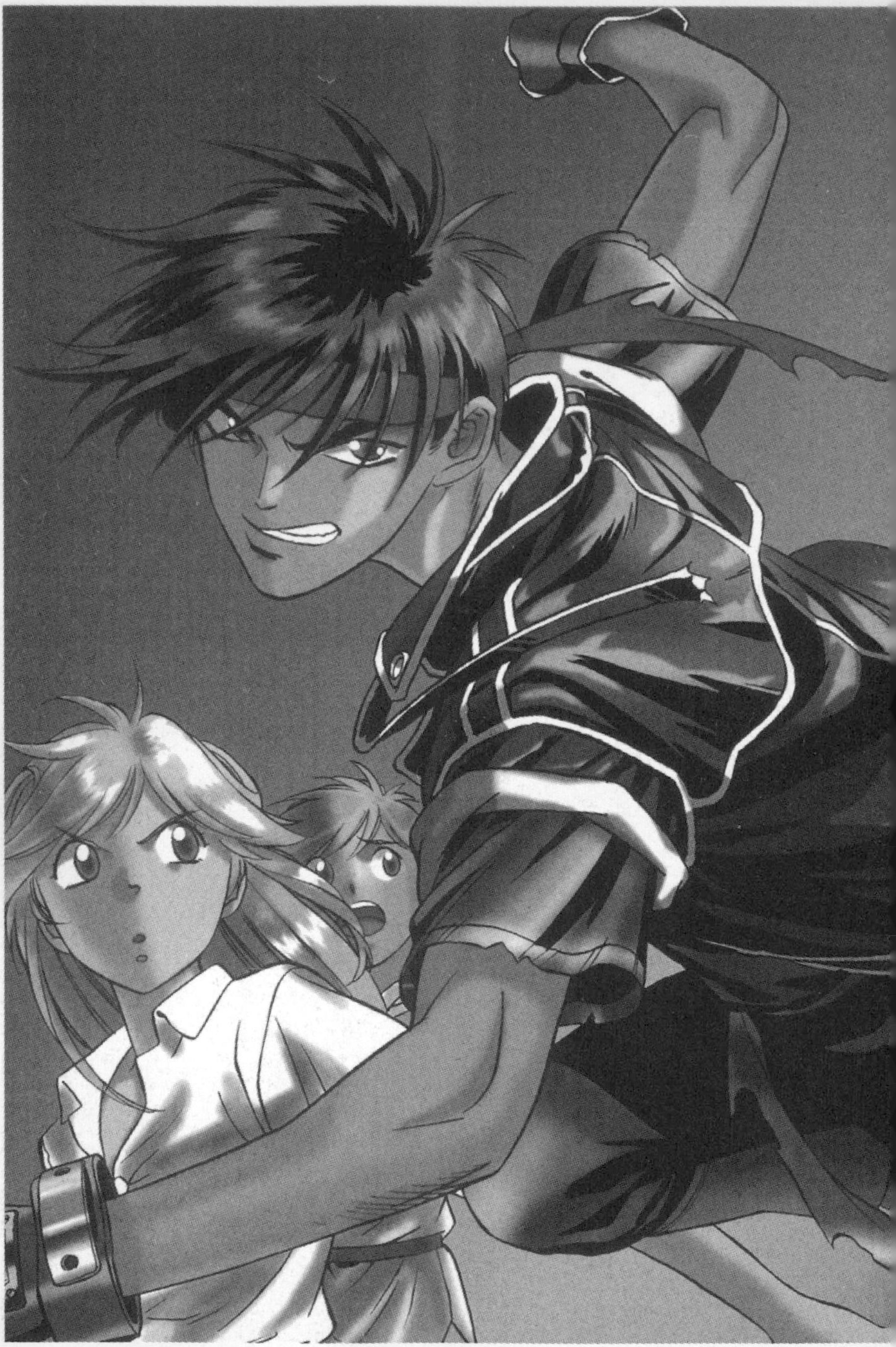

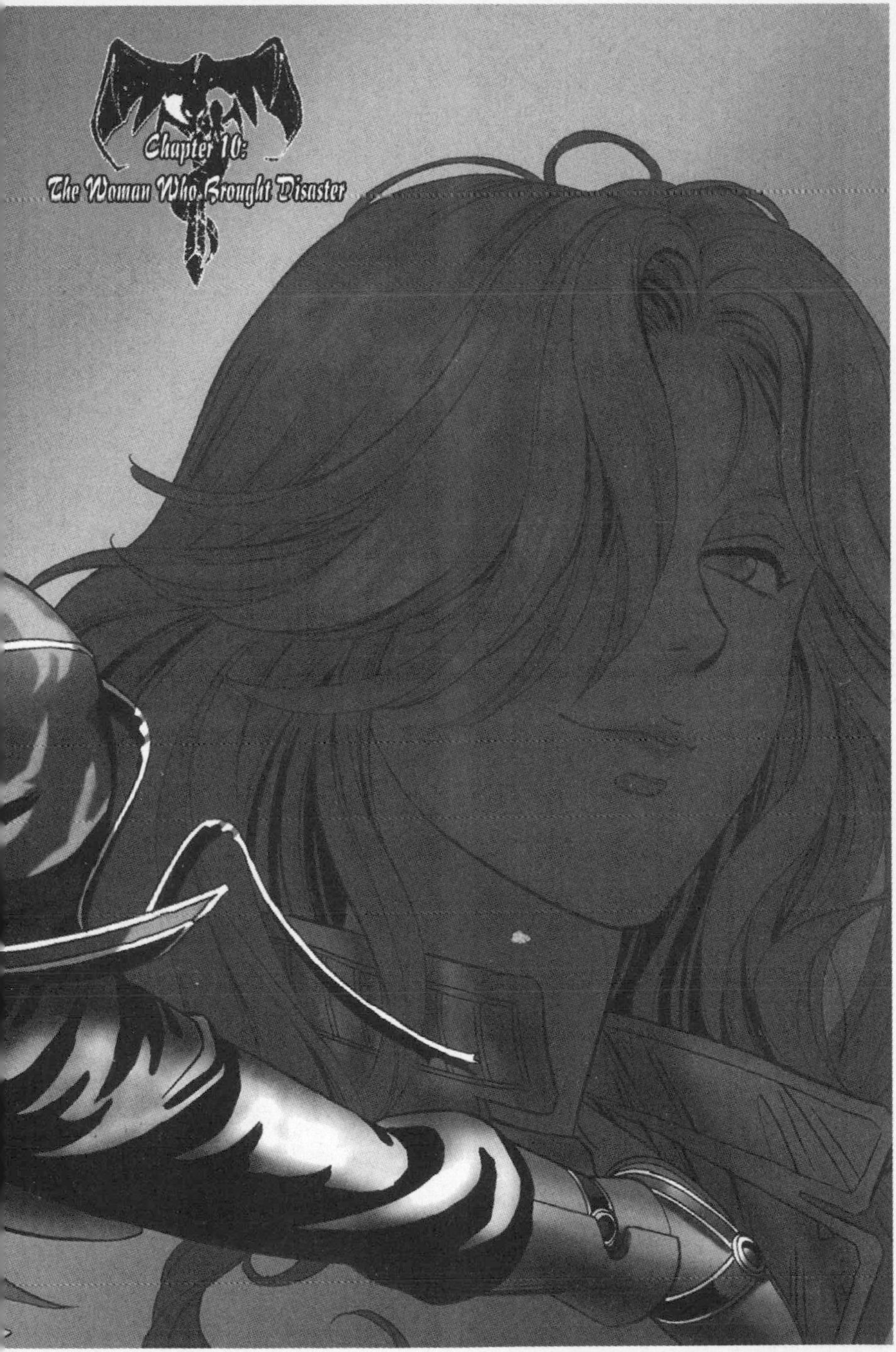
Chapter 10:
The Woman Who Brought Disaster

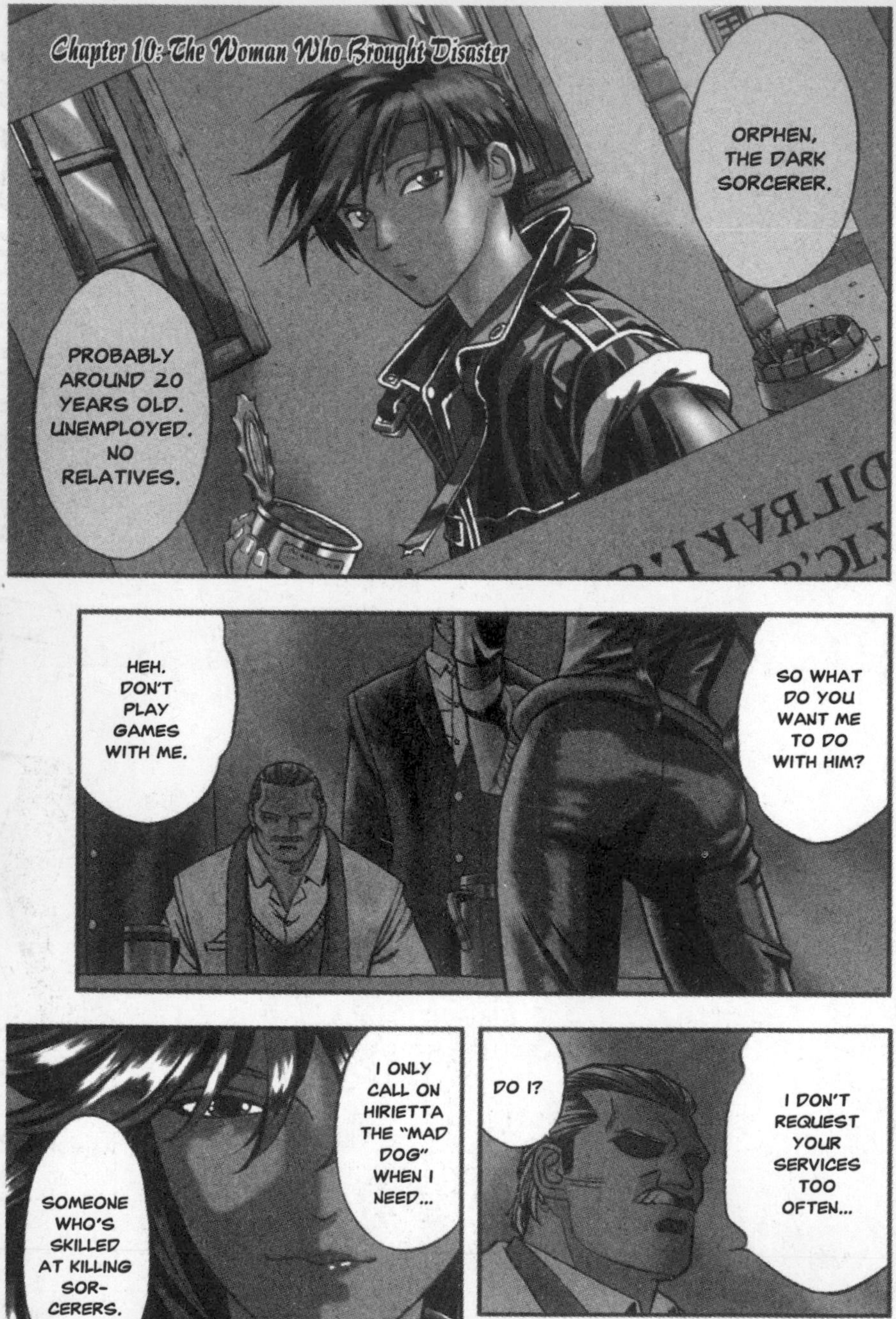
Chapter 10: The Woman Who Brought Disaster
ORPHEN, THE DARK SORCERER.
PROBABLY AROUND 20 YEARS OLD. UNEMPLOYED. NO RELATIVES.
SO WHAT DO YOU WANT ME TO DO WITH HIM?
HEH. DON'T PLAY GAMES WITH ME.
I DON'T REQUEST YOUR SERVICES TOO OFTEN...
DO I?
I ONLY CALL ON HIRIETTA THE "MAD DOG" WHEN I NEED...
SOMEONE WHO'S SKILLED AT KILLING SOR-CERERS.

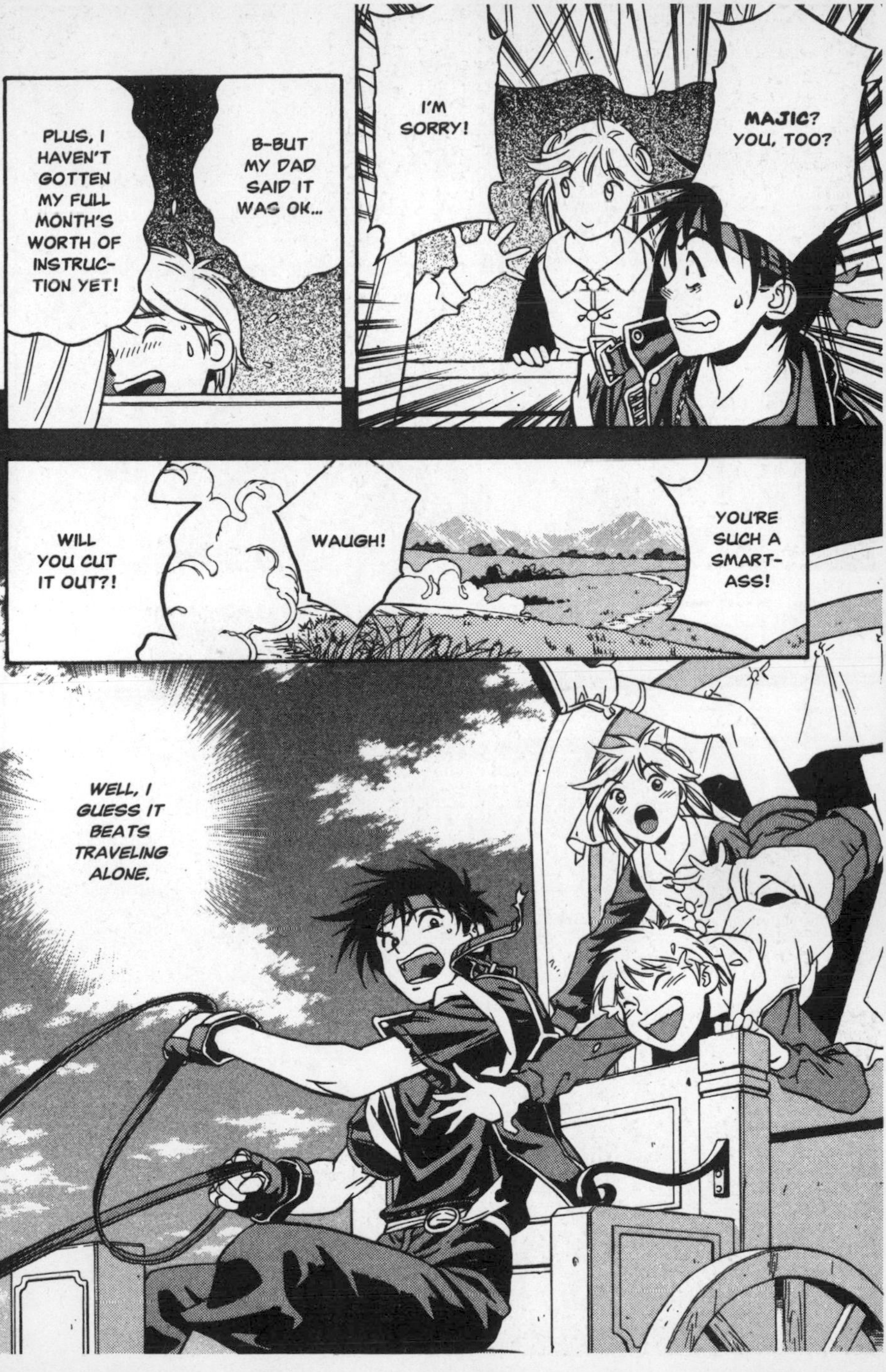
MAJIC? YOU, TOO?
I'M SORRY!
B-BUT MY DAD SAID IT WAS OK...
PLUS, I HAVEN'T GOTTEN MY FULL MONTH'S WORTH OF INSTRUC-TION YET!
YOU'RE SUCH A SMART-ASS!
WAUGH!
WILL YOU CUT IT OUT?!
WELL, I GUESS IT BEATS TRAVELING ALONE.

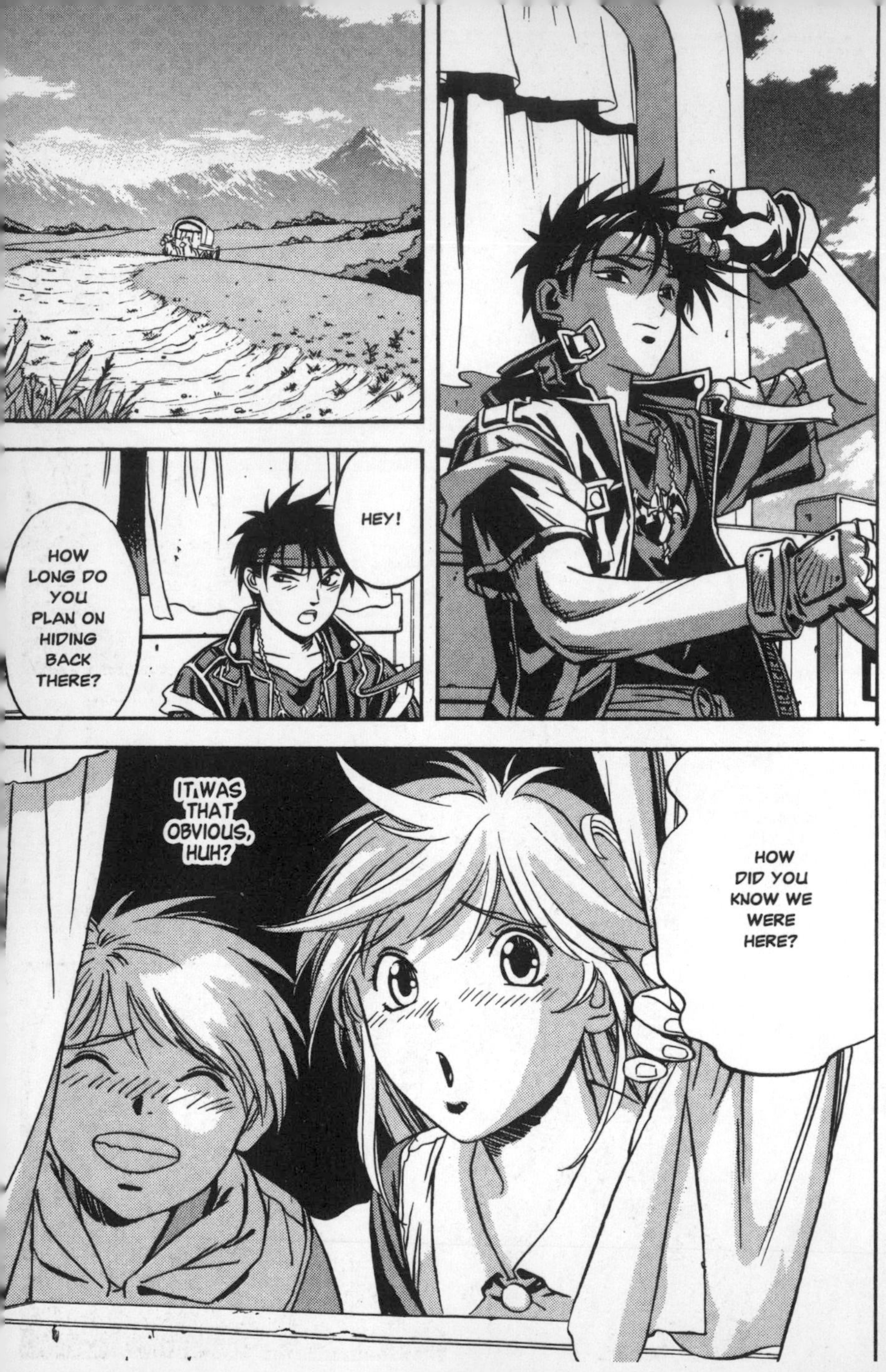
HEY!
HOW LONG DO YOU PLAN ON HIDING BACK THERE?
HOW DID YOU KNOW WE WERE HERE?
IT WAS THAT OBVIOUS, HUH?

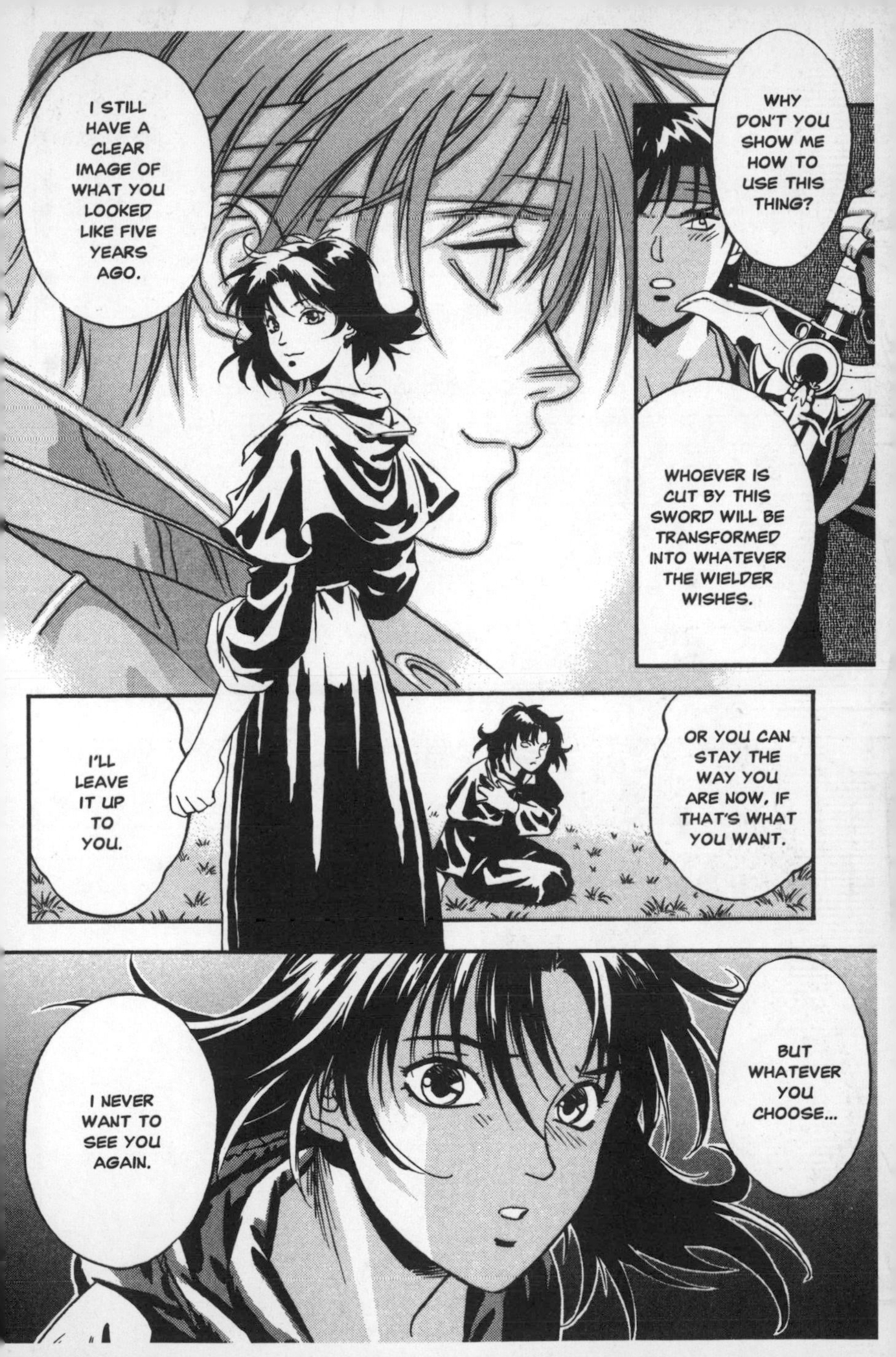
WHY DON'T YOU SHOW ME HOW TO USE THIS THING?
WHOEVER IS CUT BY THIS SWORD WILL BE TRANSFORMED INTO WHATEVER THE WIELDER WISHES.
I STILL HAVE A CLEAR IMAGE OF WHAT YOU LOOKED LIKE FIVE YEARS AGO.
OR YOU CAN STAY THE WAY YOU ARE NOW, IF THAT'S WHAT YOU WANT.
I'LL LEAVE IT UP TO YOU.
BUT WHATEVER YOU CHOOSE...
I NEVER WANT TO SEE YOU AGAIN.

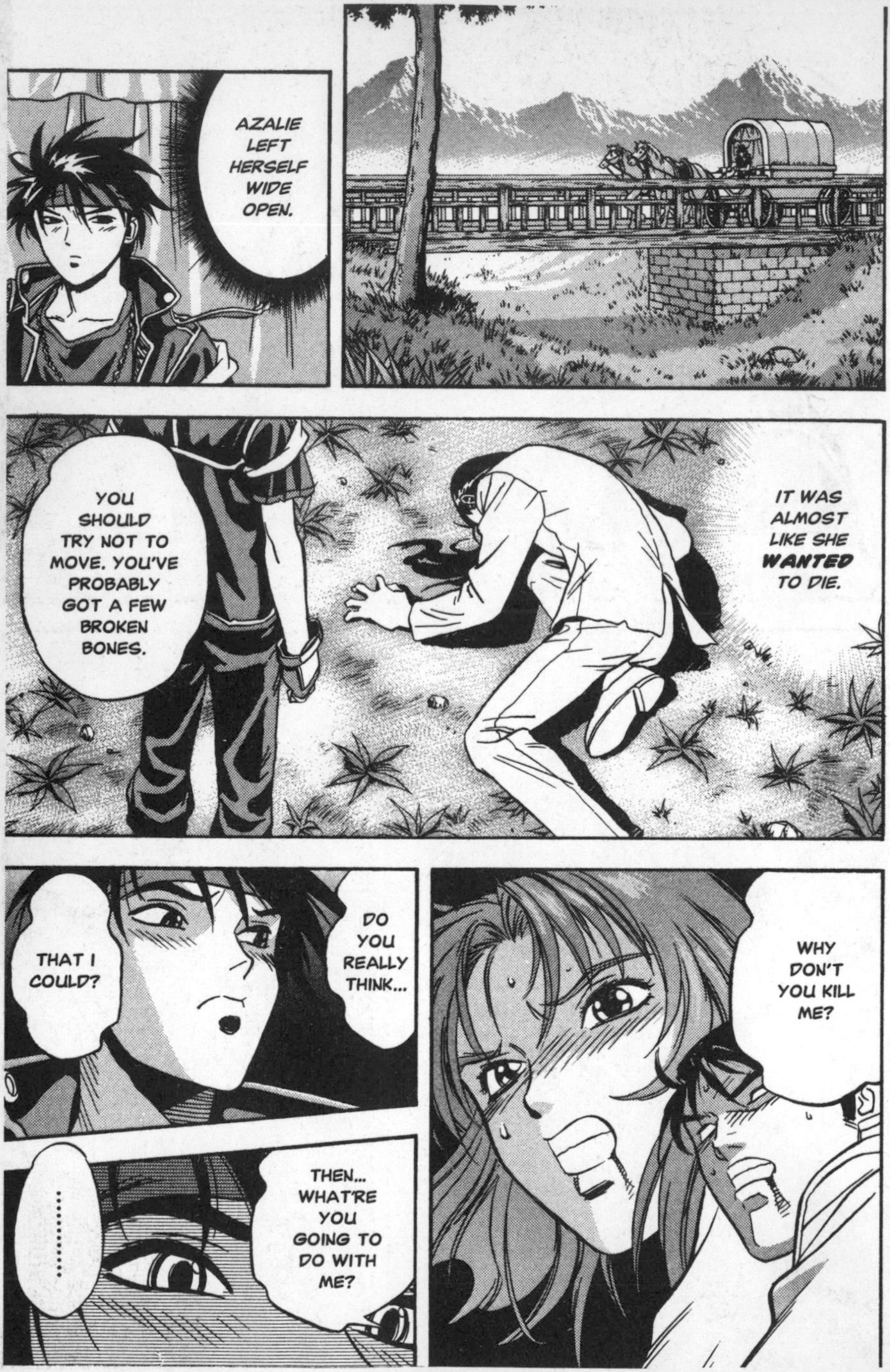

AZALIE LEFT HERSELF WIDE OPEN.
IT WAS ALMOST LIKE SHE *WANTED* TO DIE.
YOU SHOULD TRY NOT TO MOVE. YOU'VE PROBABLY GOT A FEW BROKEN BONES.
WHY DON'T YOU KILL ME?
DO YOU REALLY THINK...
THAT I COULD?
THEN... WHAT'RE YOU GOING TO DO WITH ME?
......

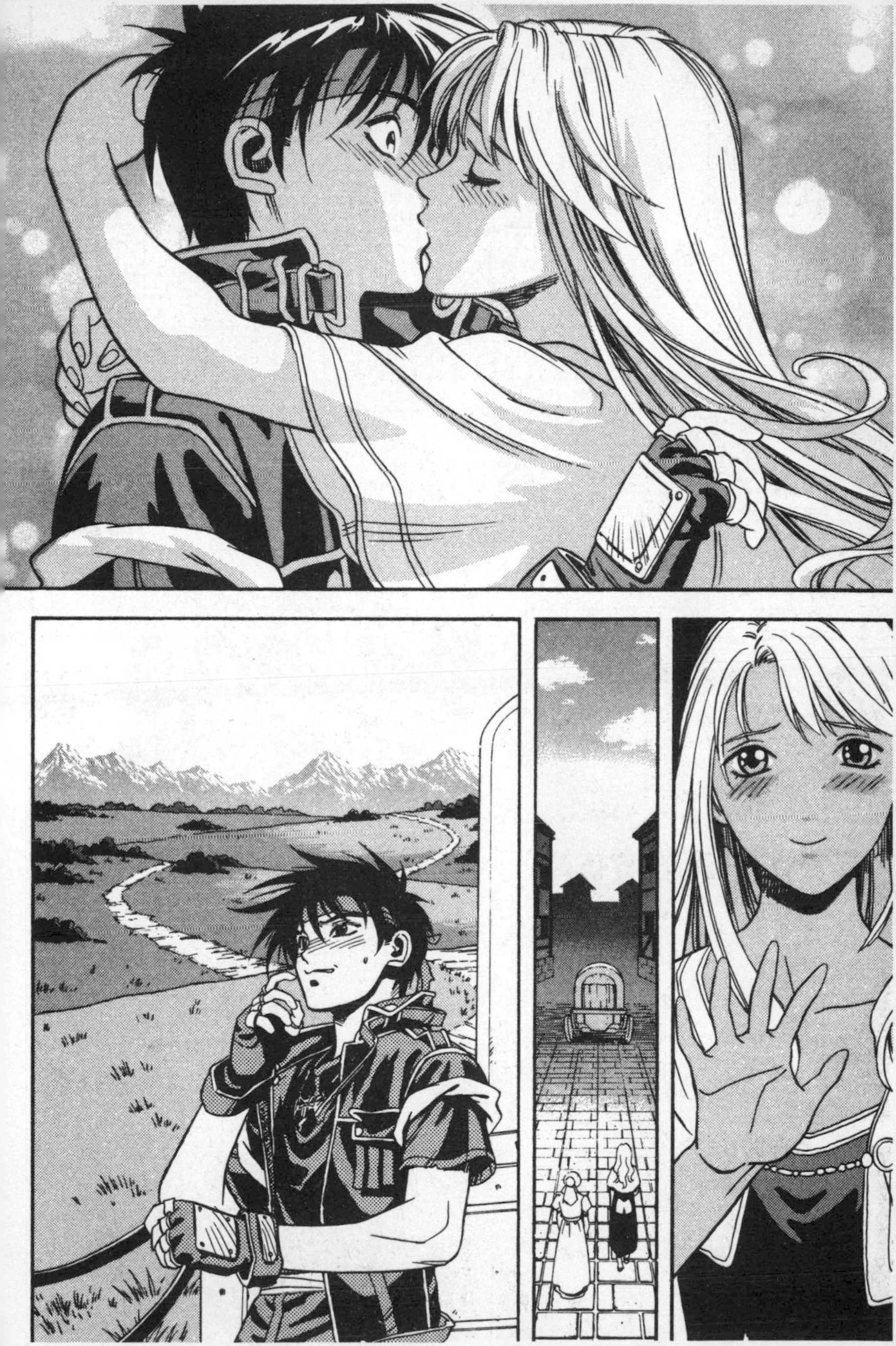

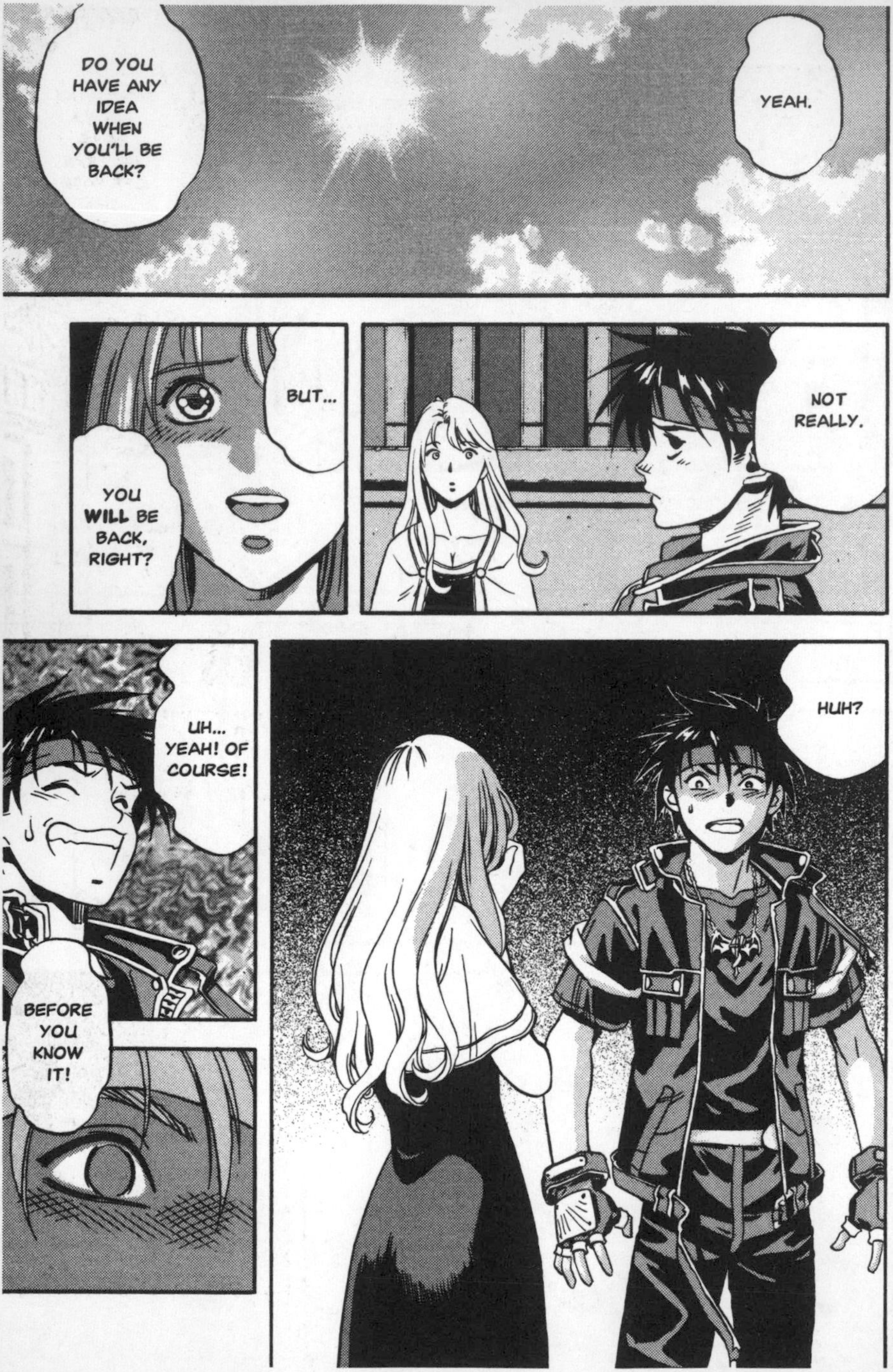
YEAH.
DO YOU HAVE ANY IDEA WHEN YOU'LL BE BACK?
NOT REALLY.
BUT...
YOU **WILL** BE BACK, RIGHT?
HUH?
UH... YEAH! OF COURSE!
BEFORE YOU KNOW IT!

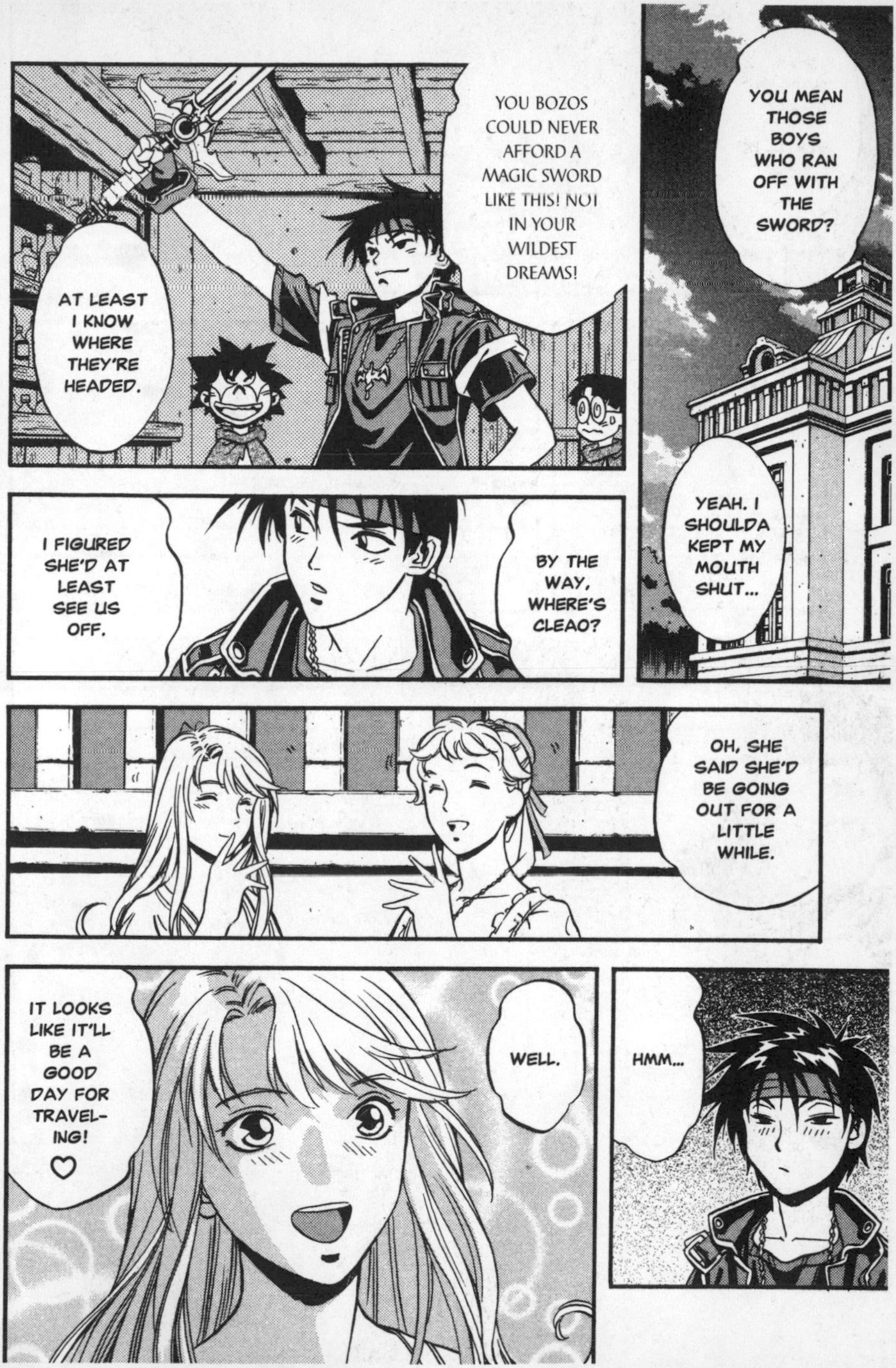

YOU BOZOS COULD NEVER AFFORD A MAGIC SWORD LIKE THIS! NOT IN YOUR WILDEST DREAMS!
AT LEAST I KNOW WHERE THEY'RE HEADED.
YOU MEAN THOSE BOYS WHO RAN OFF WITH THE SWORD?
YEAH. I SHOULDA KEPT MY MOUTH SHUT...
BY THE WAY, WHERE'S CLEAO?
I FIGURED SHE'D AT LEAST SEE US OFF.
OH, SHE SAID SHE'D BE GOING OUT FOR A LITTLE WHILE.
HMM...
WELL.
IT LOOKS LIKE IT'LL BE A GOOD DAY FOR TRAVEL-ING! ♡

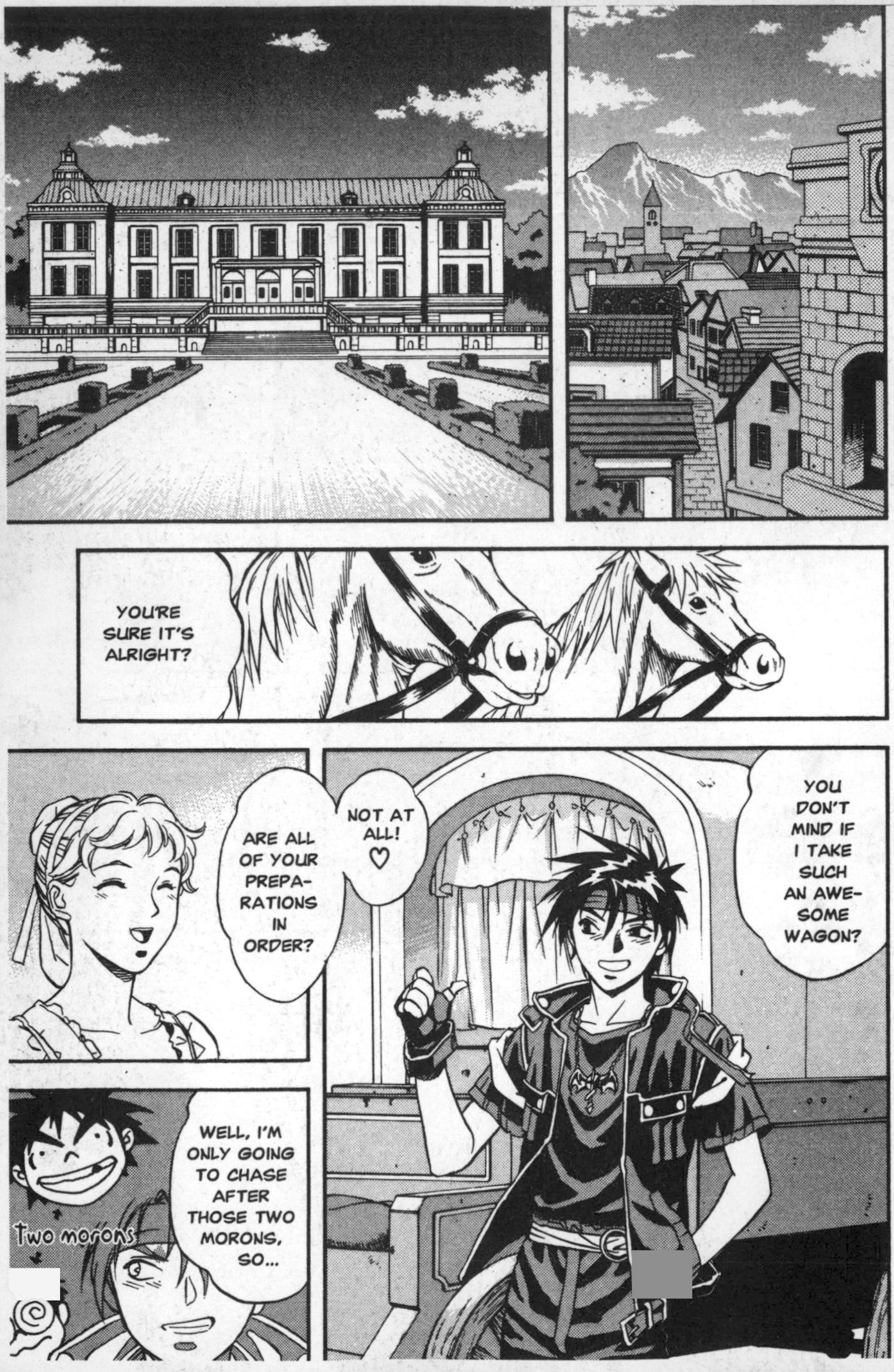
YOU'RE SURE IT'S ALRIGHT?
YOU DON'T MIND IF I TAKE SUCH AN AWE-SOME WAGON?
NOT AT ALL! ♡
ARE ALL OF YOUR PREPA-RATIONS IN ORDER?
WELL, I'M ONLY GOING TO CHASE AFTER THOSE TWO MORONS, SO...
Two morons

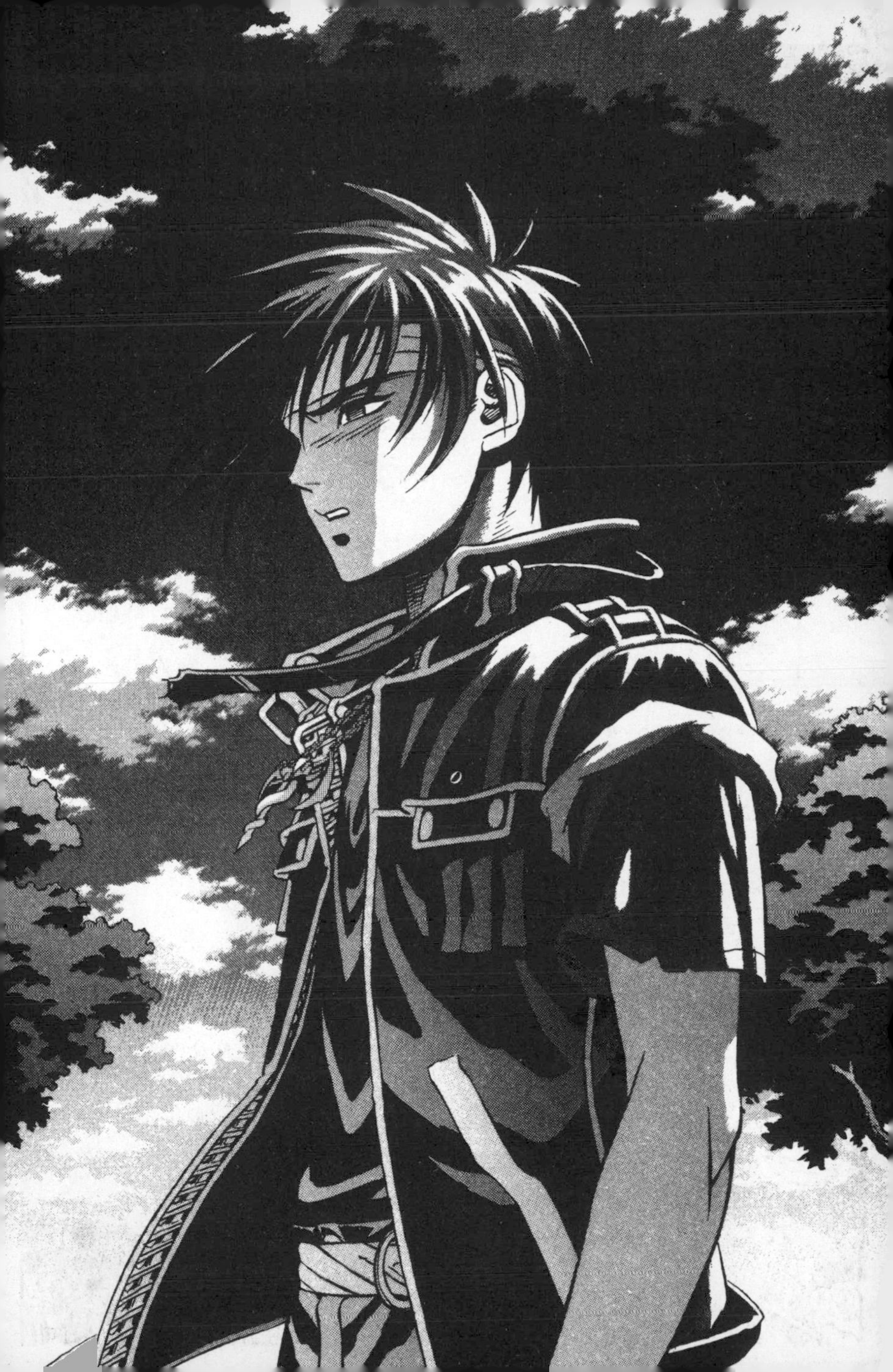

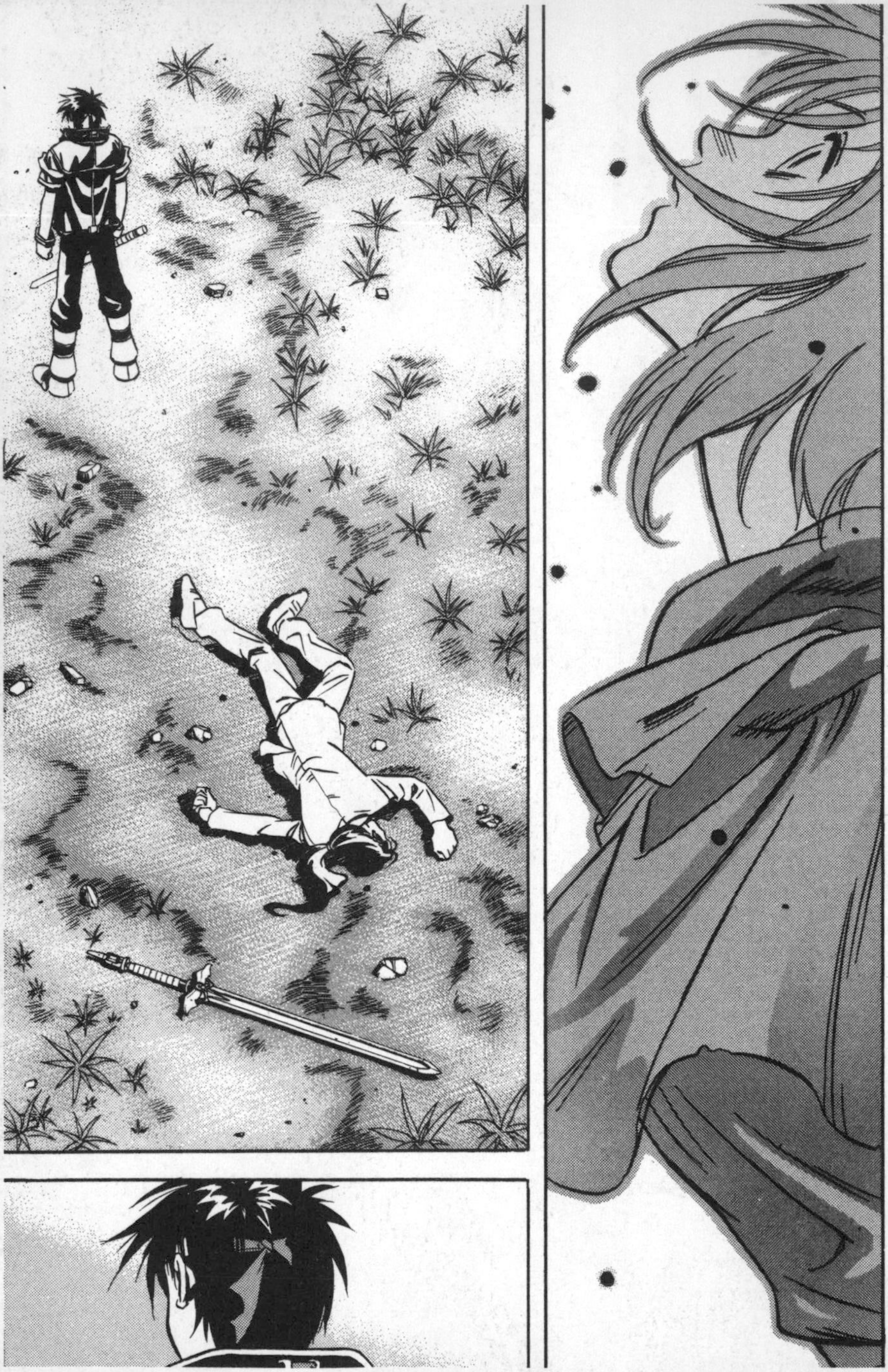

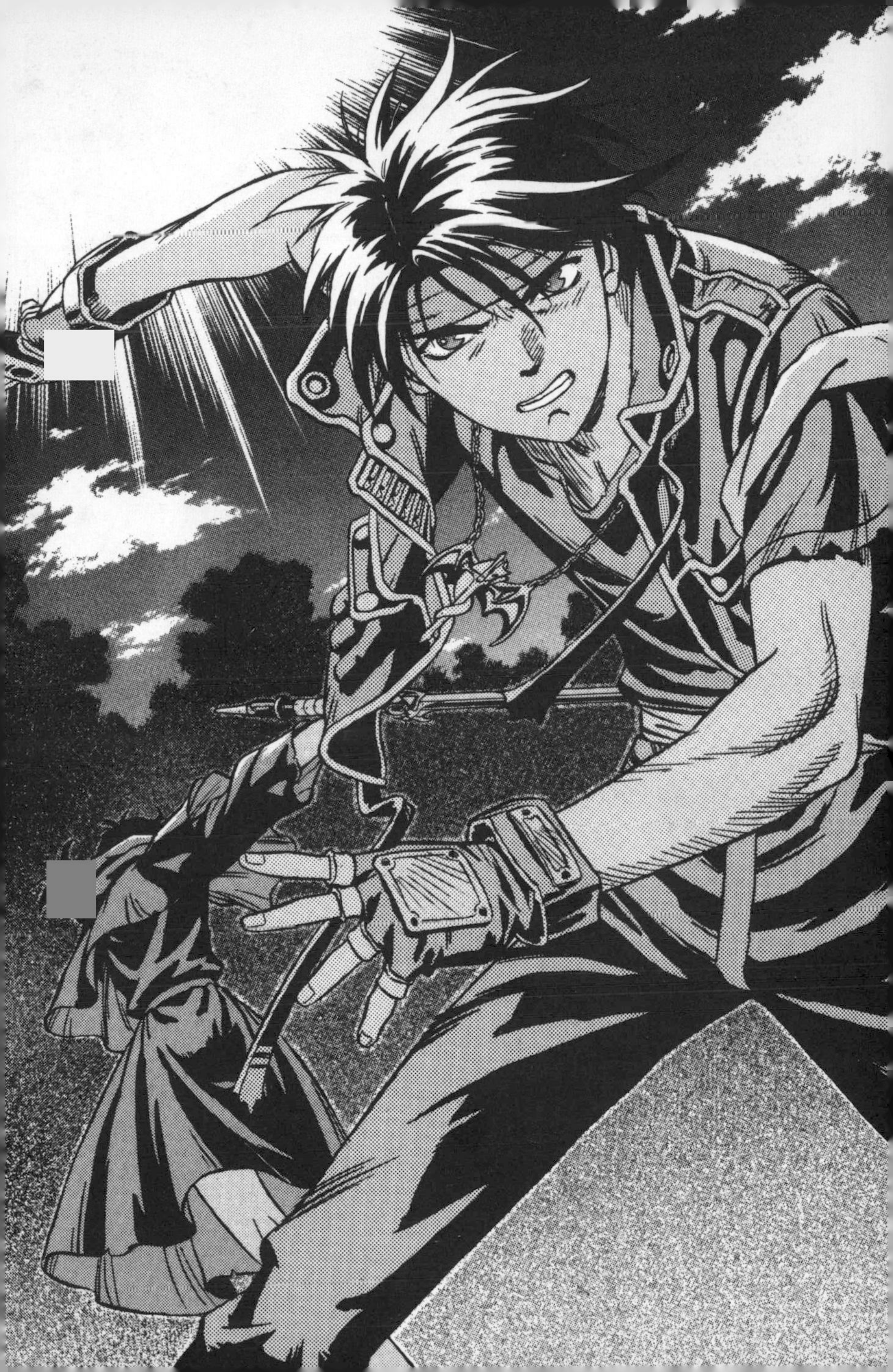

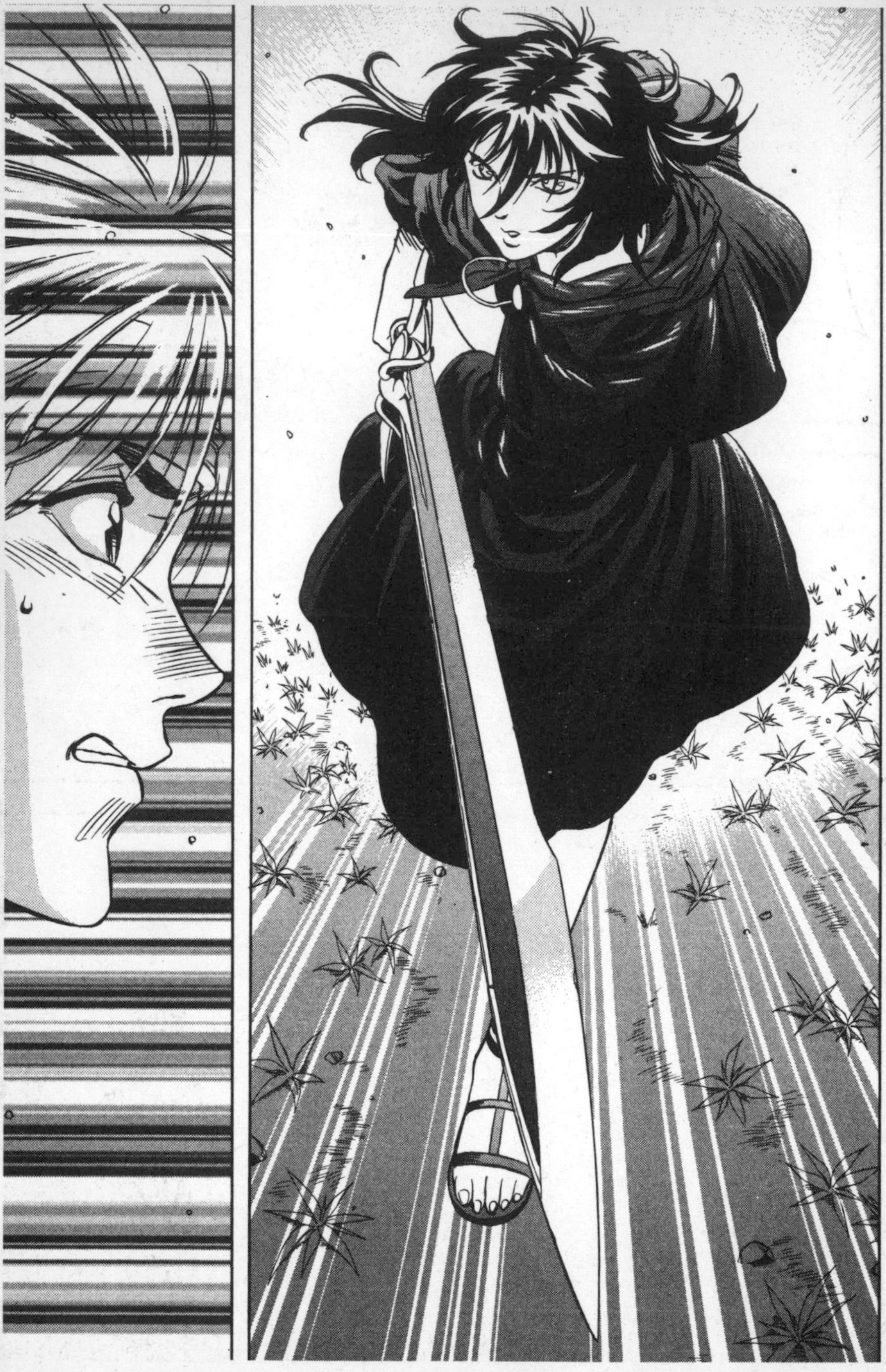

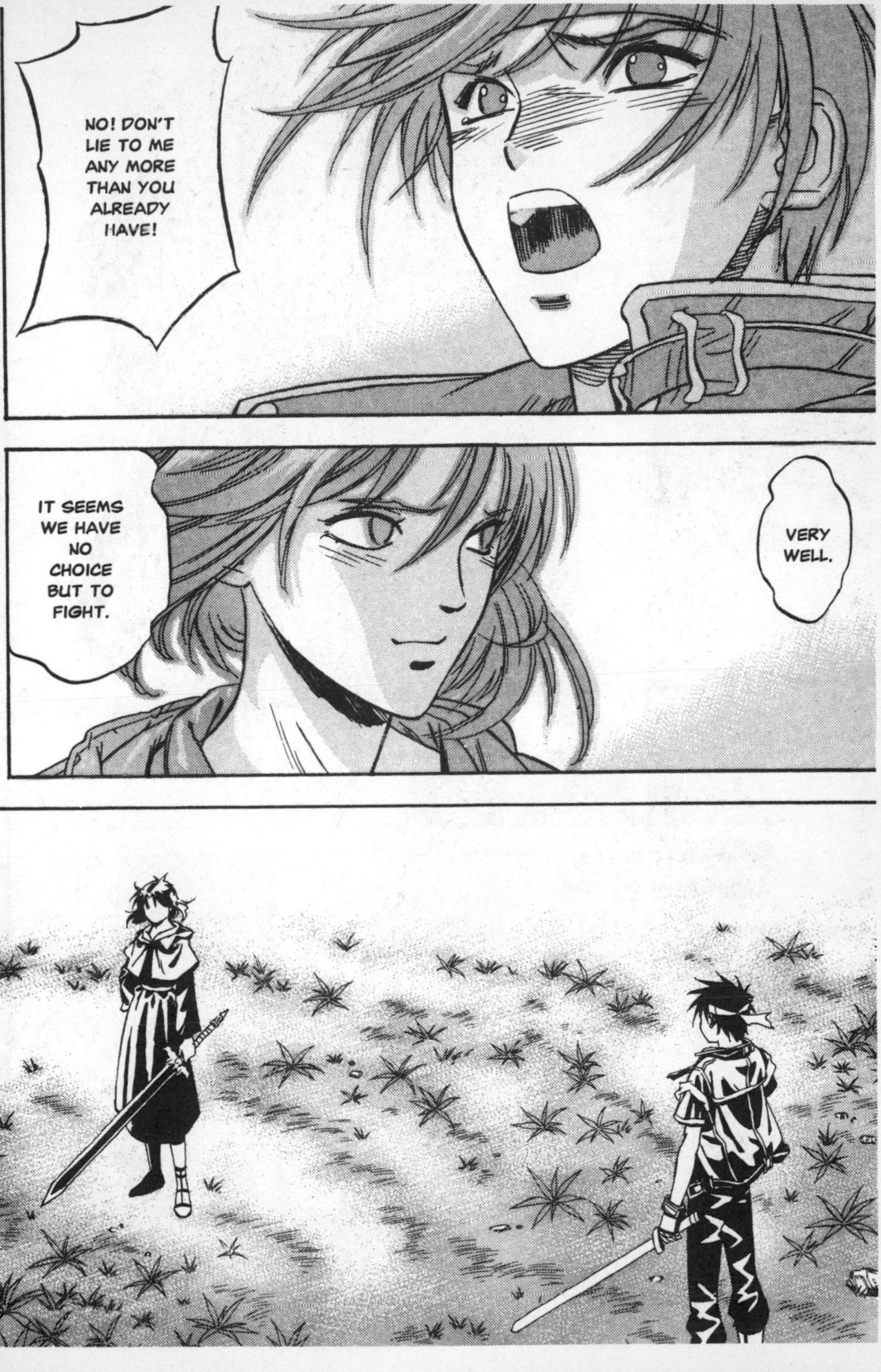
NO! DON'T LIE TO ME ANY MORE THAN YOU ALREADY HAVE!
VERY WELL.
IT SEEMS WE HAVE NO CHOICE BUT TO FIGHT.

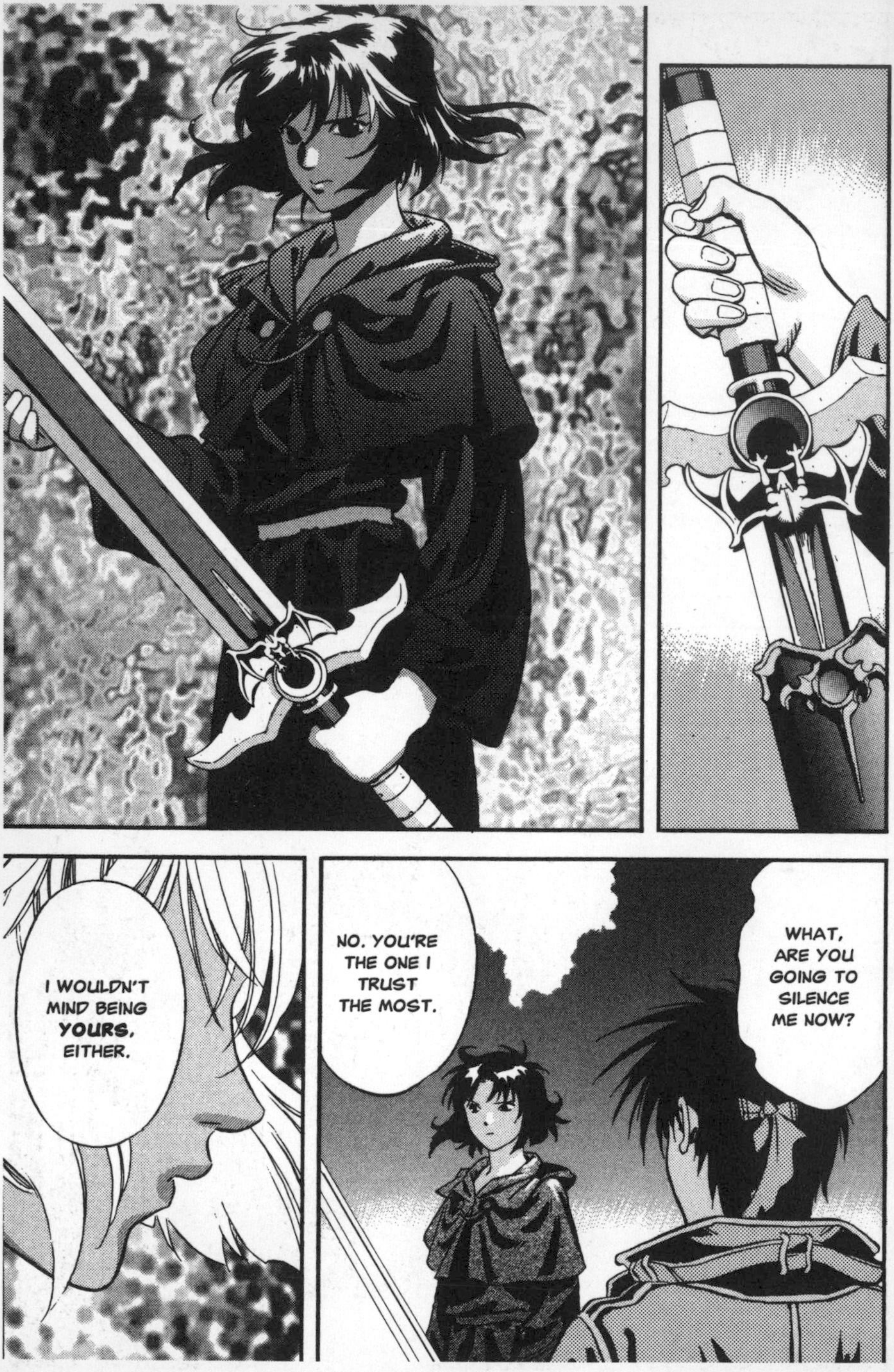
WHAT, ARE YOU GOING TO SILENCE ME NOW?
NO. YOU'RE THE ONE I TRUST THE MOST.
I WOULDN'T MIND BEING **YOURS,** EITHER.

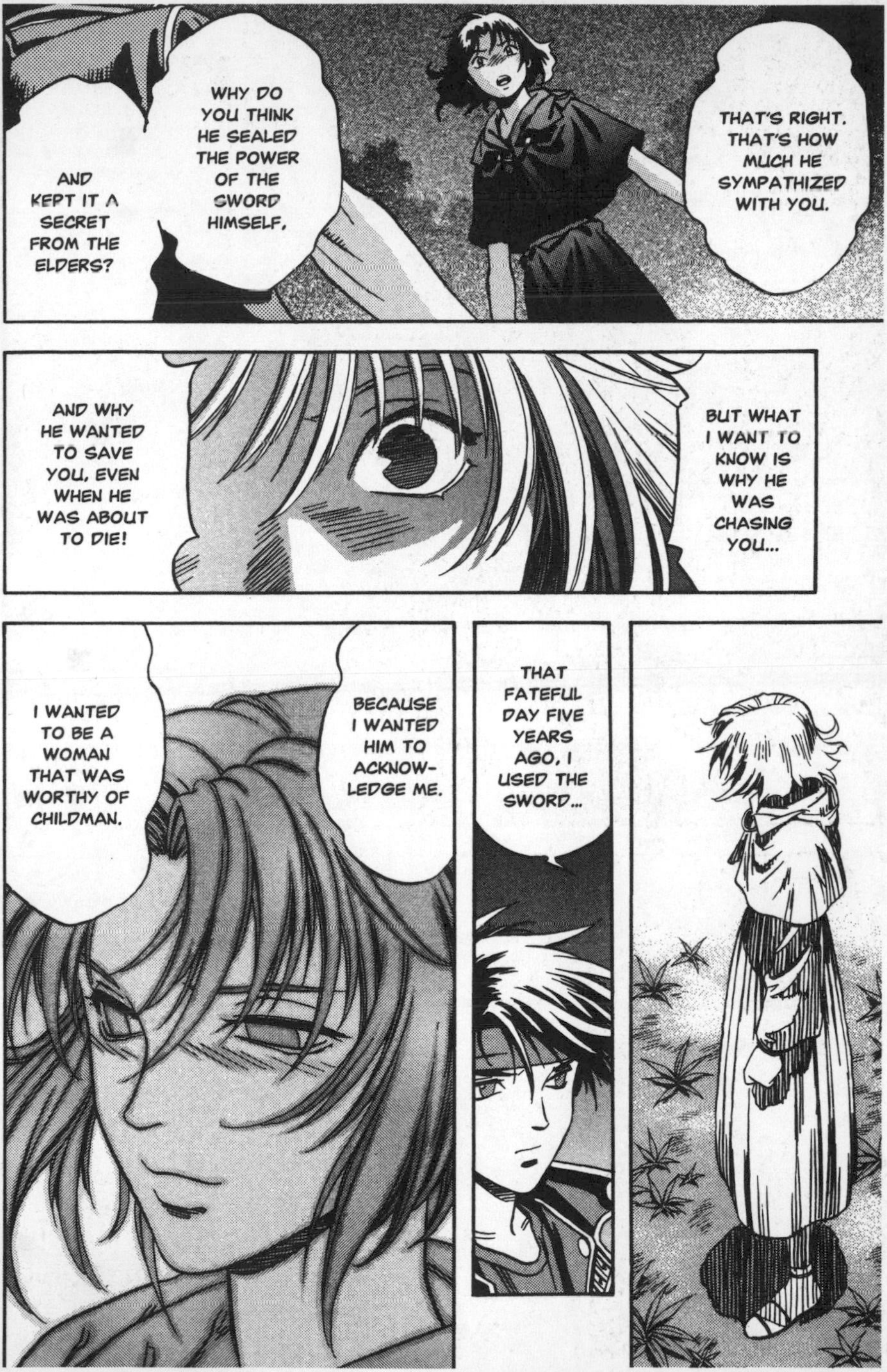
THAT'S RIGHT. THAT'S HOW MUCH HE SYMPATHIZED WITH YOU.
WHY DO YOU THINK HE SEALED THE POWER OF THE SWORD HIMSELF,
AND KEPT IT A SECRET FROM THE ELDERS?
BUT WHAT I WANT TO KNOW IS WHY HE WAS CHASING YOU...
AND WHY HE WANTED TO SAVE YOU, EVEN WHEN HE WAS ABOUT TO DIE!
THAT FATEFUL DAY FIVE YEARS AGO, I USED THE SWORD...
BECAUSE I WANTED HIM TO ACKNOW-LEDGE ME.
I WANTED TO BE A WOMAN THAT WAS WORTHY OF CHILDMAN.

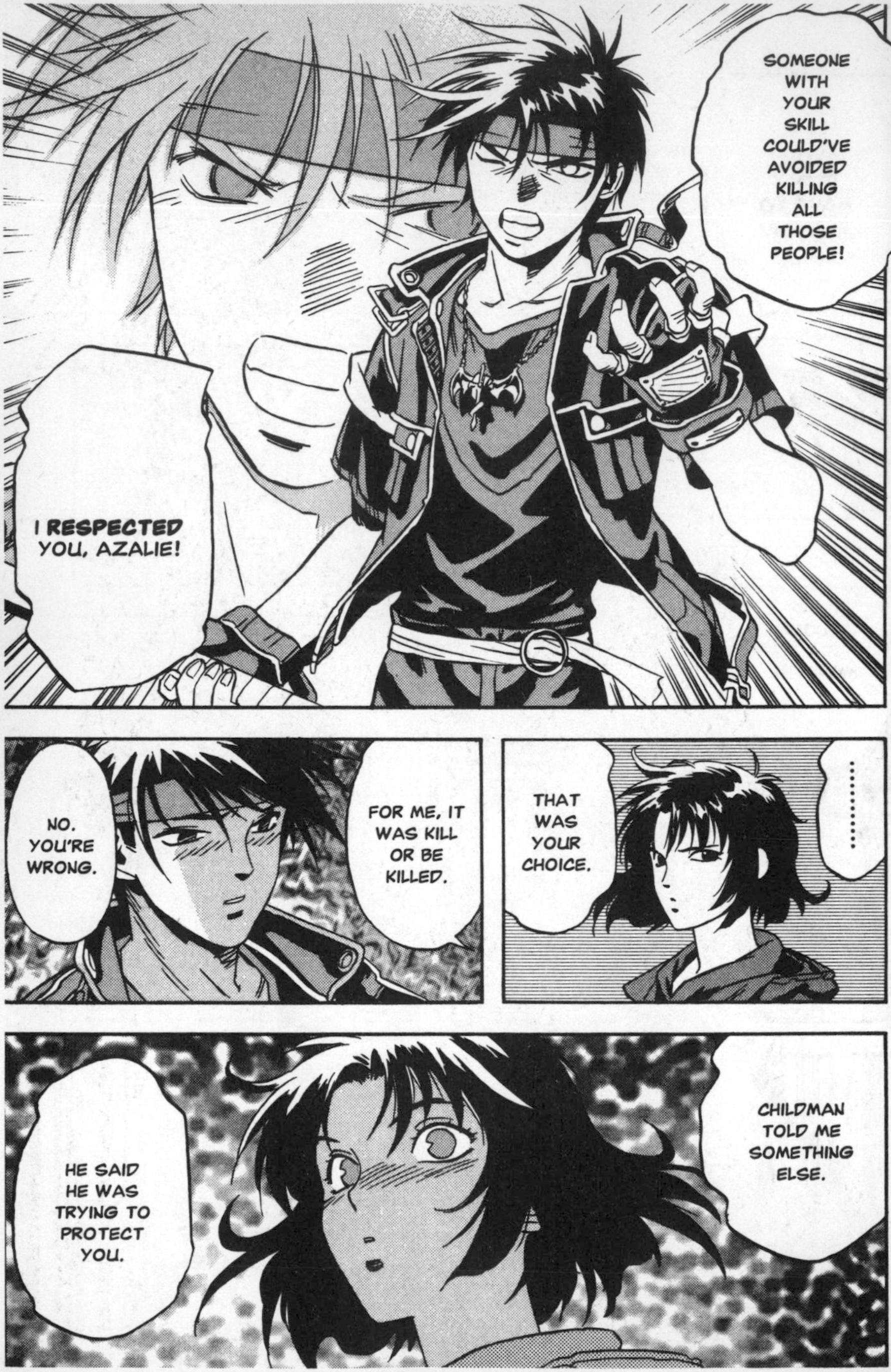
SOMEONE WITH YOUR SKILL COULD'VE AVOIDED KILLING ALL THOSE PEOPLE!
I RESPECTED YOU, AZALIE!
......
THAT WAS YOUR CHOICE.
FOR ME, IT WAS KILL OR BE KILLED.
NO. YOU'RE WRONG.
CHILDMAN TOLD ME SOMETHING ELSE.
HE SAID HE WAS TRYING TO PROTECT YOU.

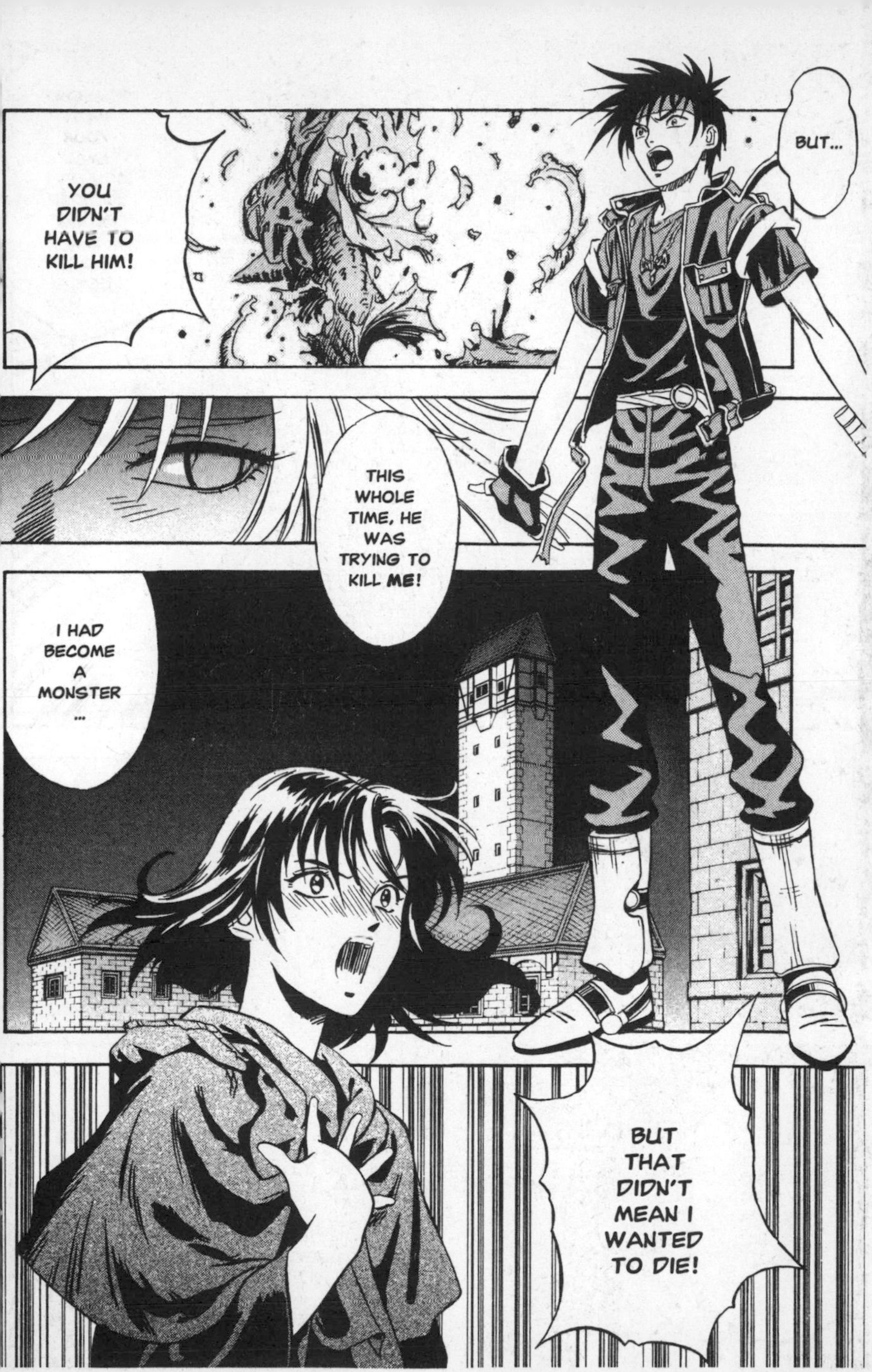
BUT...
YOU DIDN'T HAVE TO KILL HIM!
THIS WHOLE TIME, HE WAS TRYING TO KILL ME!
I HAD BECOME A MONSTER ...
BUT THAT DIDN'T MEAN I WANTED TO DIE!

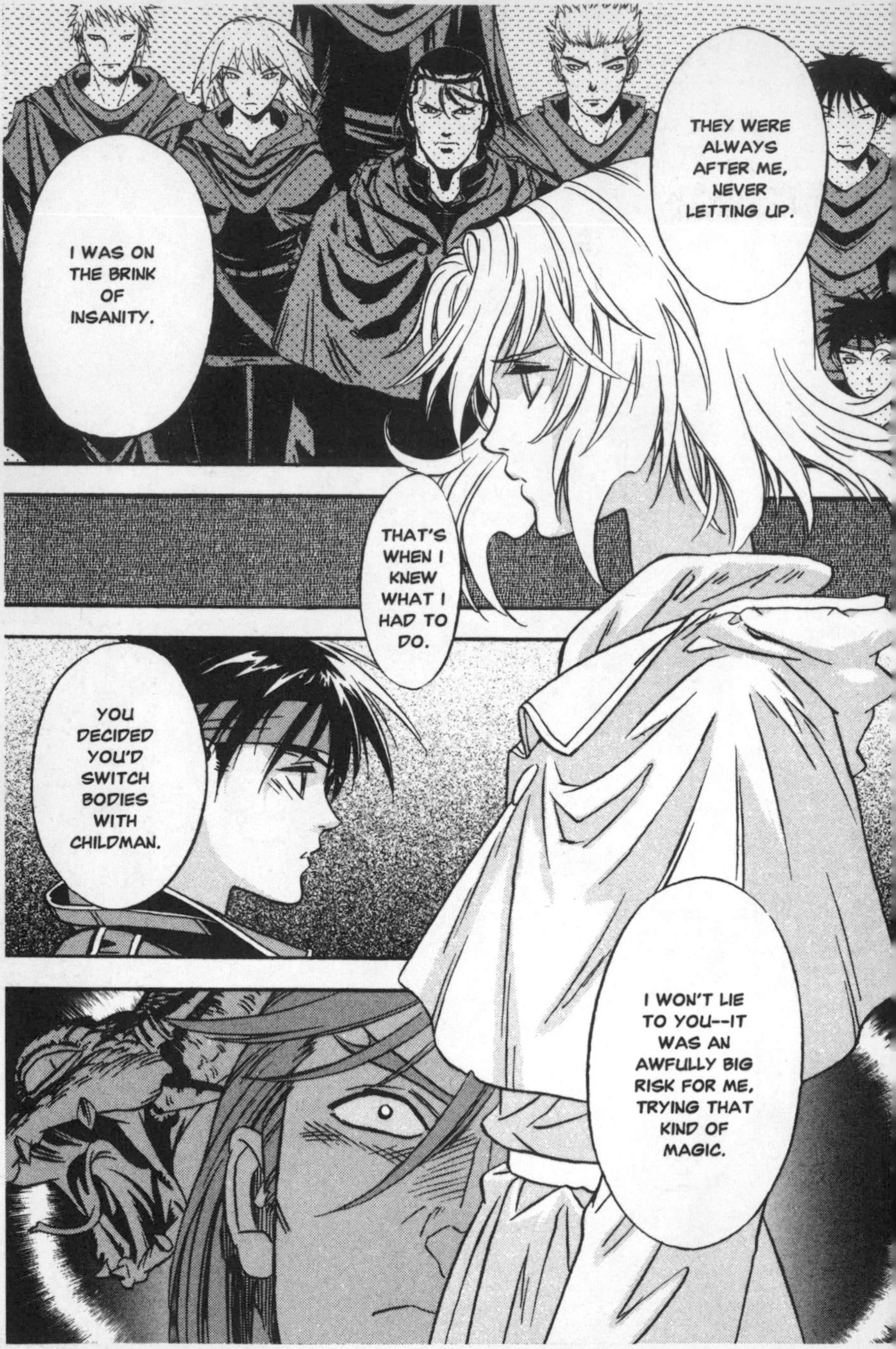
THEY WERE ALWAYS AFTER ME, NEVER LETTING UP.
I WAS ON THE BRINK OF INSANITY.
THAT'S WHEN I KNEW WHAT I HAD TO DO.
YOU DECIDED YOU'D SWITCH BODIES WITH CHILDMAN.
I WON'T LIE TO YOU--IT WAS AN AWFULLY BIG RISK FOR ME, TRYING THAT KIND OF MAGIC.

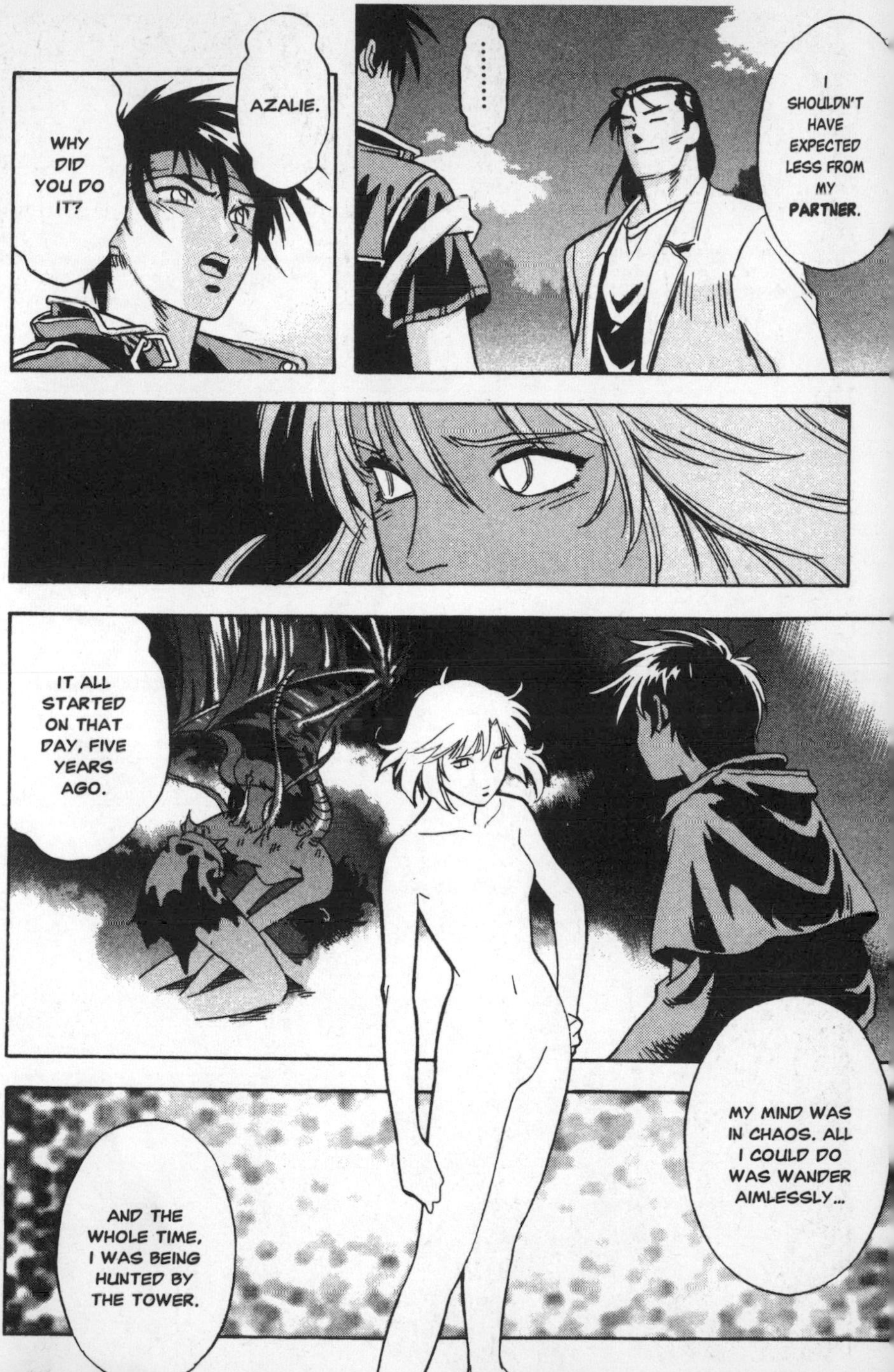
I SHOULDN'T HAVE EXPECTED LESS FROM MY PARTNER.
......
AZALIE.
WHY DID YOU DO IT?
IT ALL STARTED ON THAT DAY, FIVE YEARS AGO.
MY MIND WAS IN CHAOS. ALL I COULD DO WAS WANDER AIMLESSLY...
AND THE WHOLE TIME, I WAS BEING HUNTED BY THE TOWER.

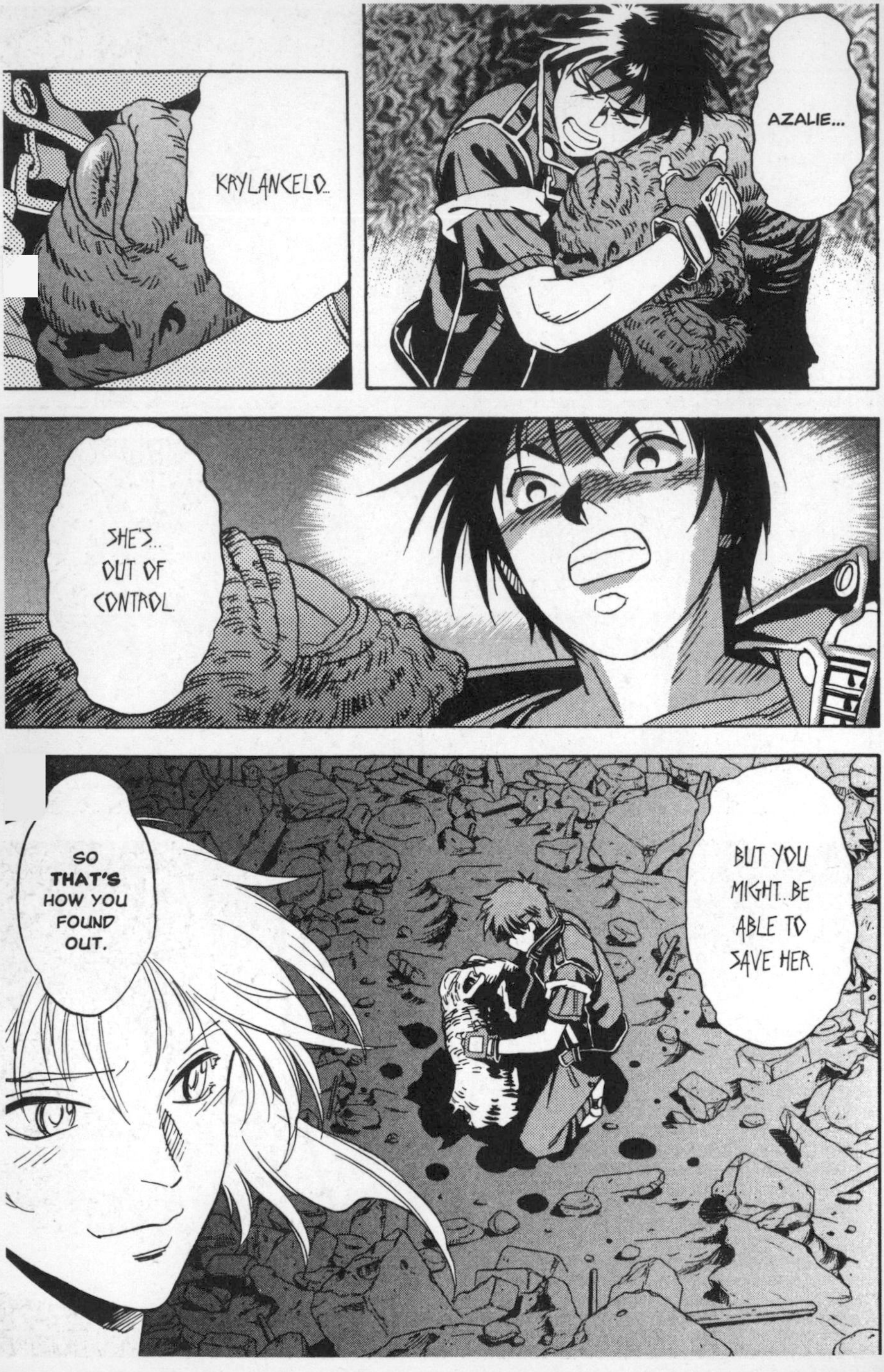
AZALIE...
KRYLANCELO...
SHE'S... OUT OF CONTROL.
BUT YOU MIGHT...BE ABLE TO SAVE HER.
SO **THAT'S** HOW YOU FOUND OUT.

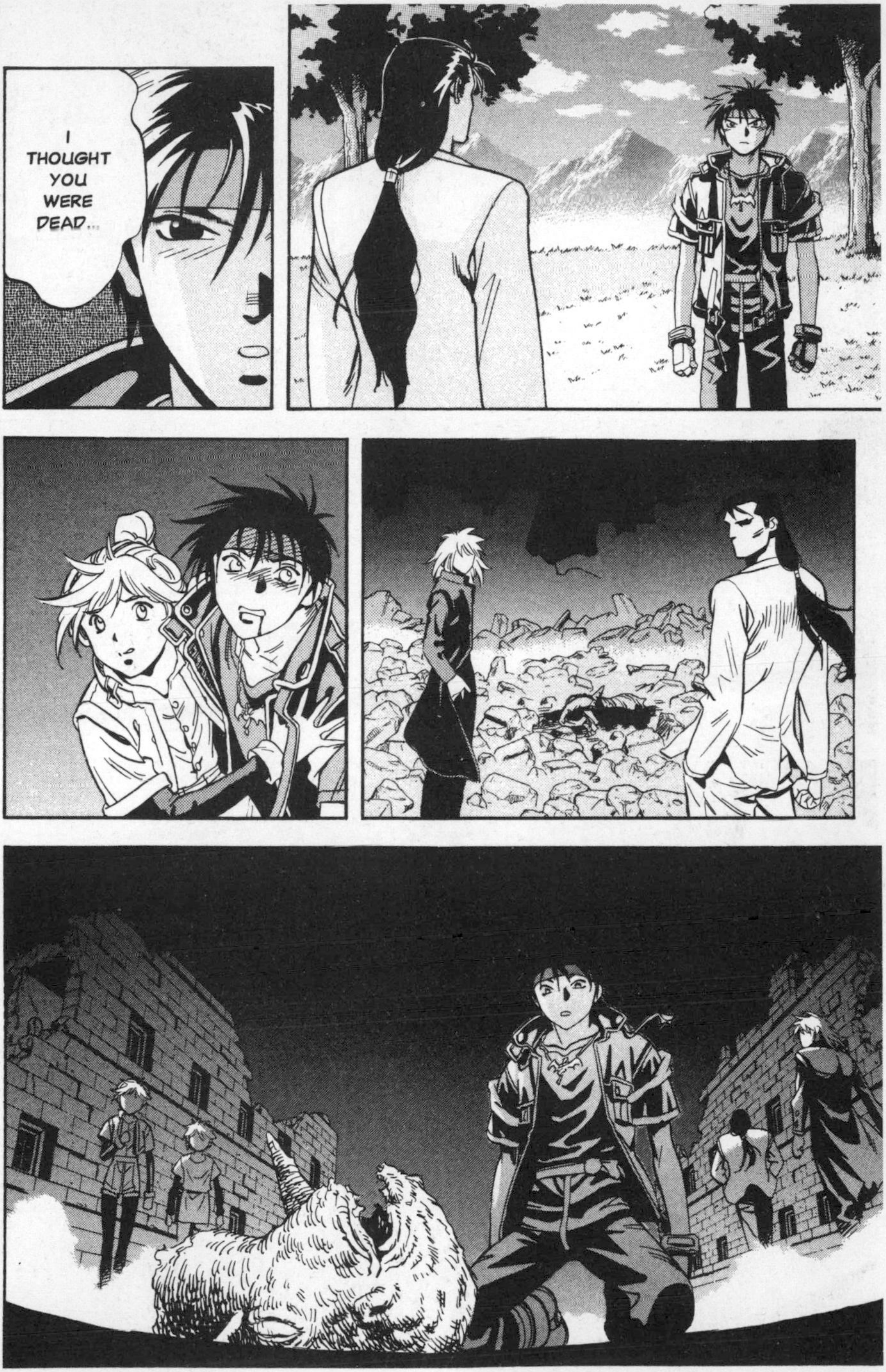
I THOUGHT YOU WERE DEAD...

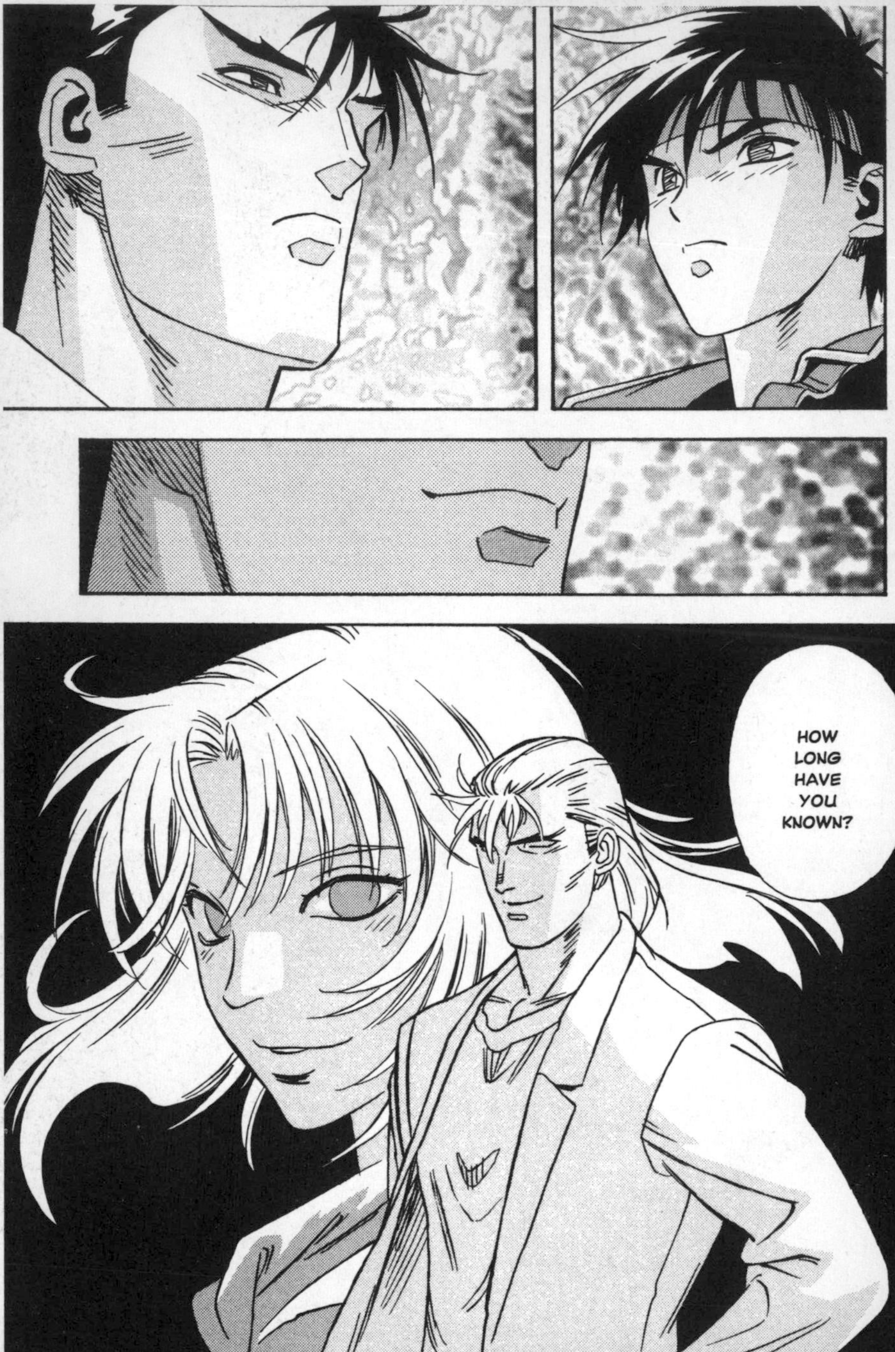
HOW LONG HAVE YOU KNOWN?

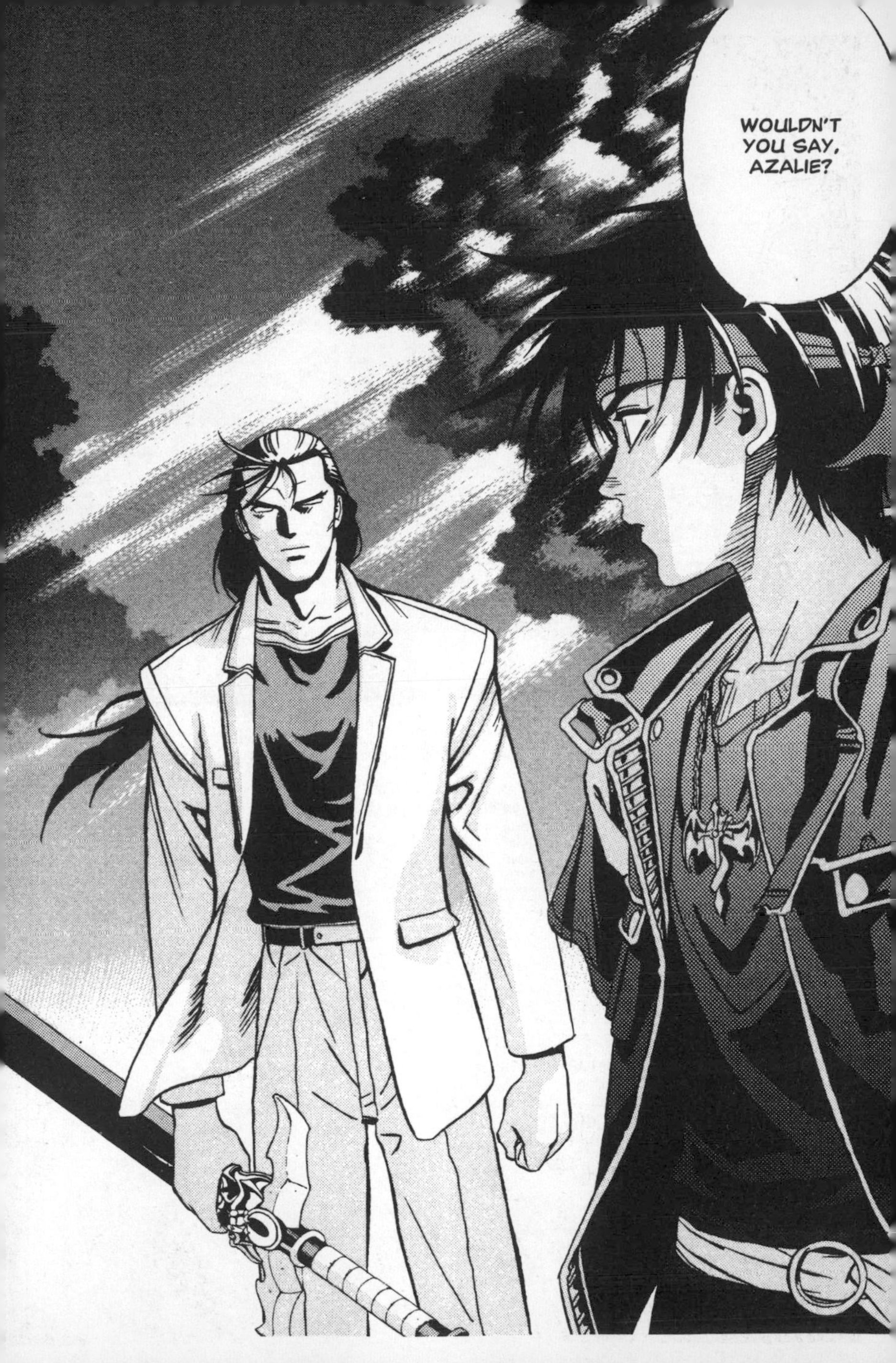
WOULDN'T YOU SAY, AZALIE?

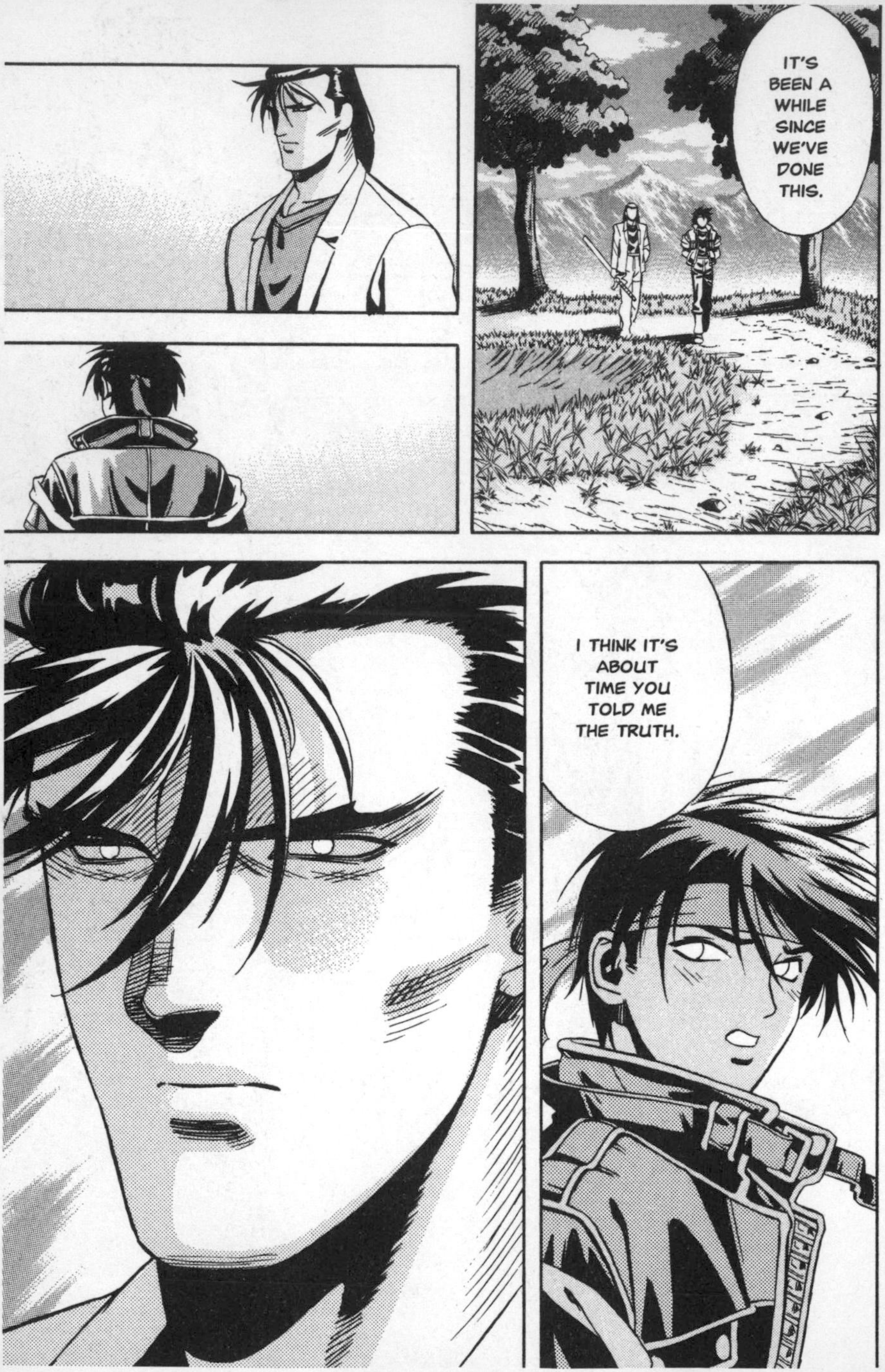
IT'S BEEN A WHILE SINCE WE'VE DONE THIS.
I THINK IT'S ABOUT TIME YOU TOLD ME THE TRUTH.

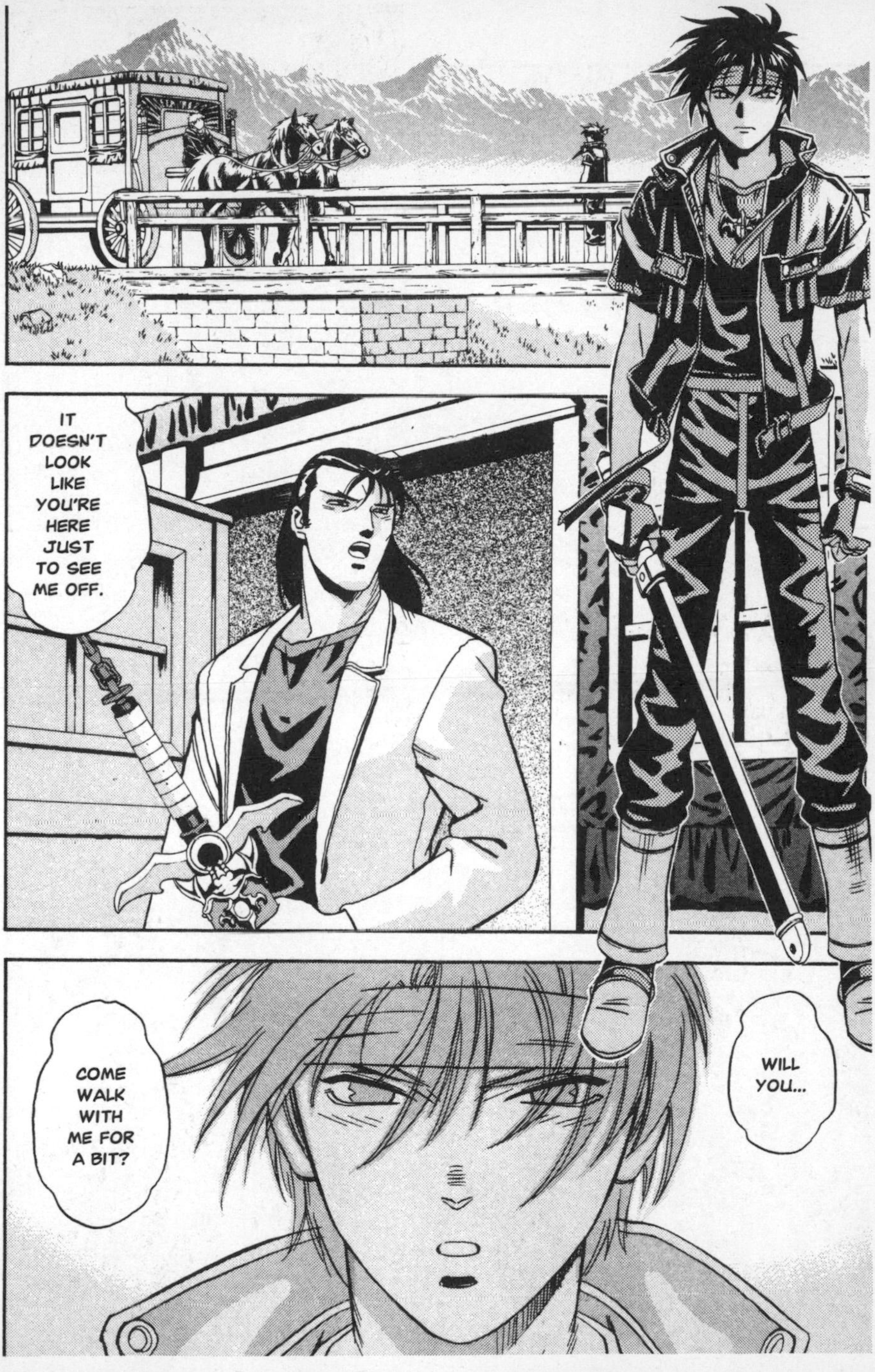
IT DOESN'T LOOK LIKE YOU'RE HERE JUST TO SEE ME OFF.
WILL YOU...
COME WALK WITH ME FOR A BIT?

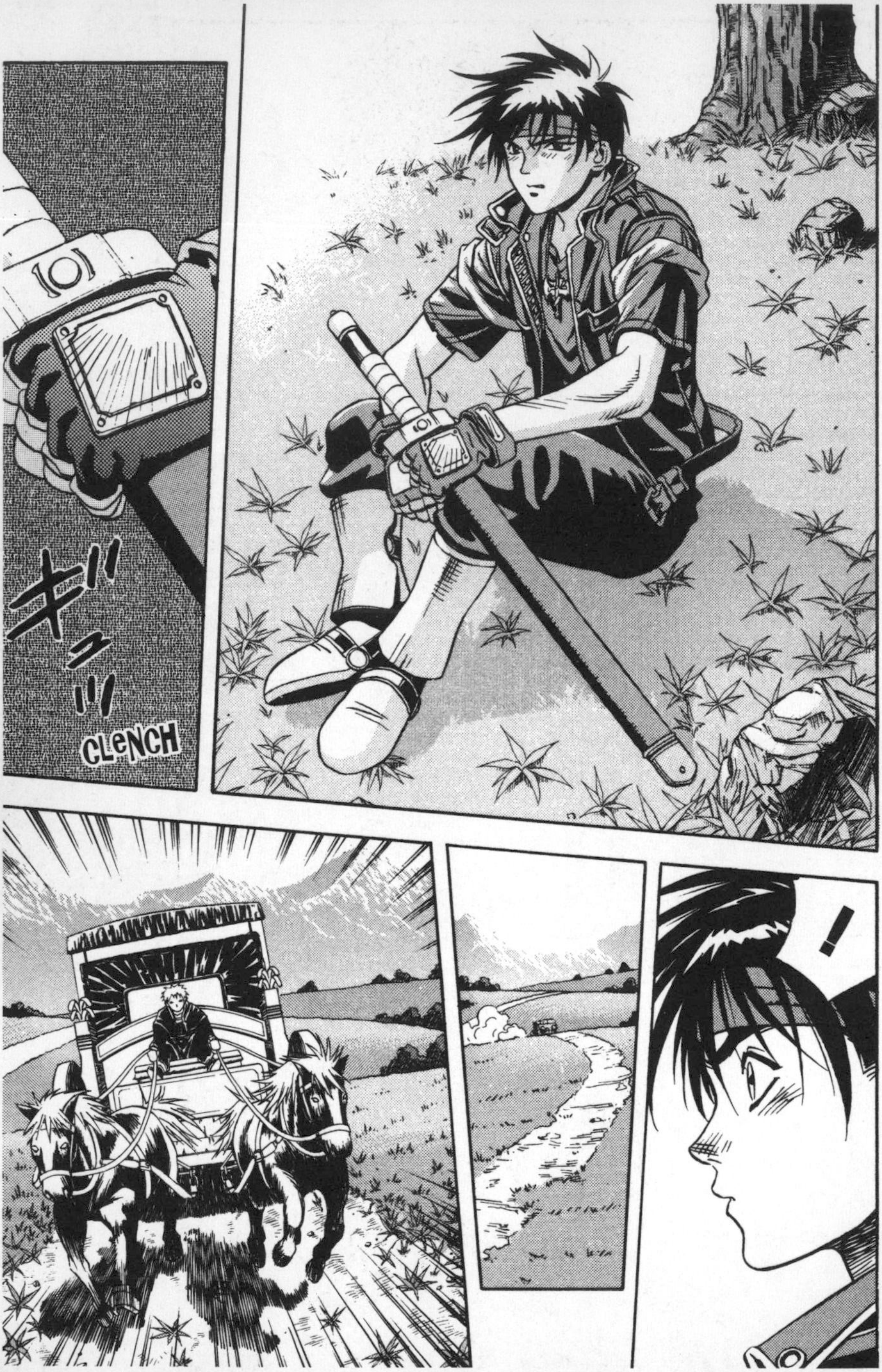
ギュッ
CLENCH
!

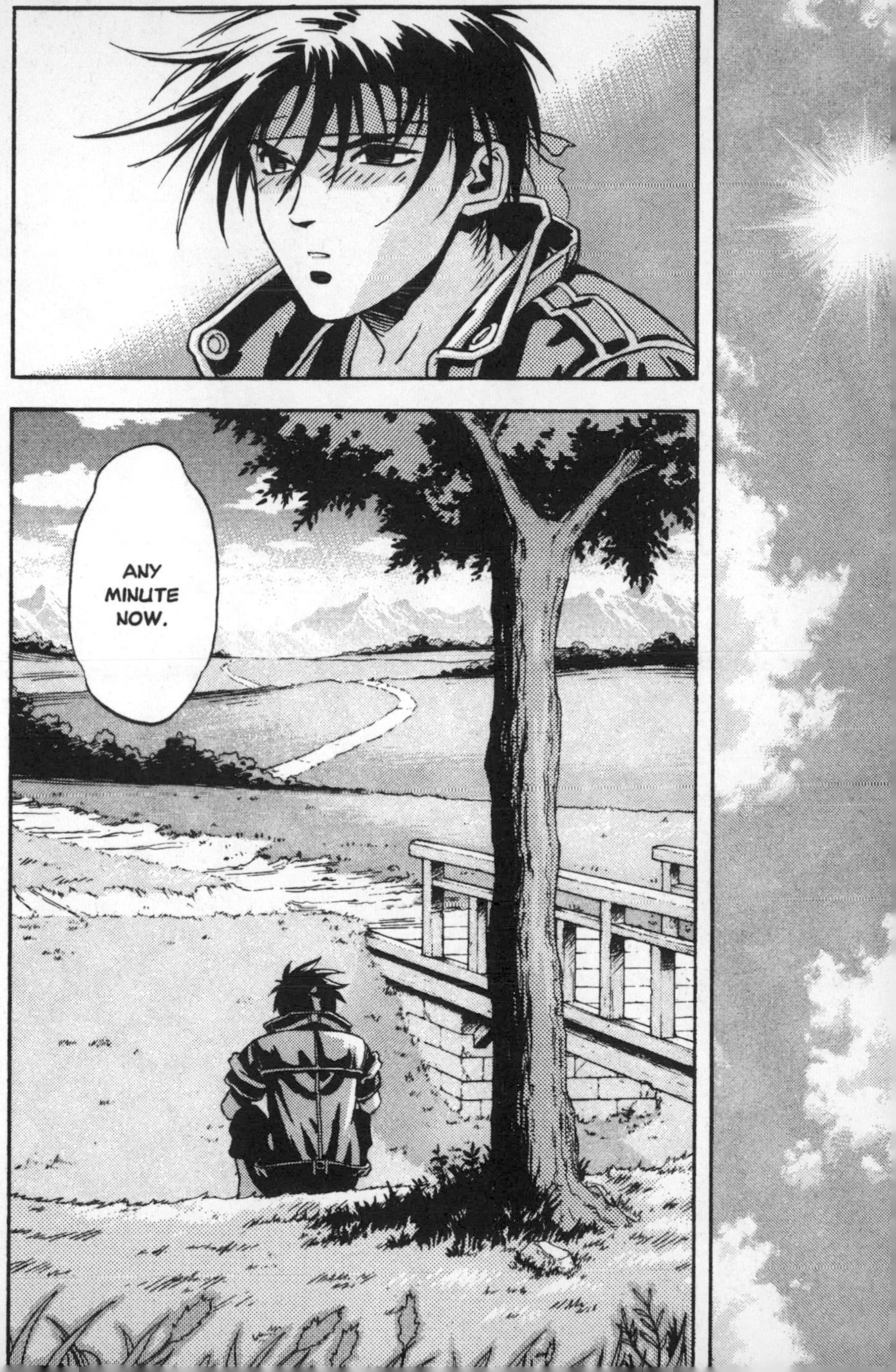
ANY MINUTE NOW.

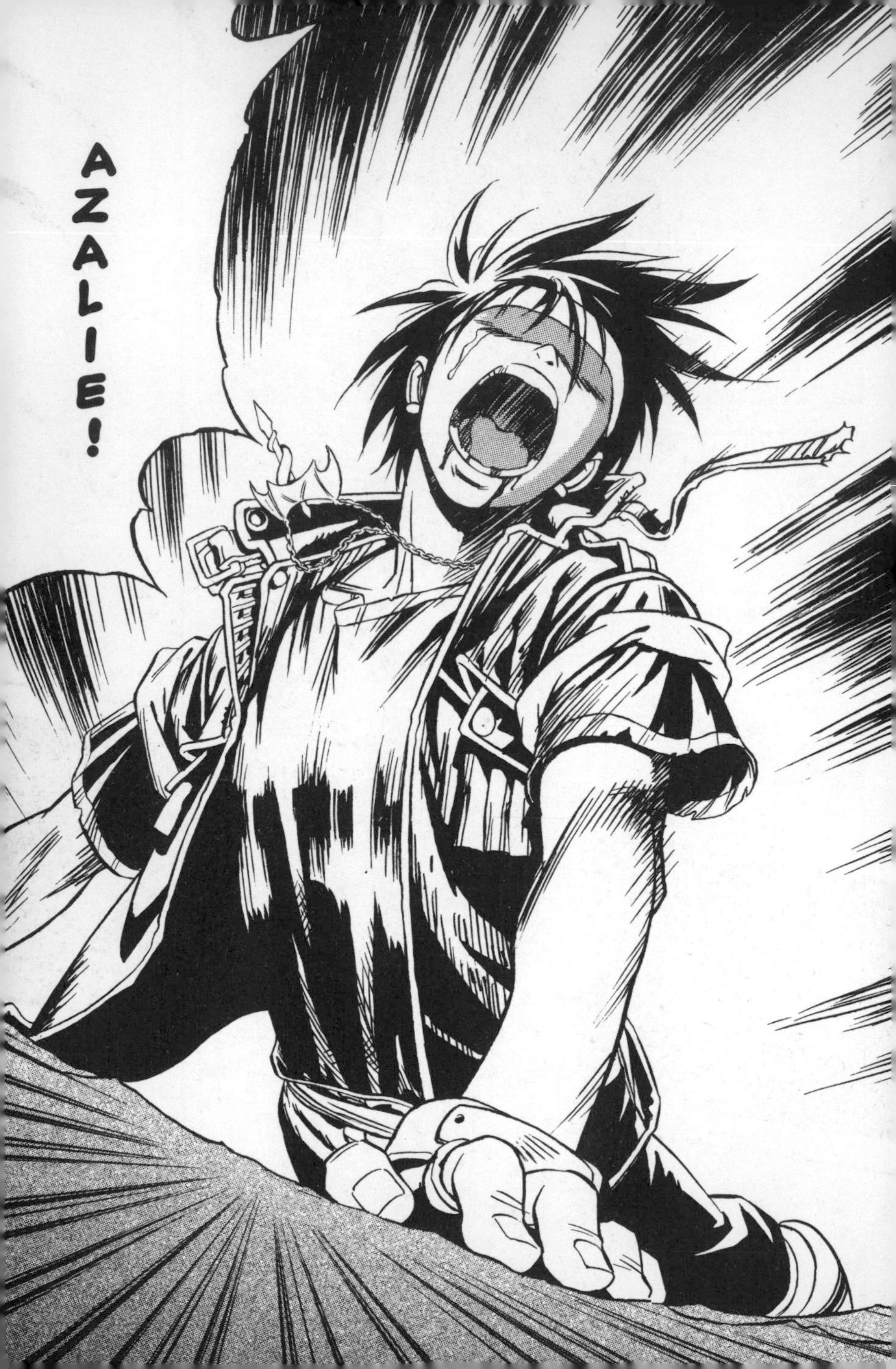
AZALIE!

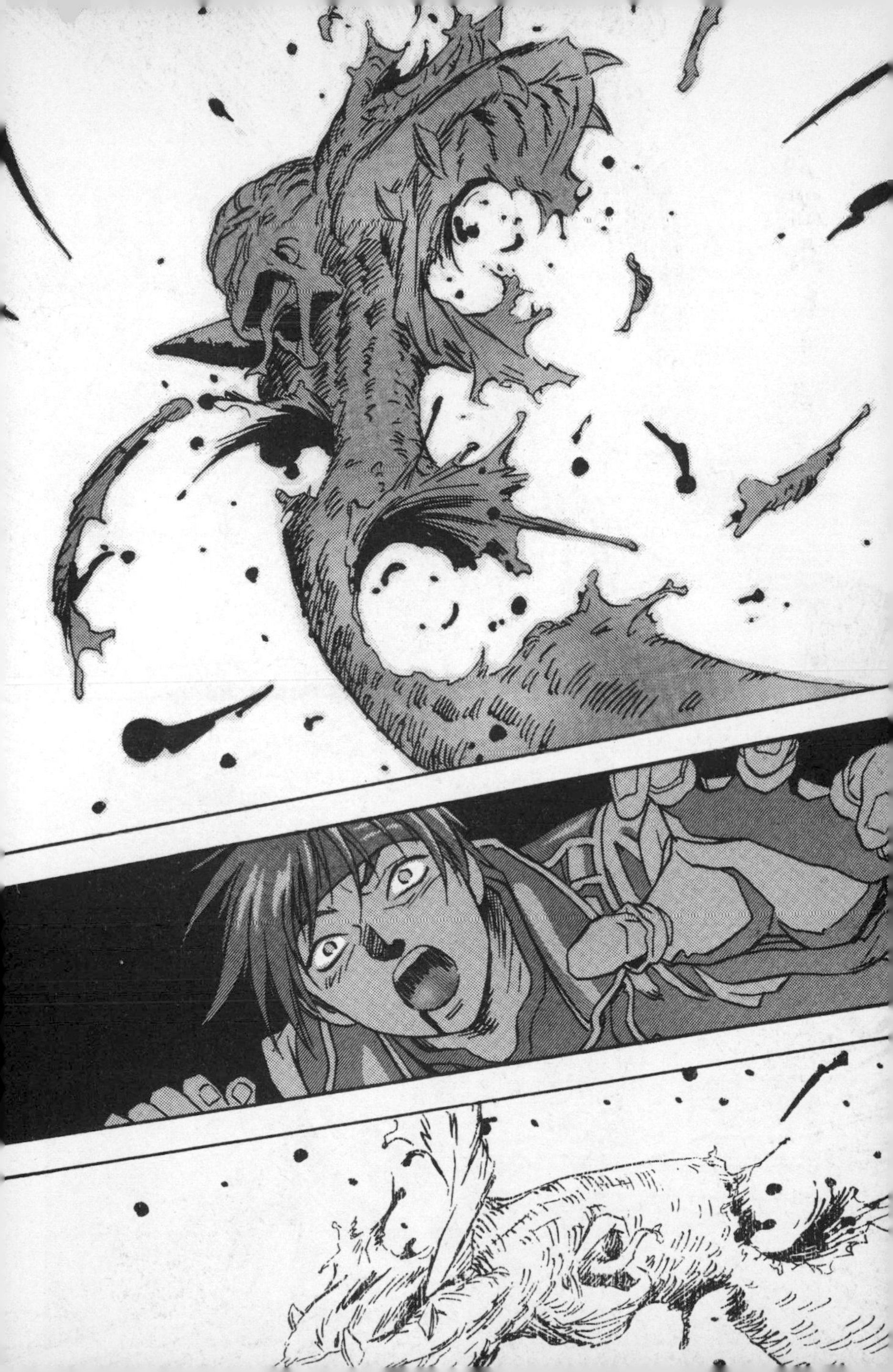

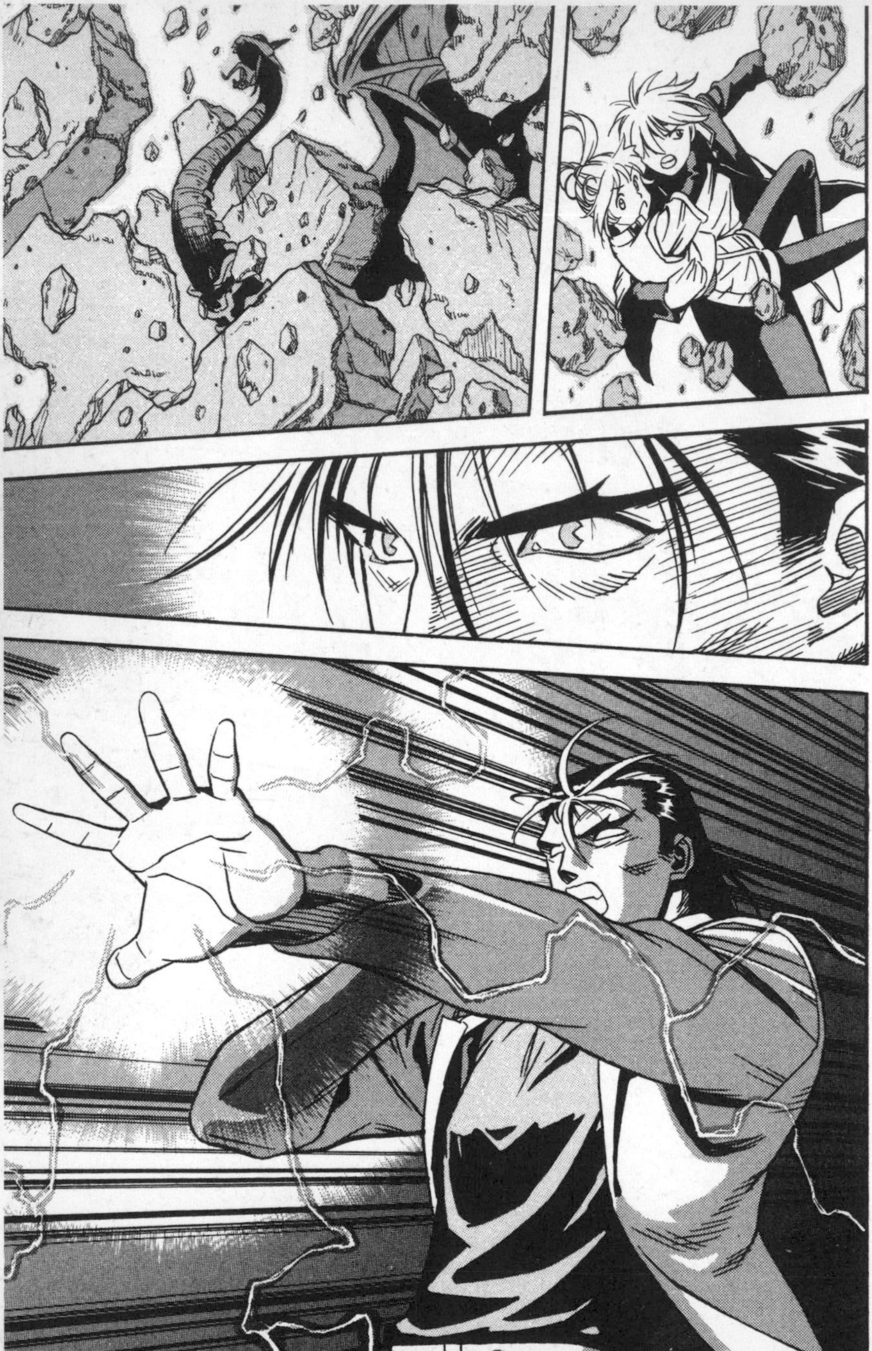

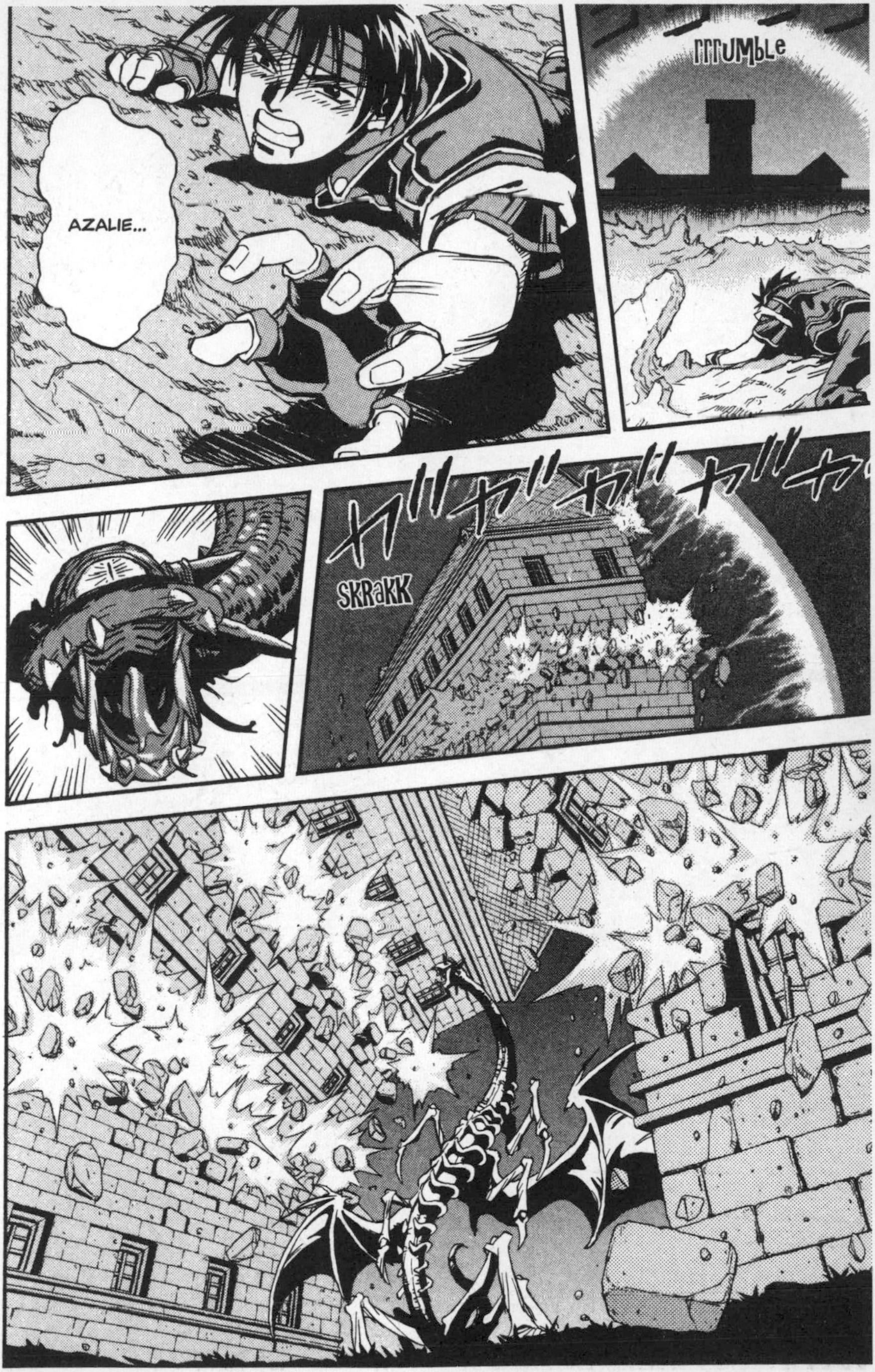
rrrUMbLe
AZALIE...
SKRaKK

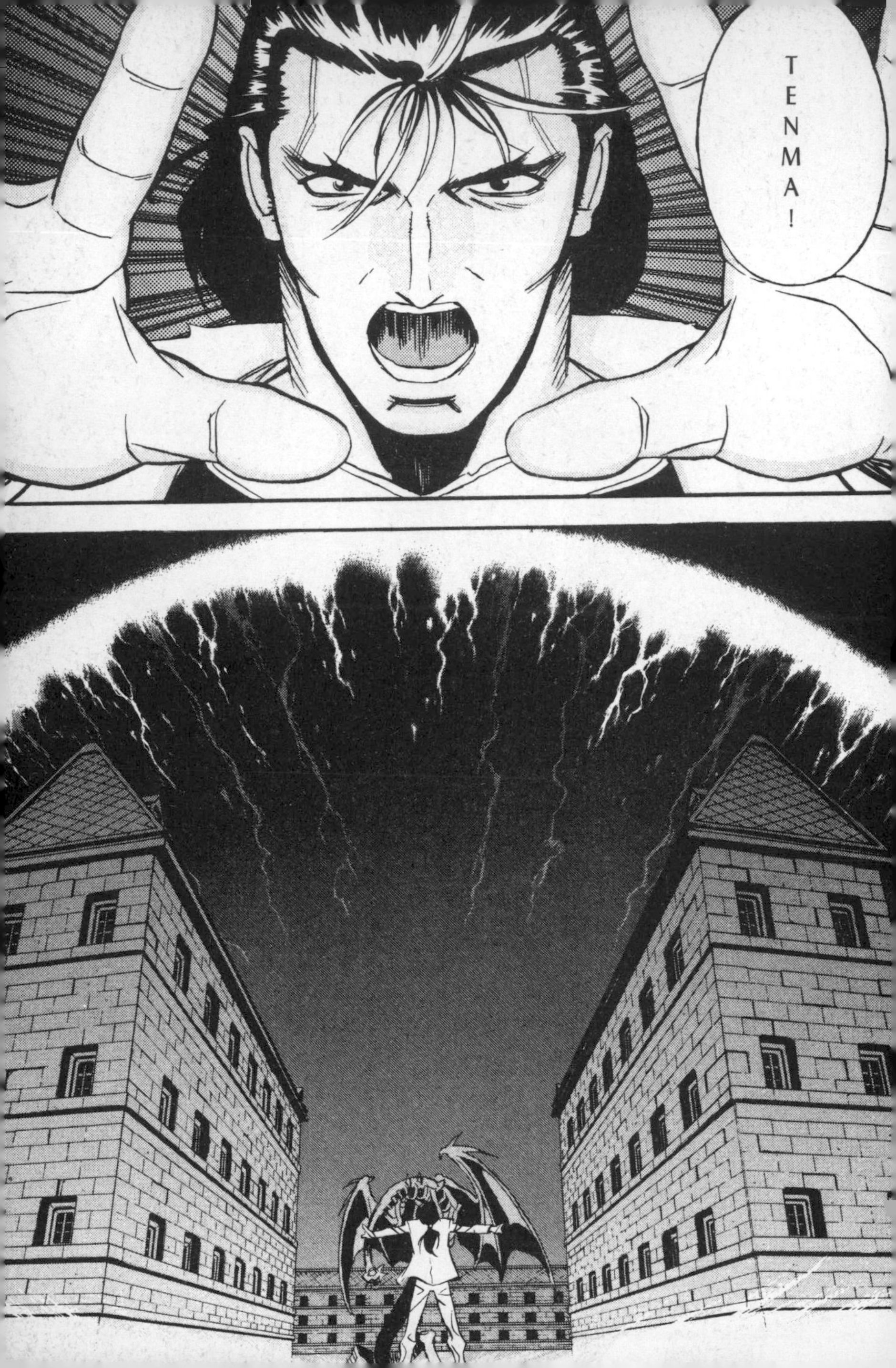
TENMA!

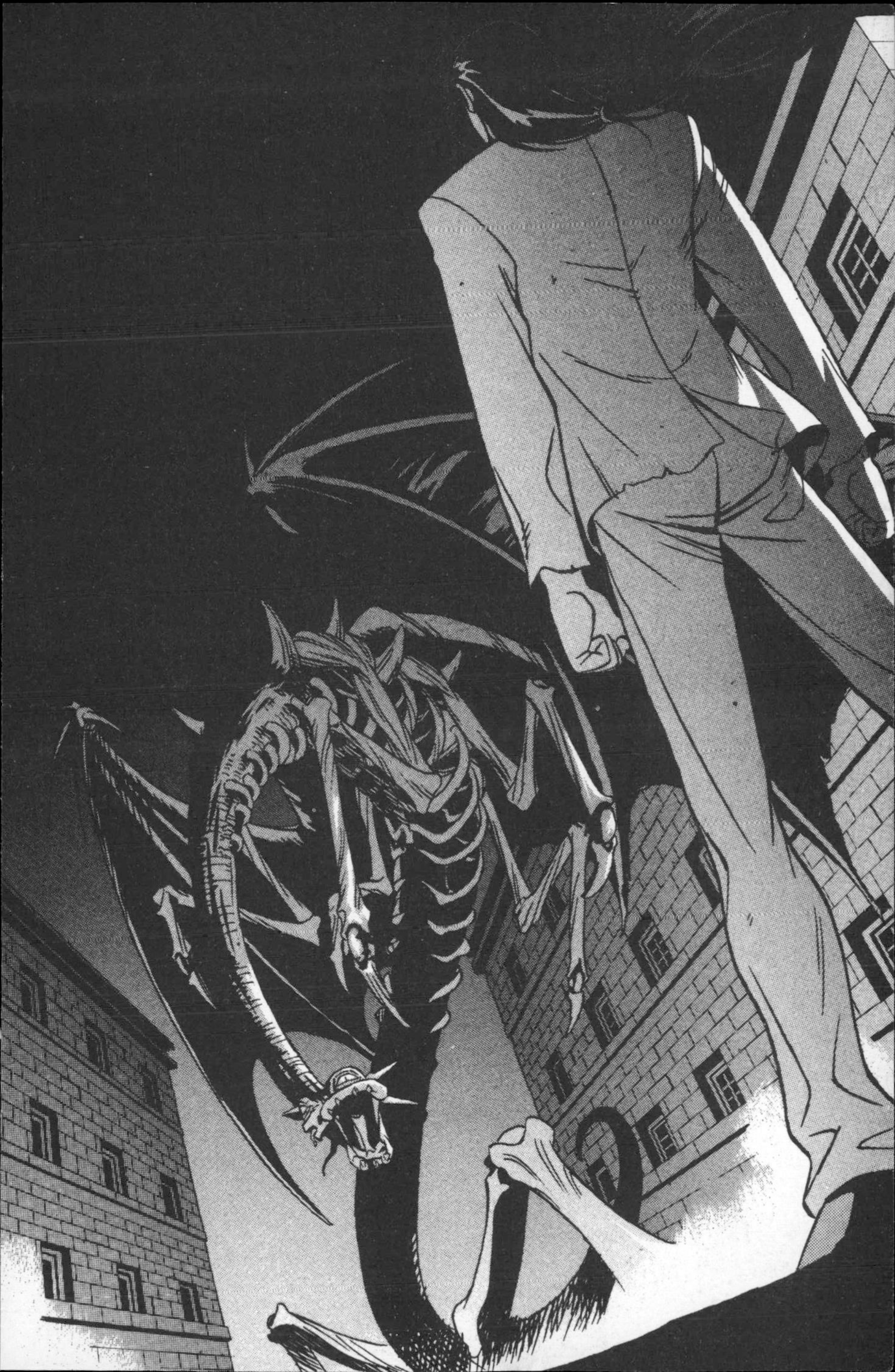

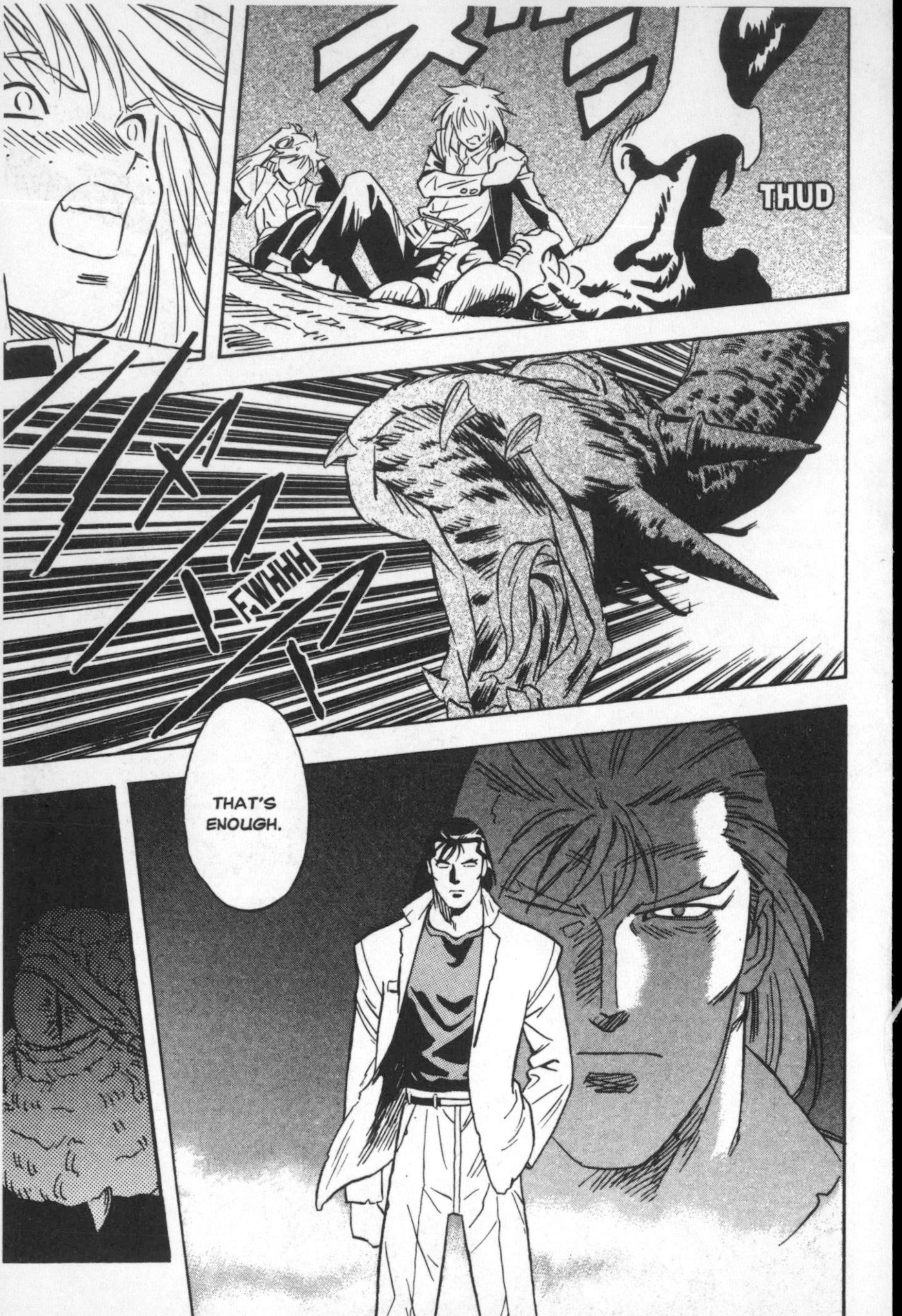
THUD
F.WHHH
THAT'S ENOUGH.

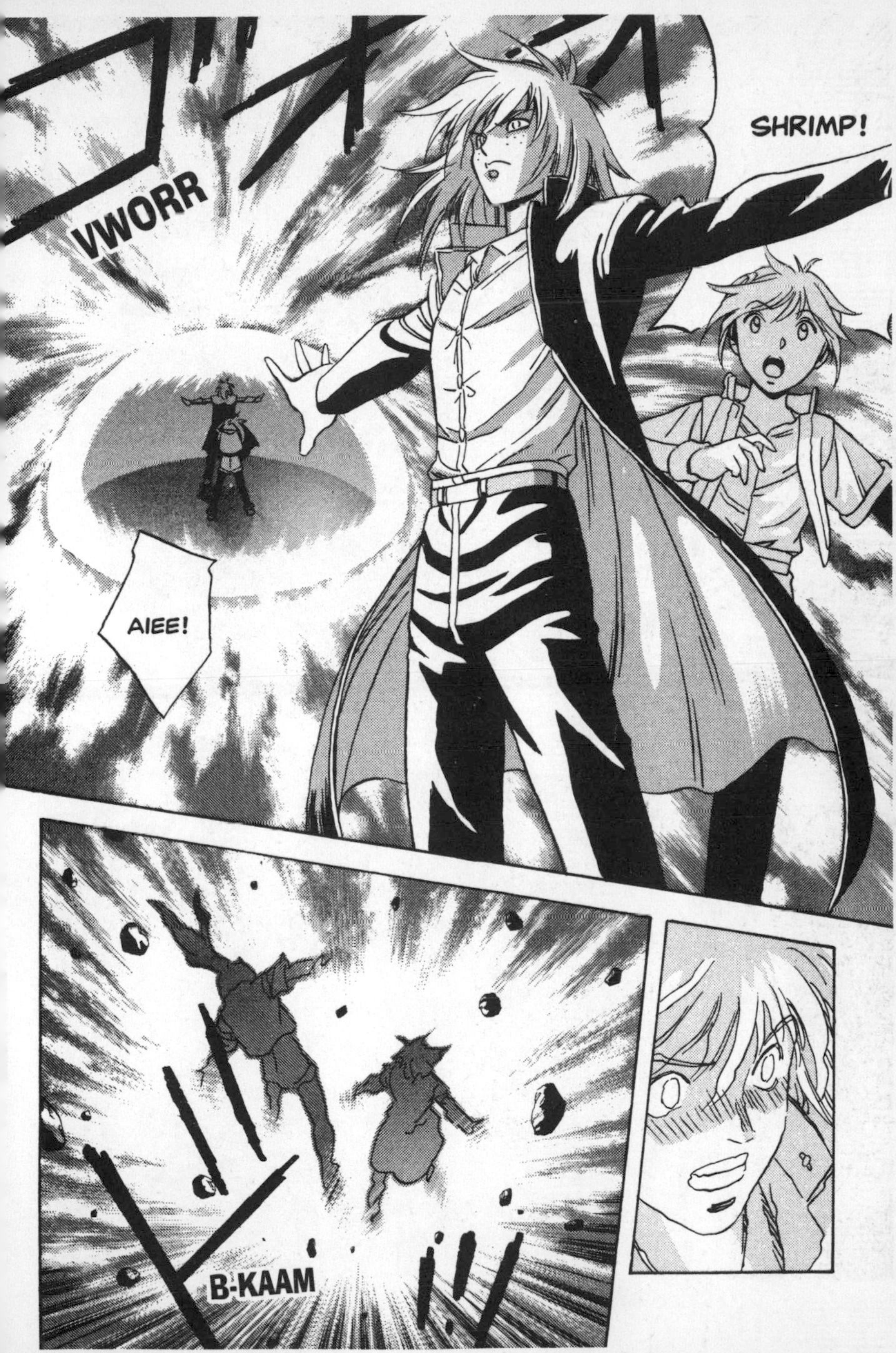

SHRIMP!
VWORR
AIEE!
B-KAAM

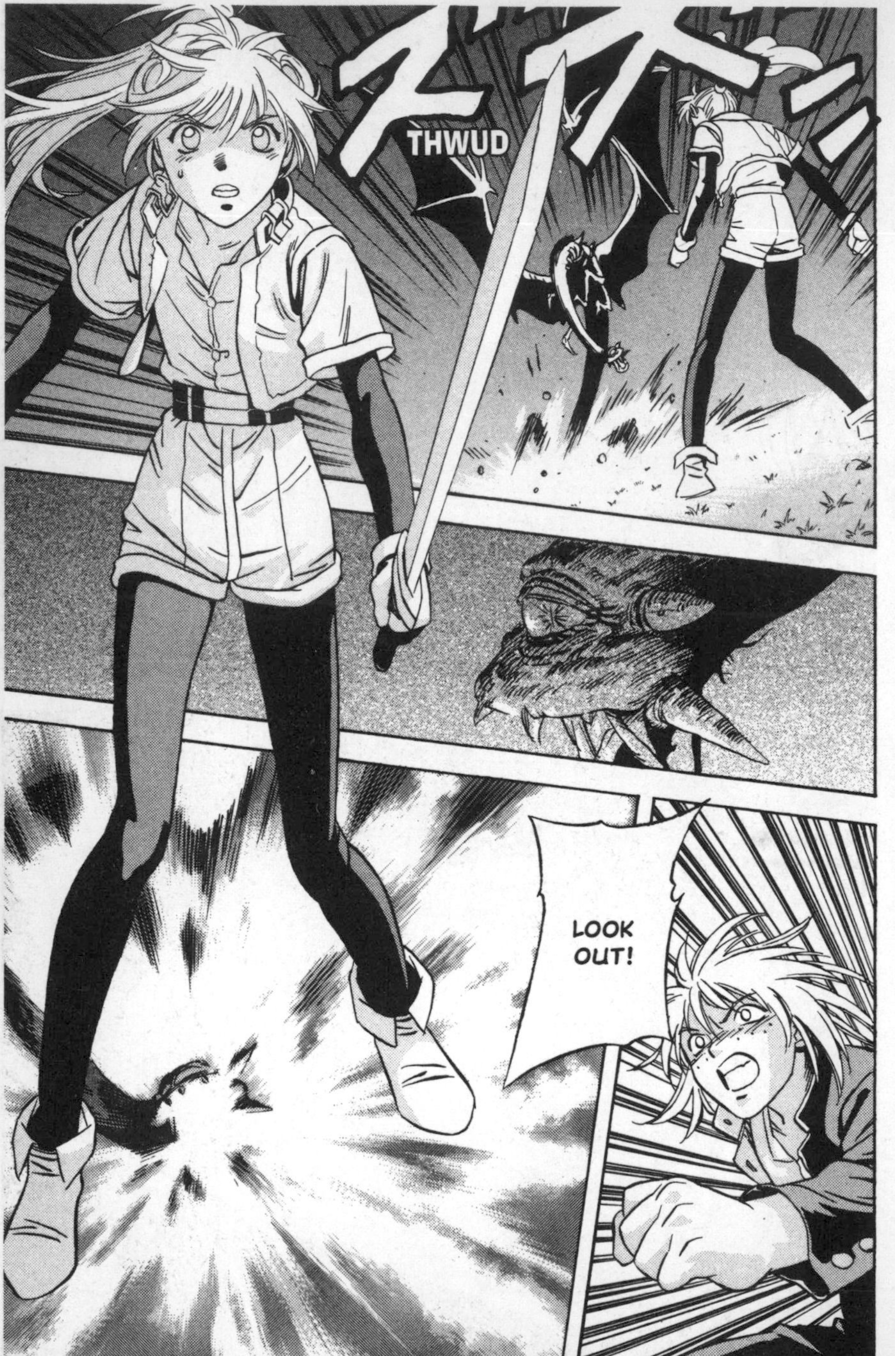
THWUD
LOOK OUT!

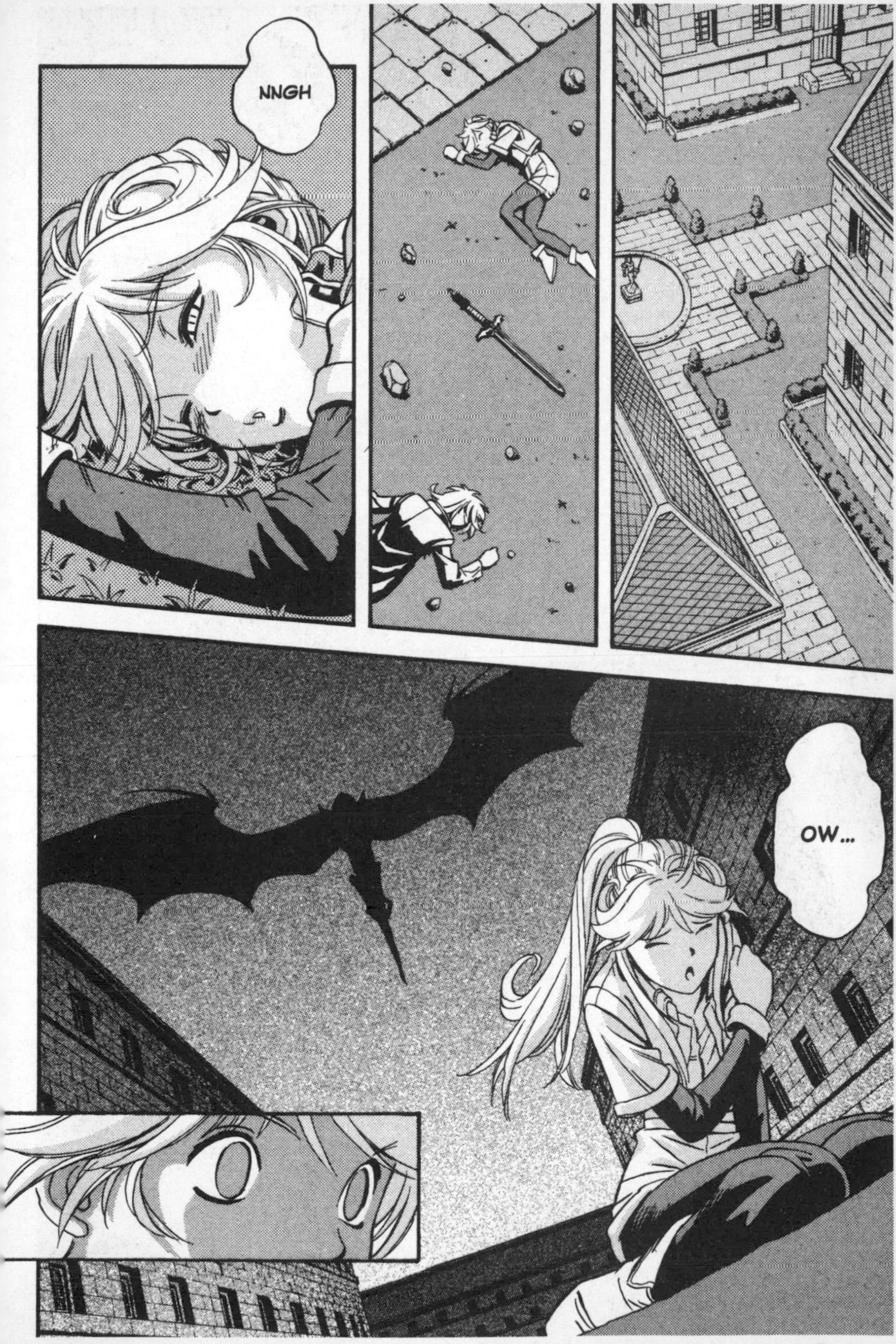
NNGH
OW...

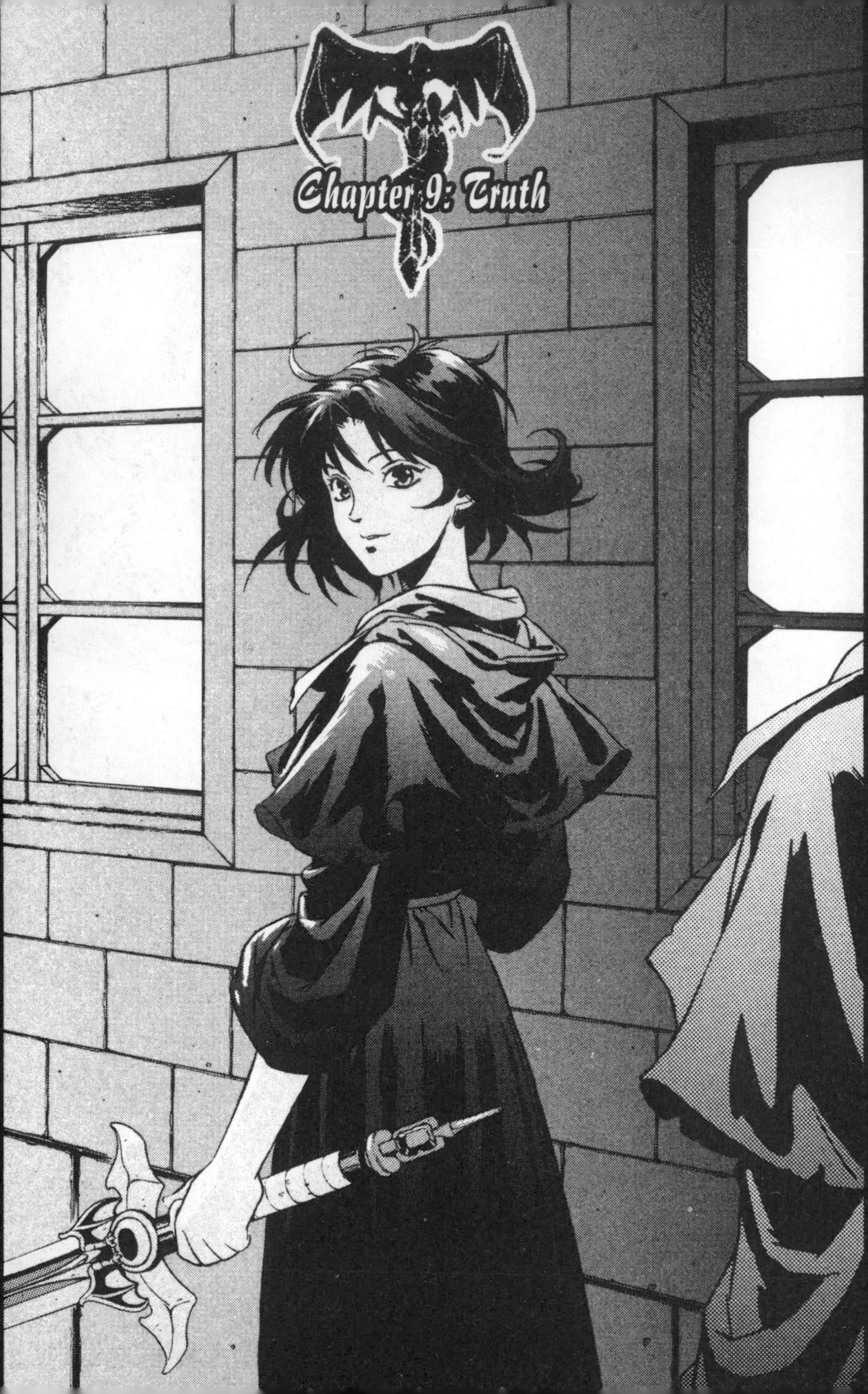
Chapter 9: Truth

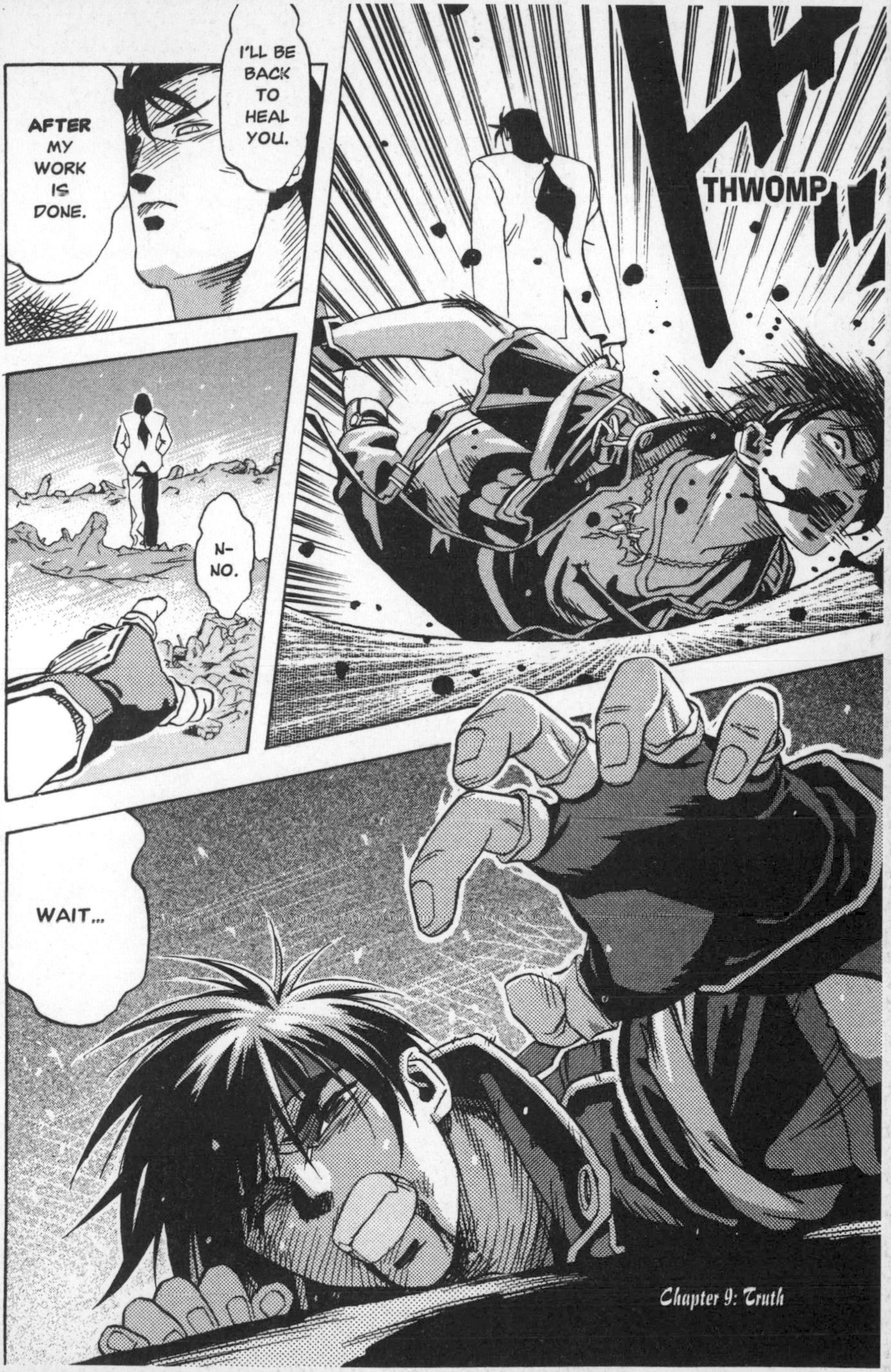
I'LL BE BACK TO HEAL YOU.
AFTER MY WORK IS DONE.
THWOMP
N-NO.
WAIT...
Chapter 9: Truth

ΘRPHEN

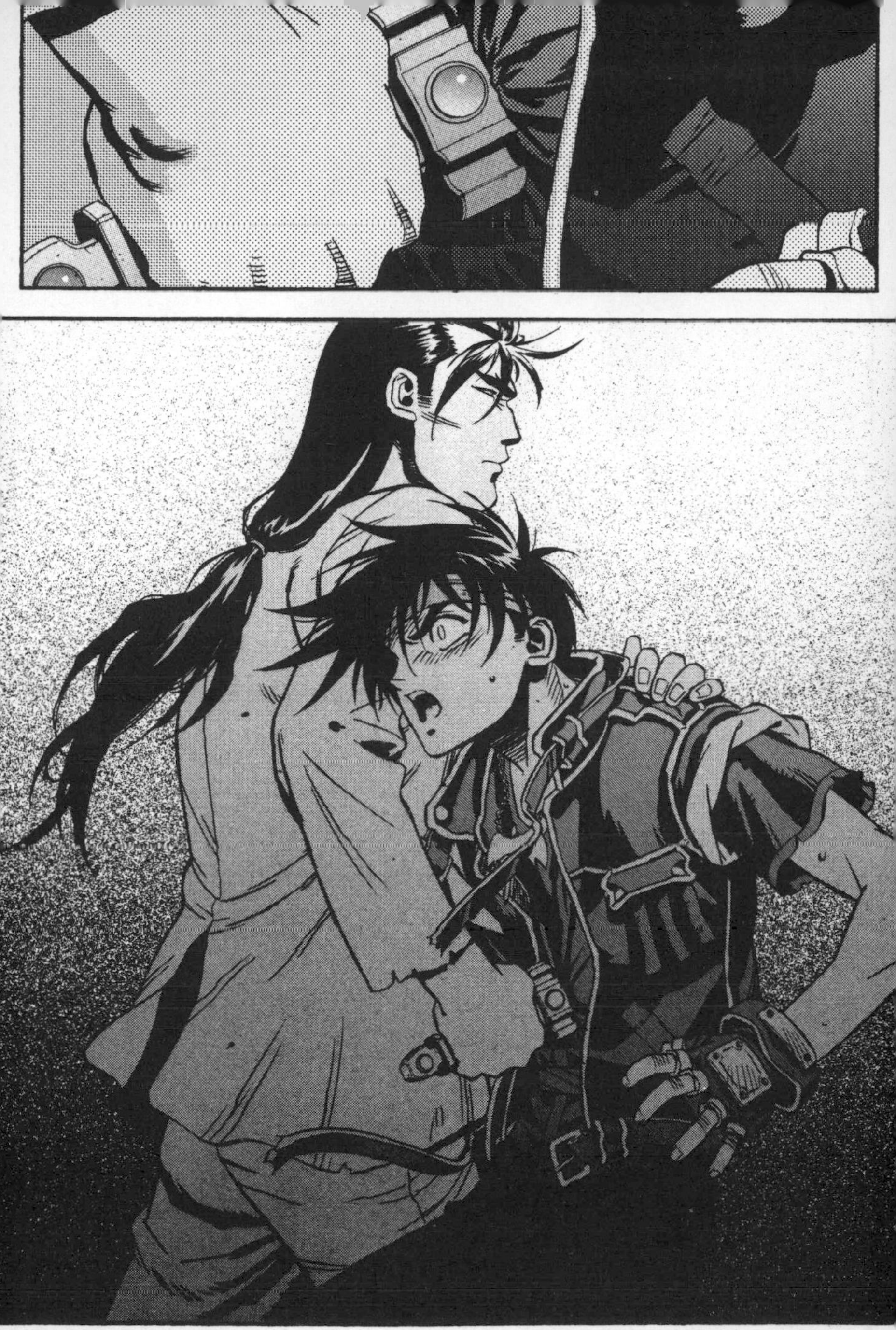

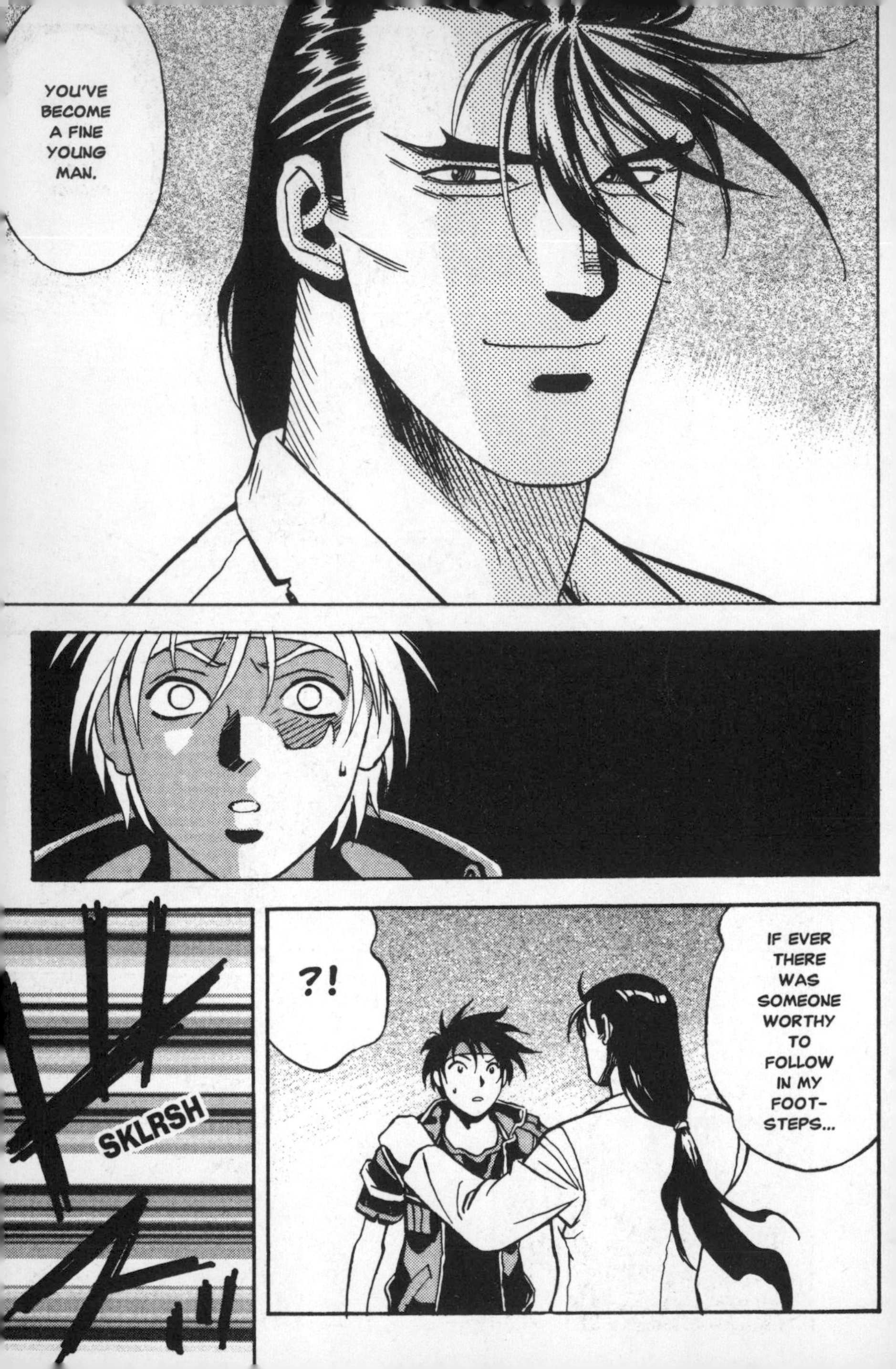
YOU'VE BECOME A FINE YOUNG MAN.
?!
IF EVER THERE WAS SOMEONE WORTHY TO FOLLOW IN MY FOOT-STEPS...
SKLRSH

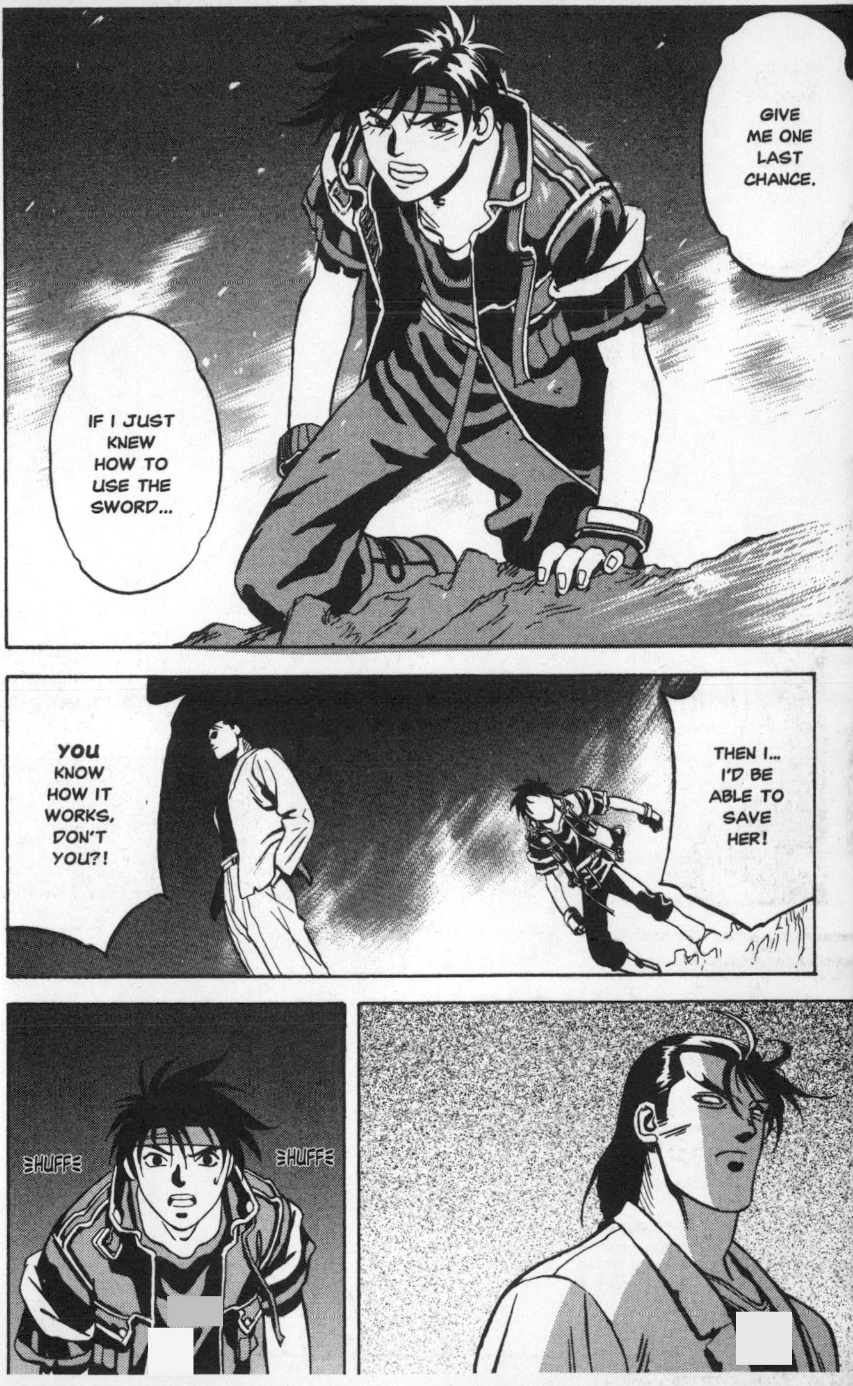
GIVE ME ONE LAST CHANCE.
IF I JUST KNEW HOW TO USE THE SWORD...
THEN I... I'D BE ABLE TO SAVE HER!
YOU KNOW HOW IT WORKS, DON'T YOU?!
HUFF
HUFF

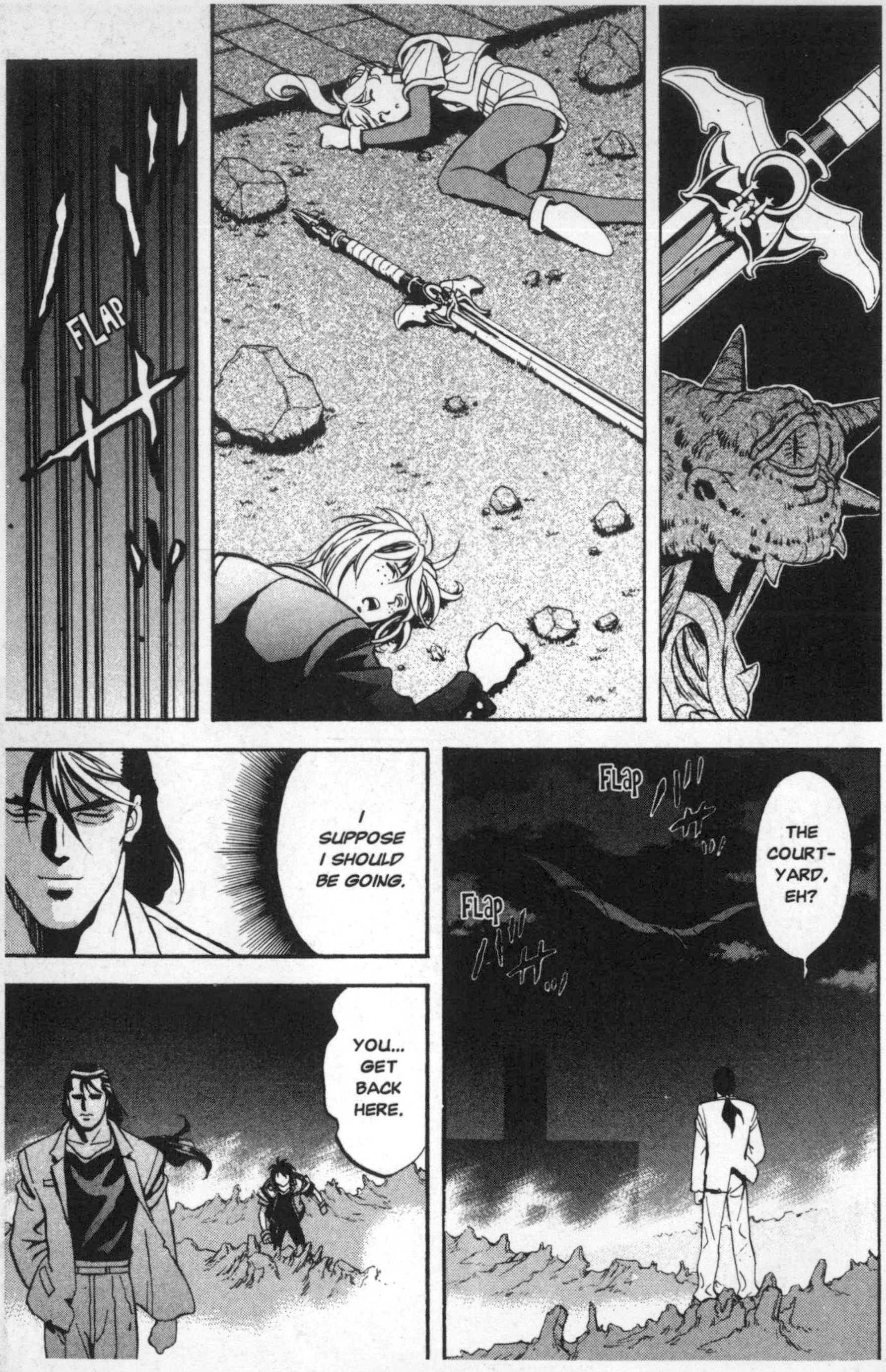
FLAP
I SUPPOSE I SHOULD BE GOING.
FLAP
FLAP
THE COURT-YARD, EH?
YOU... GET BACK HERE.

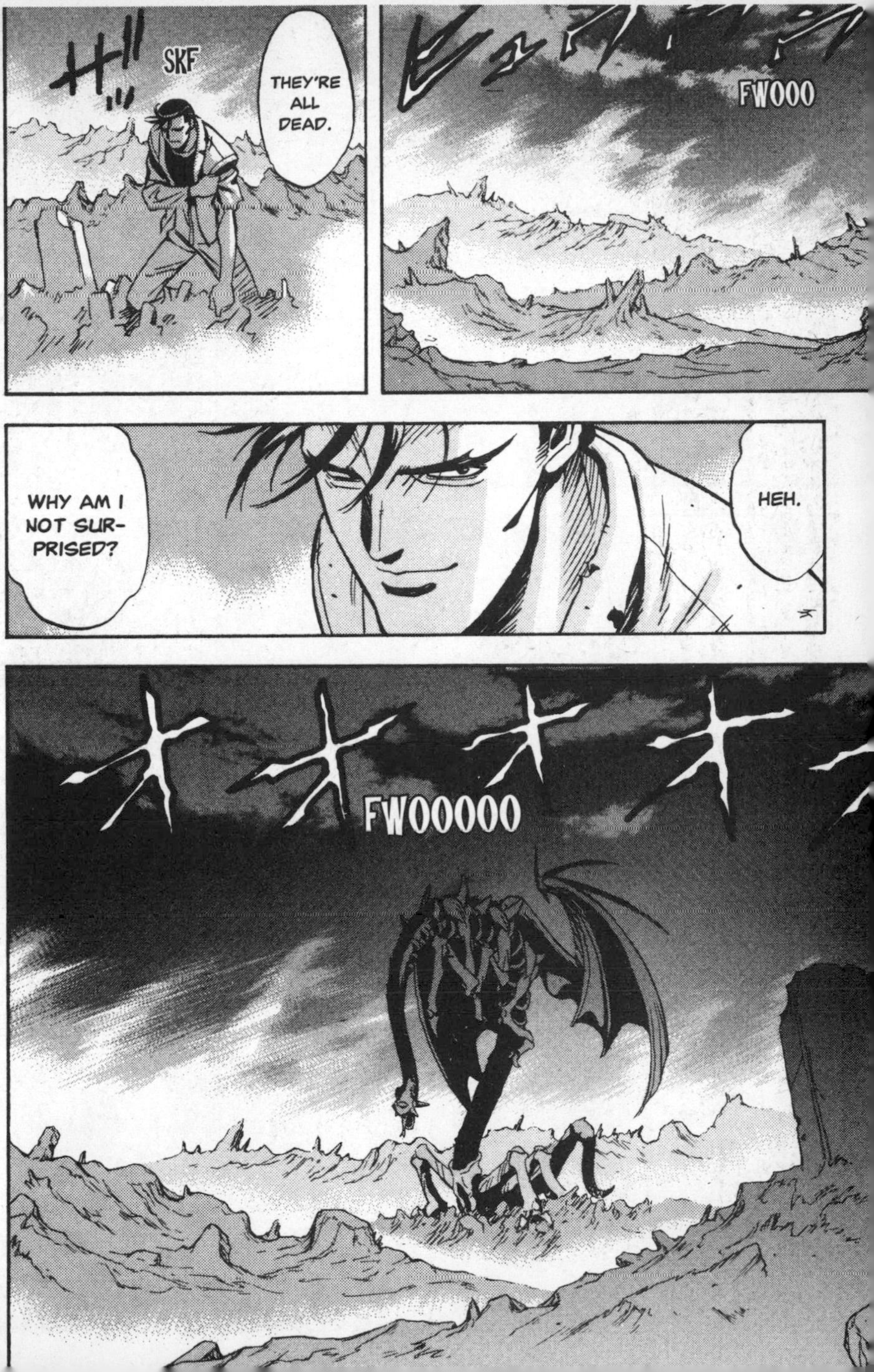
FWOOO
SKF
THEY'RE ALL DEAD.
HEH.
WHY AM I NOT SUR-PRISED?
FWOOOOO

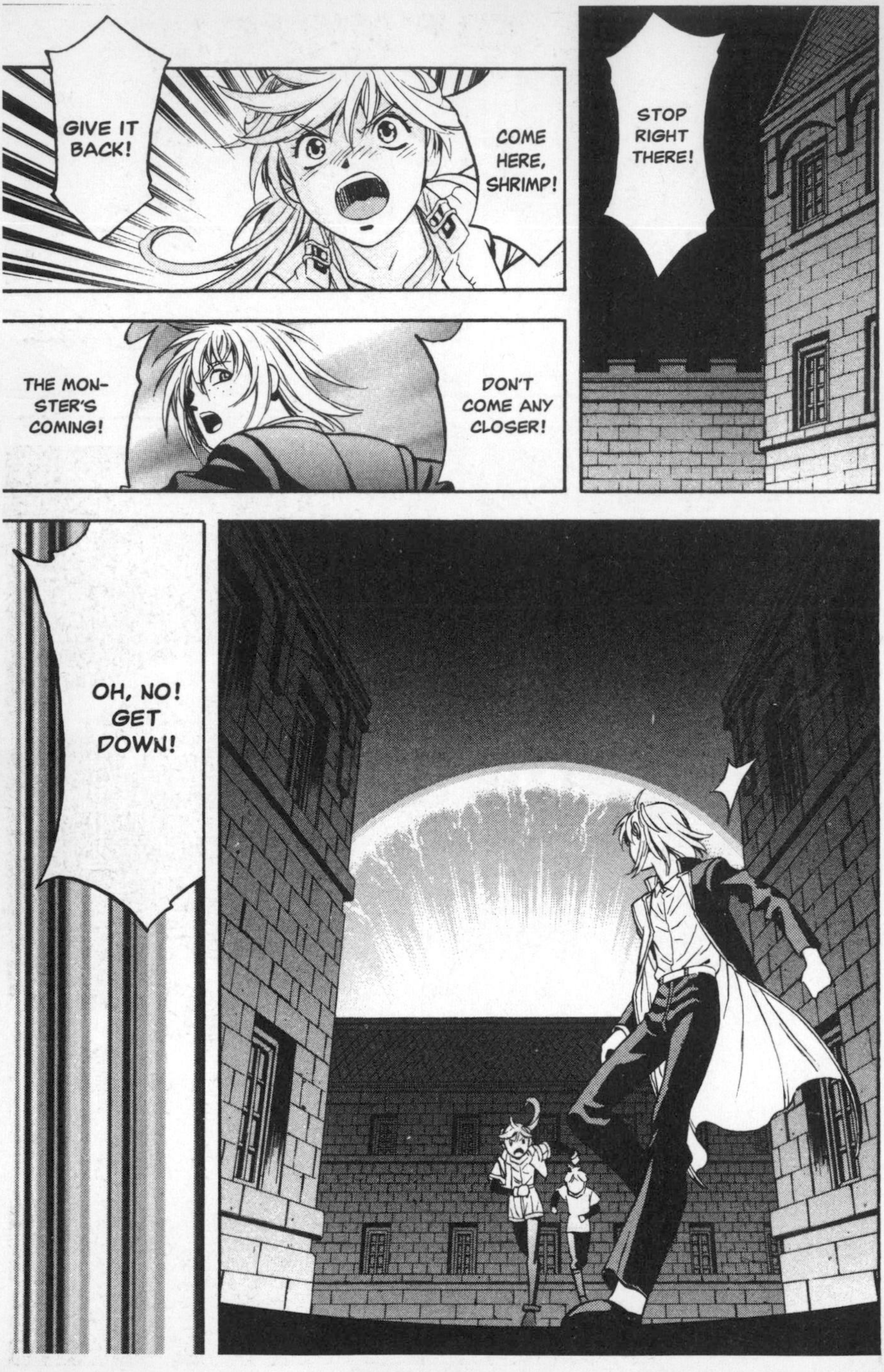
STOP RIGHT THERE!
COME HERE, SHRIMP!
GIVE IT BACK!
DON'T COME ANY CLOSER!
THE MON-STER'S COMING!
OH, NO! GET DOWN!

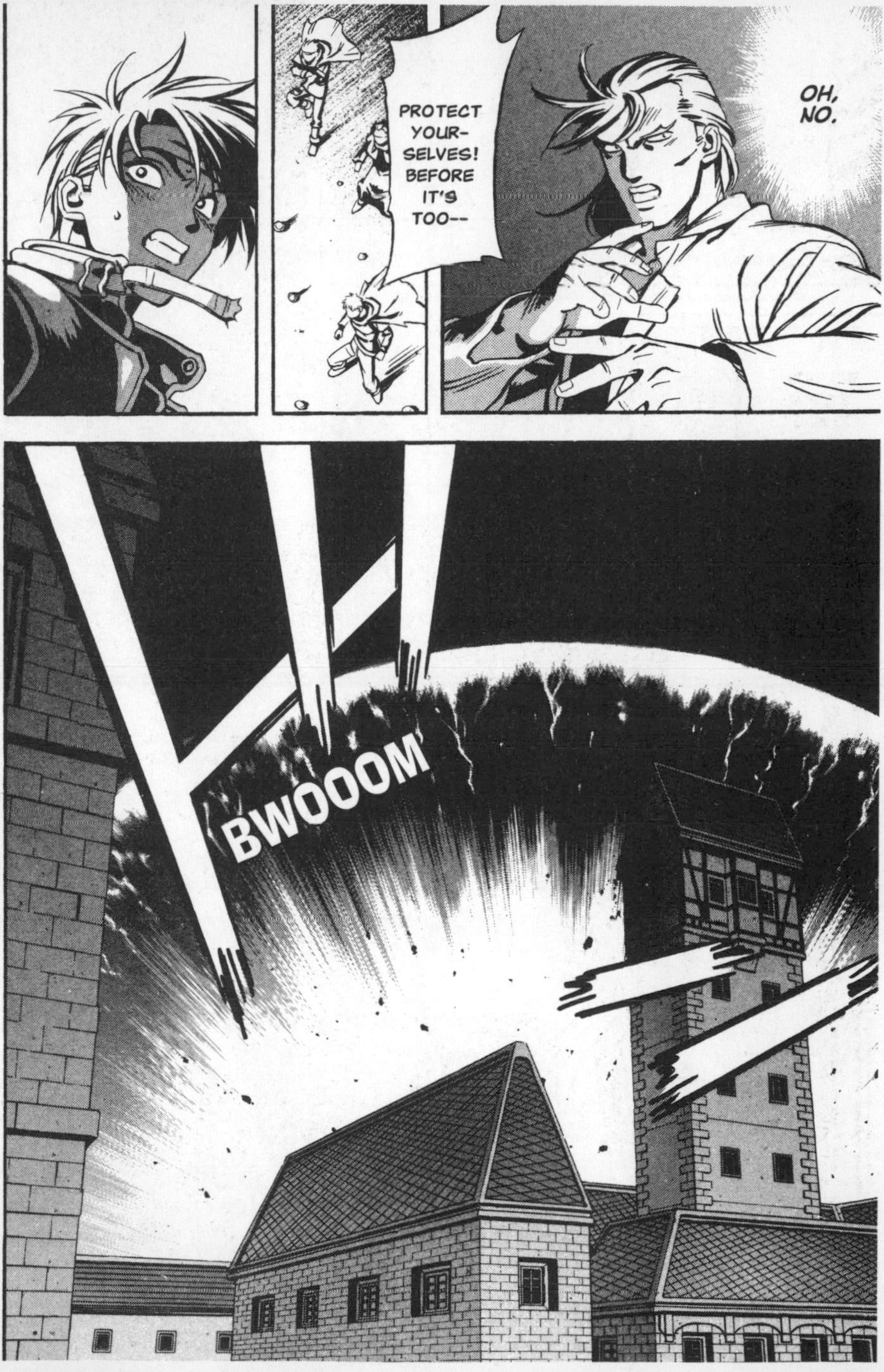
OH, NO.
PROTECT YOUR-SELVES! BEFORE IT'S TOO--
BWOOOM

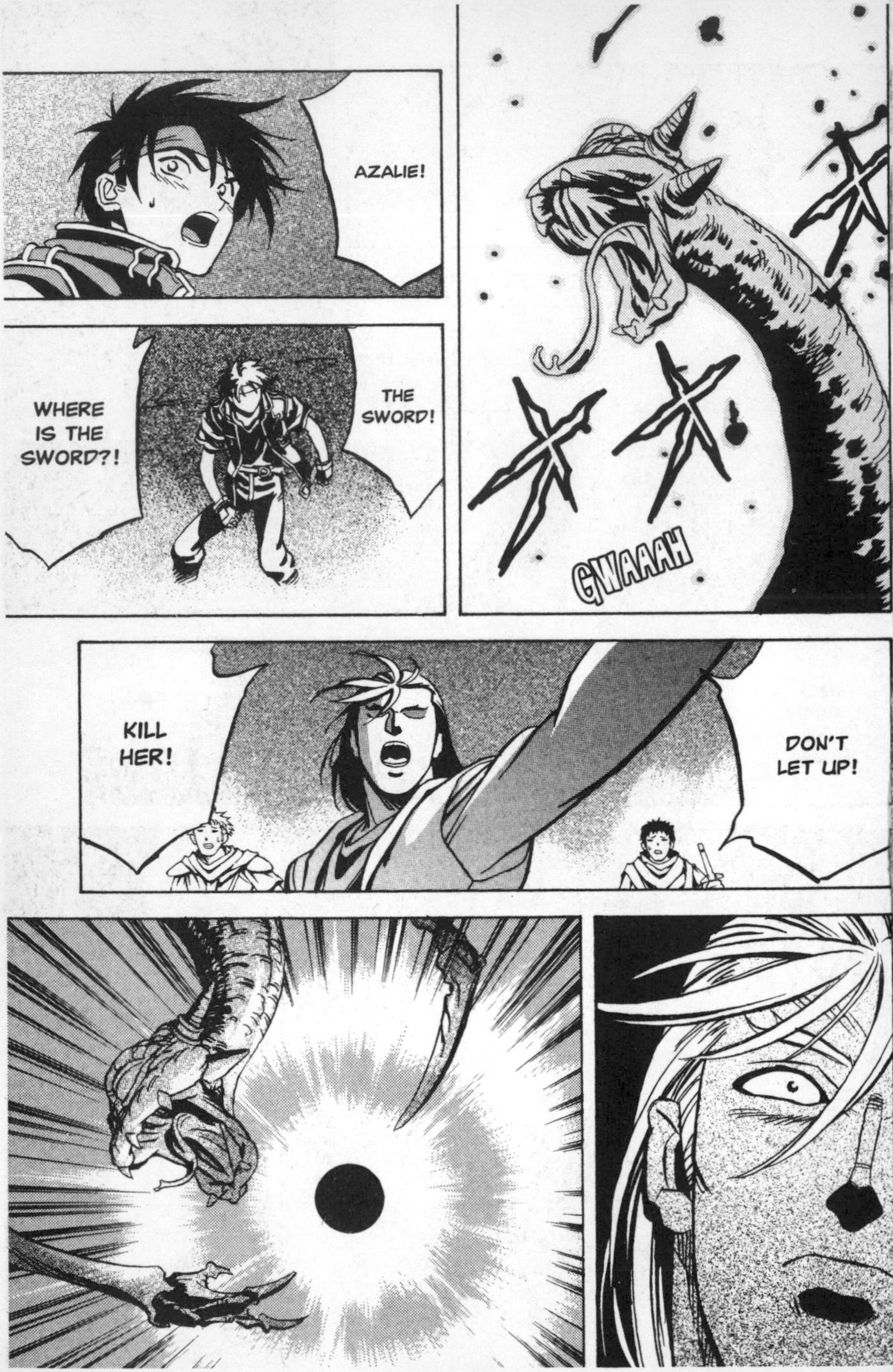

AZALIE!
WHERE IS THE SWORD?!
THE SWORD!
GWAAAH
KILL HER!
DON'T LET UP!

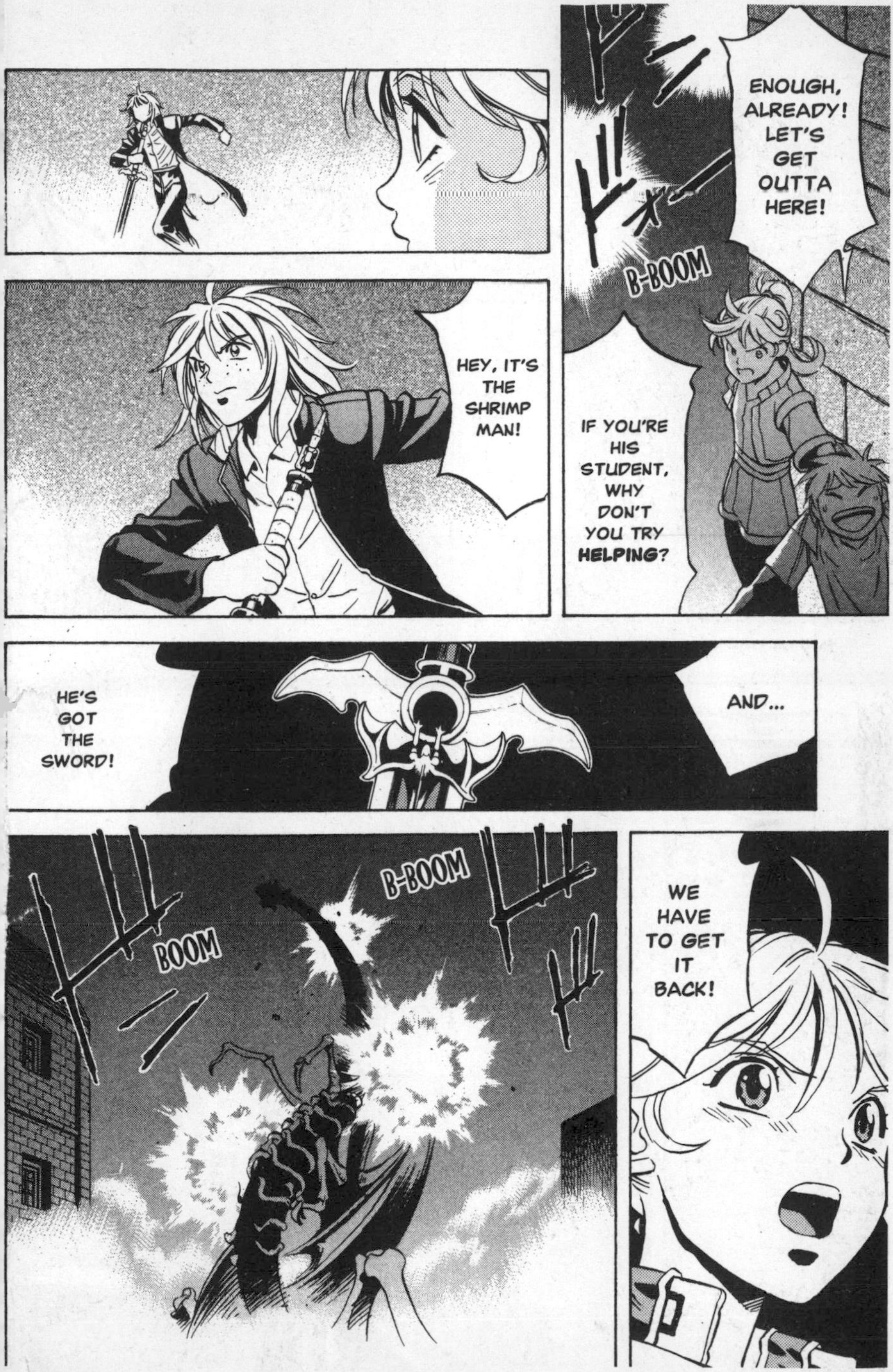
ENOUGH, ALREADY! LET'S GET OUTTA HERE!
B-BOOM
IF YOU'RE HIS STUDENT, WHY DON'T YOU TRY HELPING?
HEY, IT'S THE SHRIMP MAN!
AND...
HE'S GOT THE SWORD!
WE HAVE TO GET IT BACK!
B-BOOM
BOOM

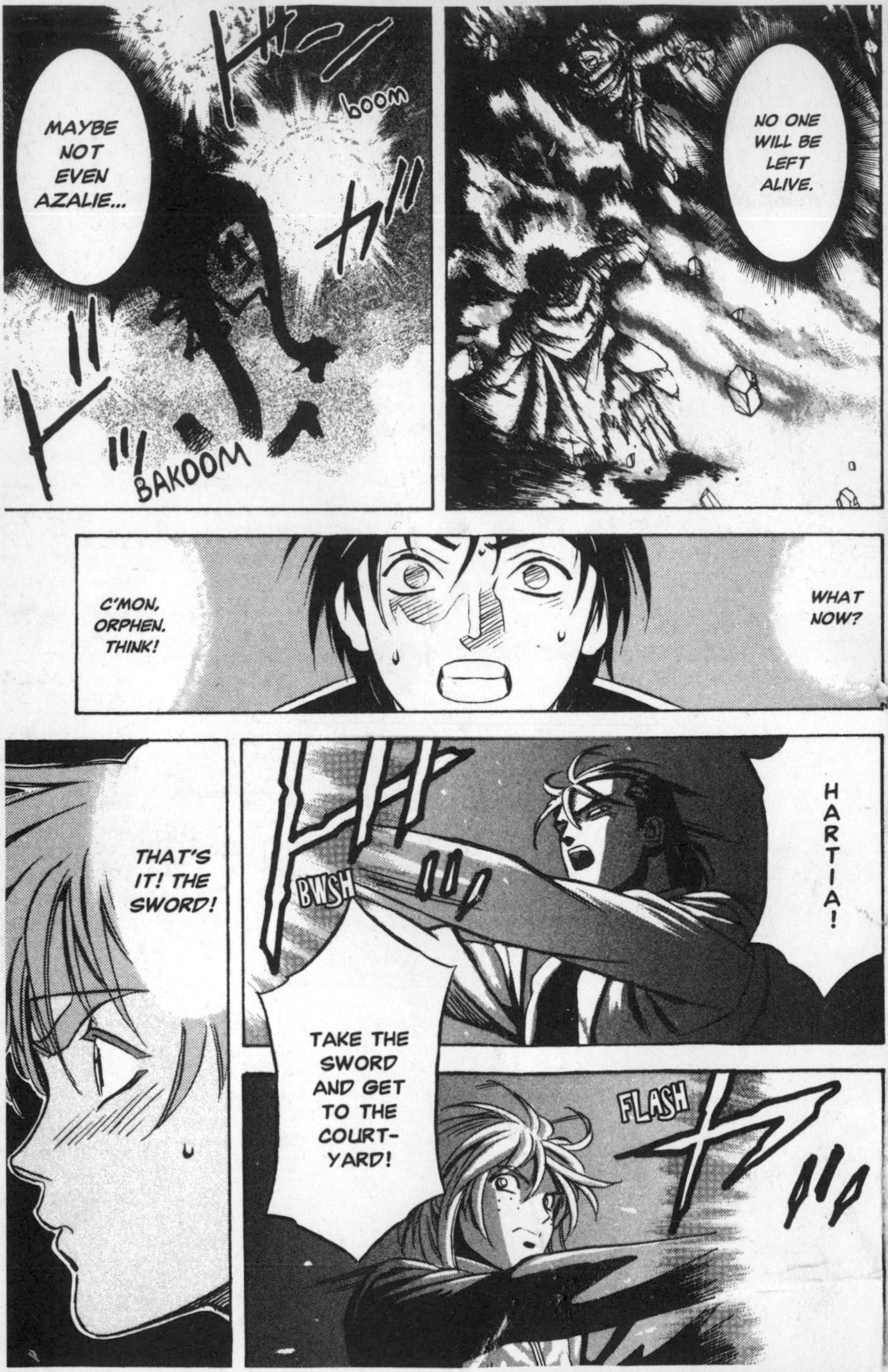
NO ONE WILL BE LEFT ALIVE.
MAYBE NOT EVEN AZALIE...
boom
BAKOOM
WHAT NOW?
C'MON, ORPHEN. THINK!
THAT'S IT! THE SWORD!
HARTIA!
BWSH
TAKE THE SWORD AND GET TO THE COURT-YARD!
FLASH

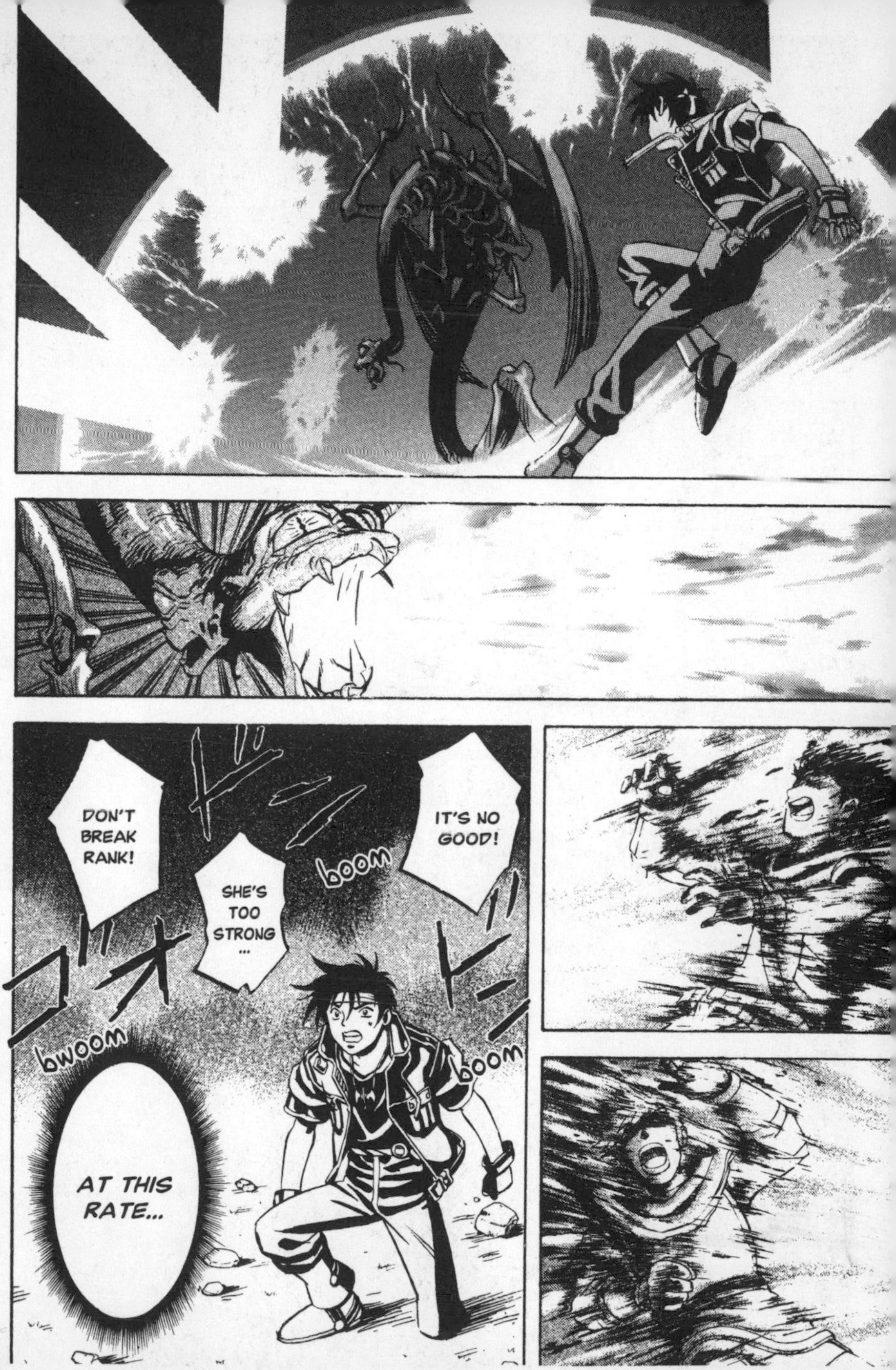
IT'S NO GOOD!
boom
DON'T BREAK RANK!
SHE'S TOO STRONG ...
boom
bwoom
AT THIS RATE...

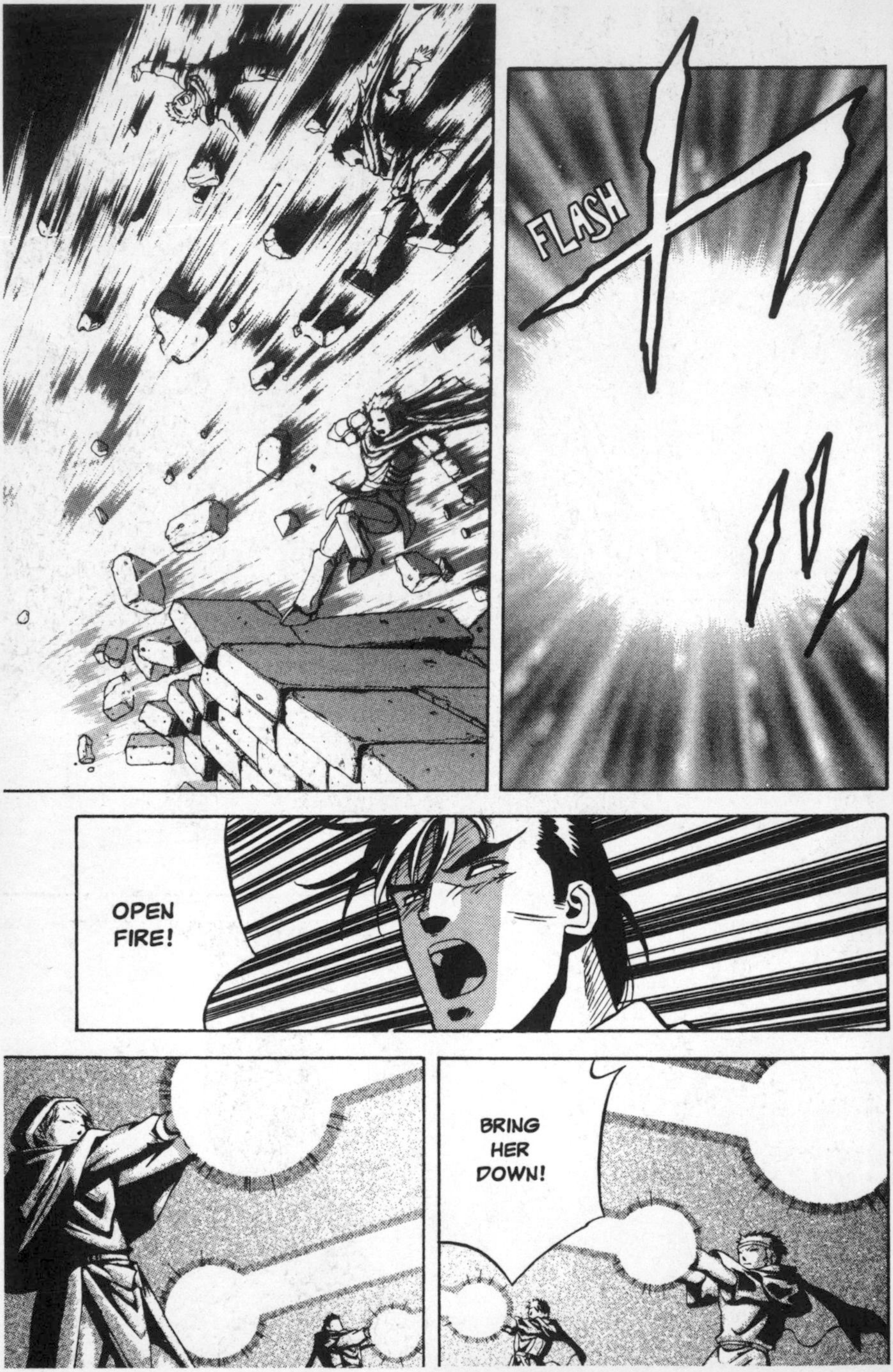
FLASH
OPEN FIRE!
BRING HER DOWN!

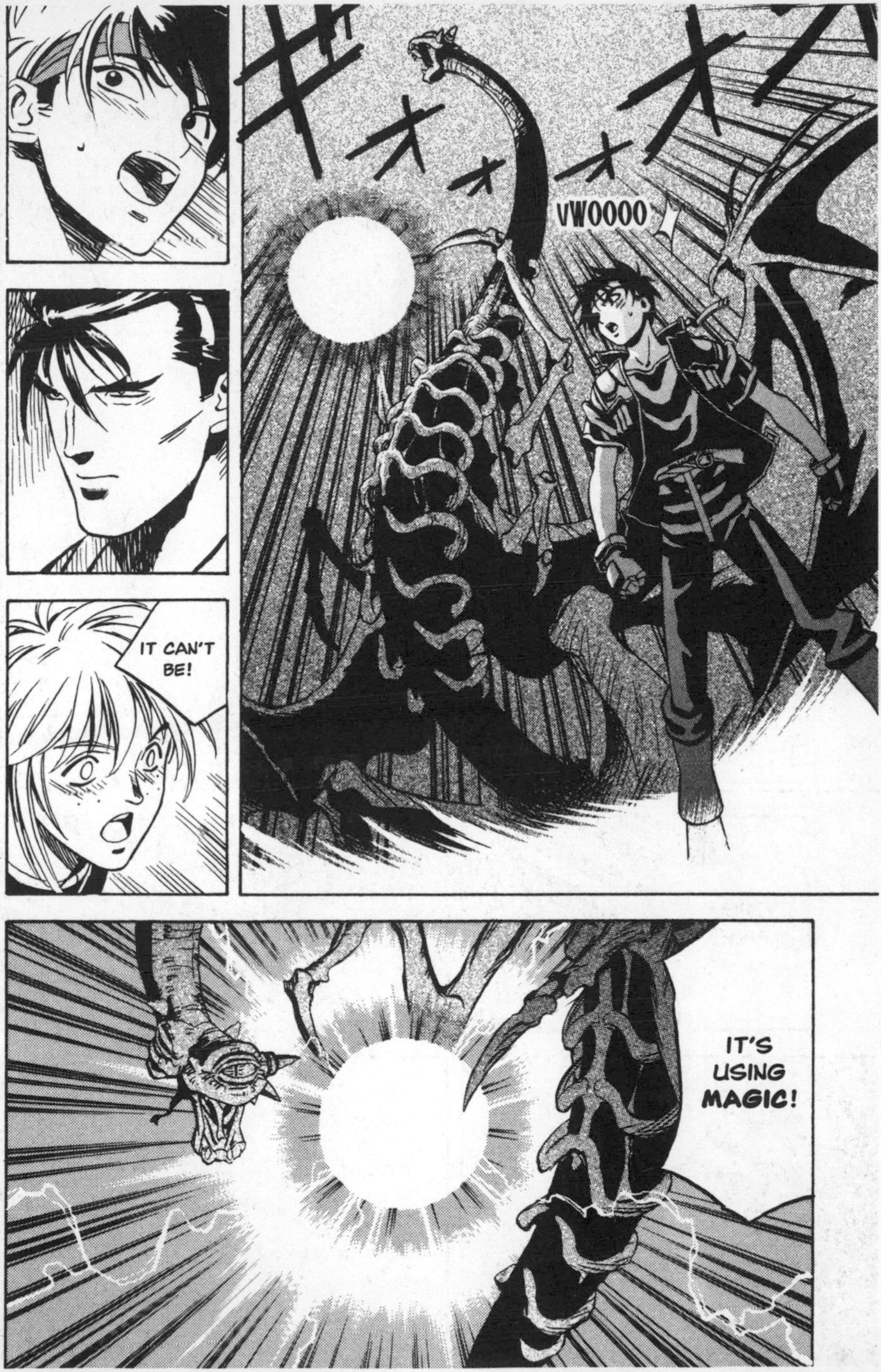
VWOOOO
IT CAN'T BE!
IT'S USING MAGIC!

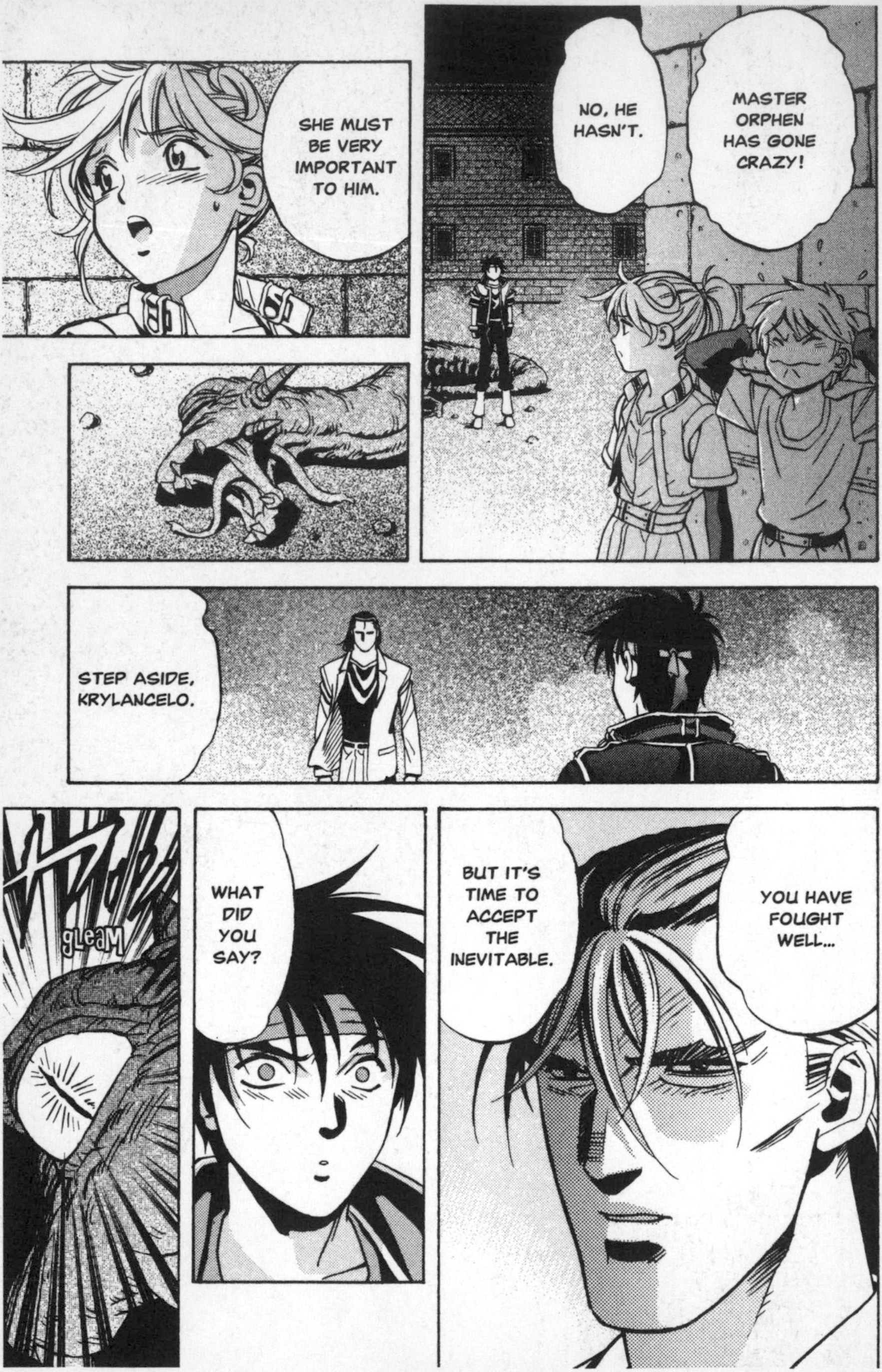
MASTER ORPHEN HAS GONE CRAZY!
NO, HE HASN'T.
SHE MUST BE VERY IMPORTANT TO HIM.
STEP ASIDE, KRYLANCELO.
YOU HAVE FOUGHT WELL...
BUT IT'S TIME TO ACCEPT THE INEVITABLE.
WHAT DID YOU SAY?
gleam

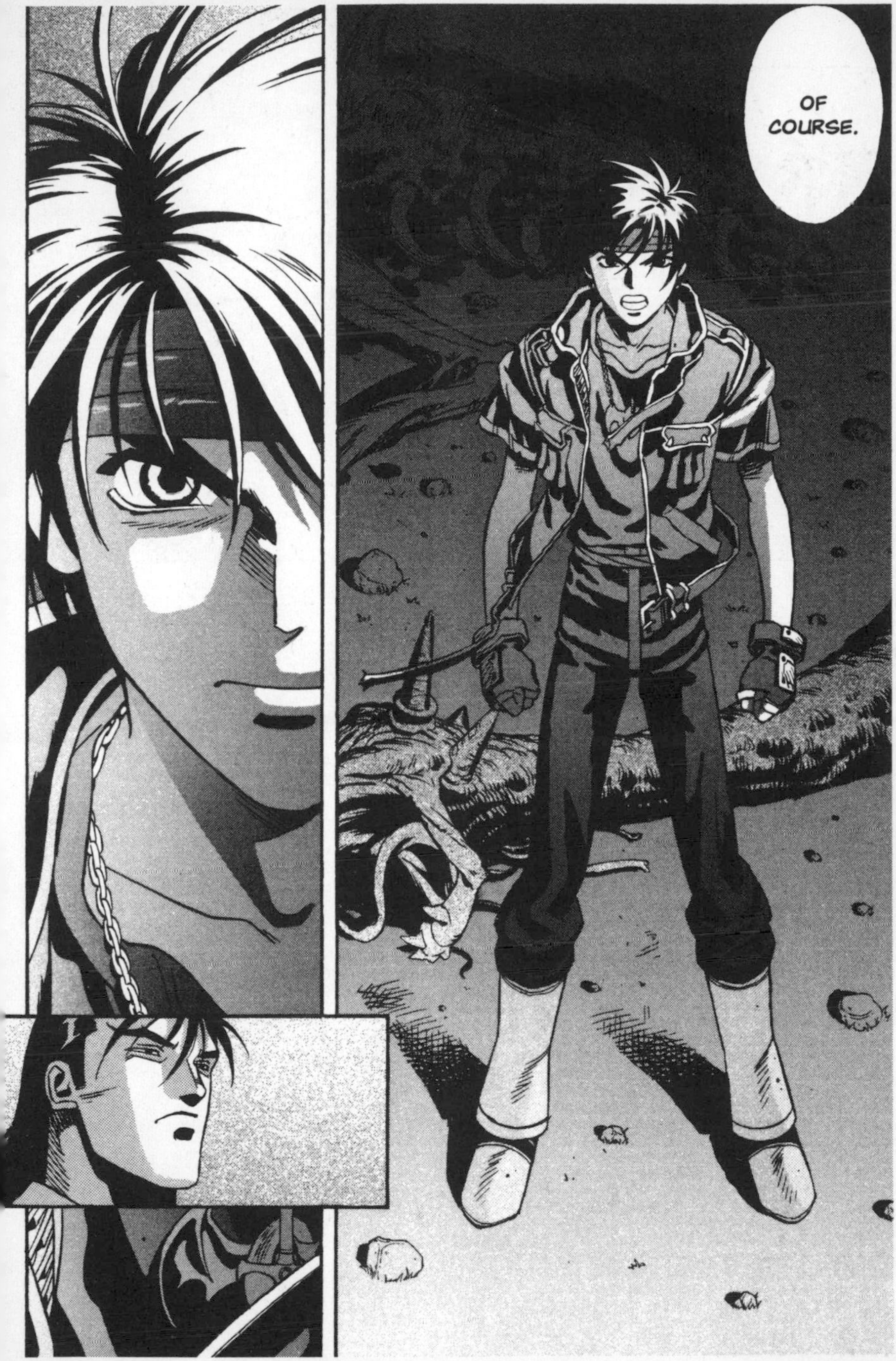
OF COURSE.

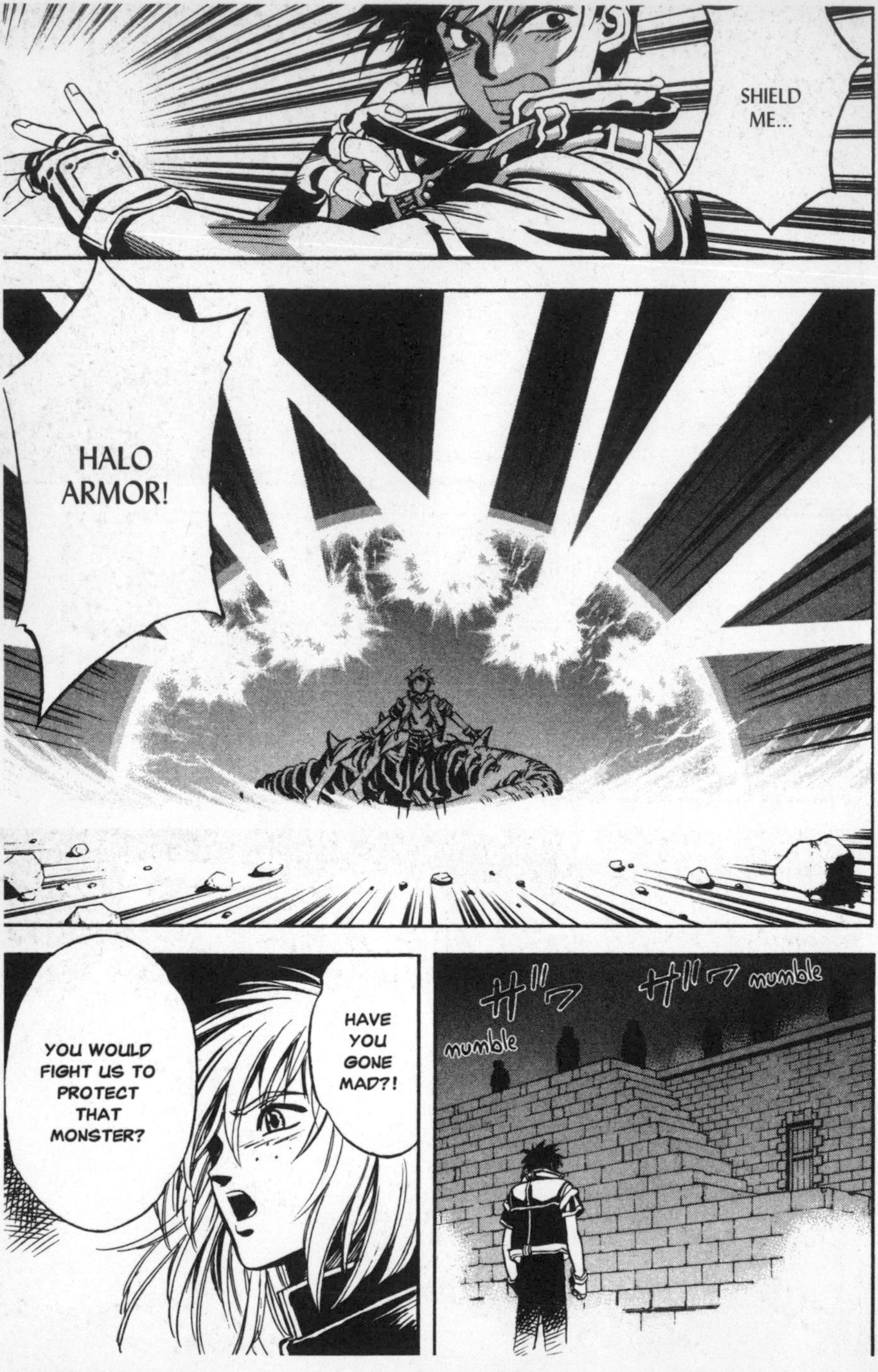
SHIELD ME...
HALO ARMOR!
HAVE YOU GONE MAD?!
YOU WOULD FIGHT US TO PROTECT THAT MONSTER?
ザワ ザワ
mumble
mumble

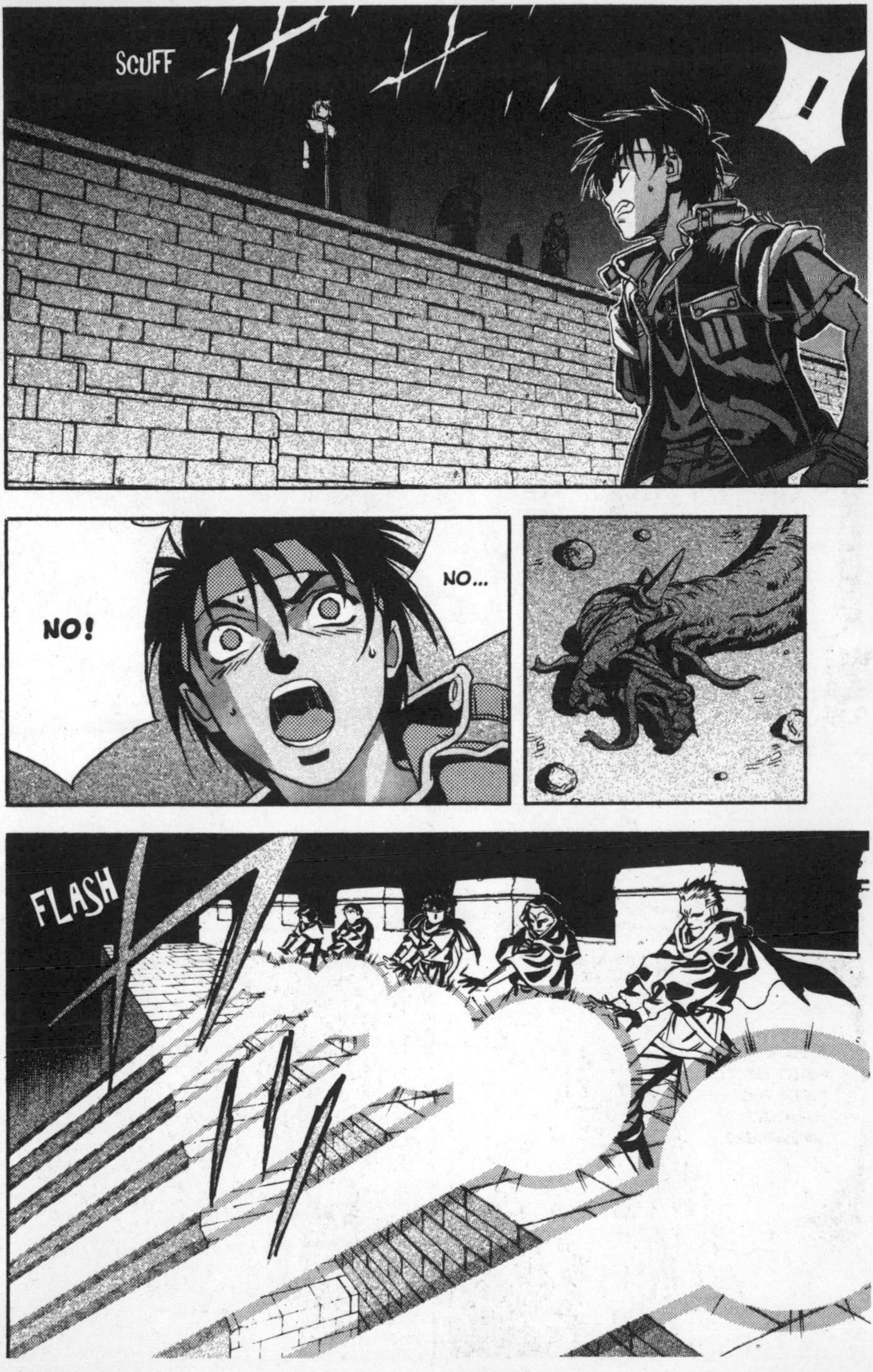
!
SCUFF
NO...
NO!
FLASH

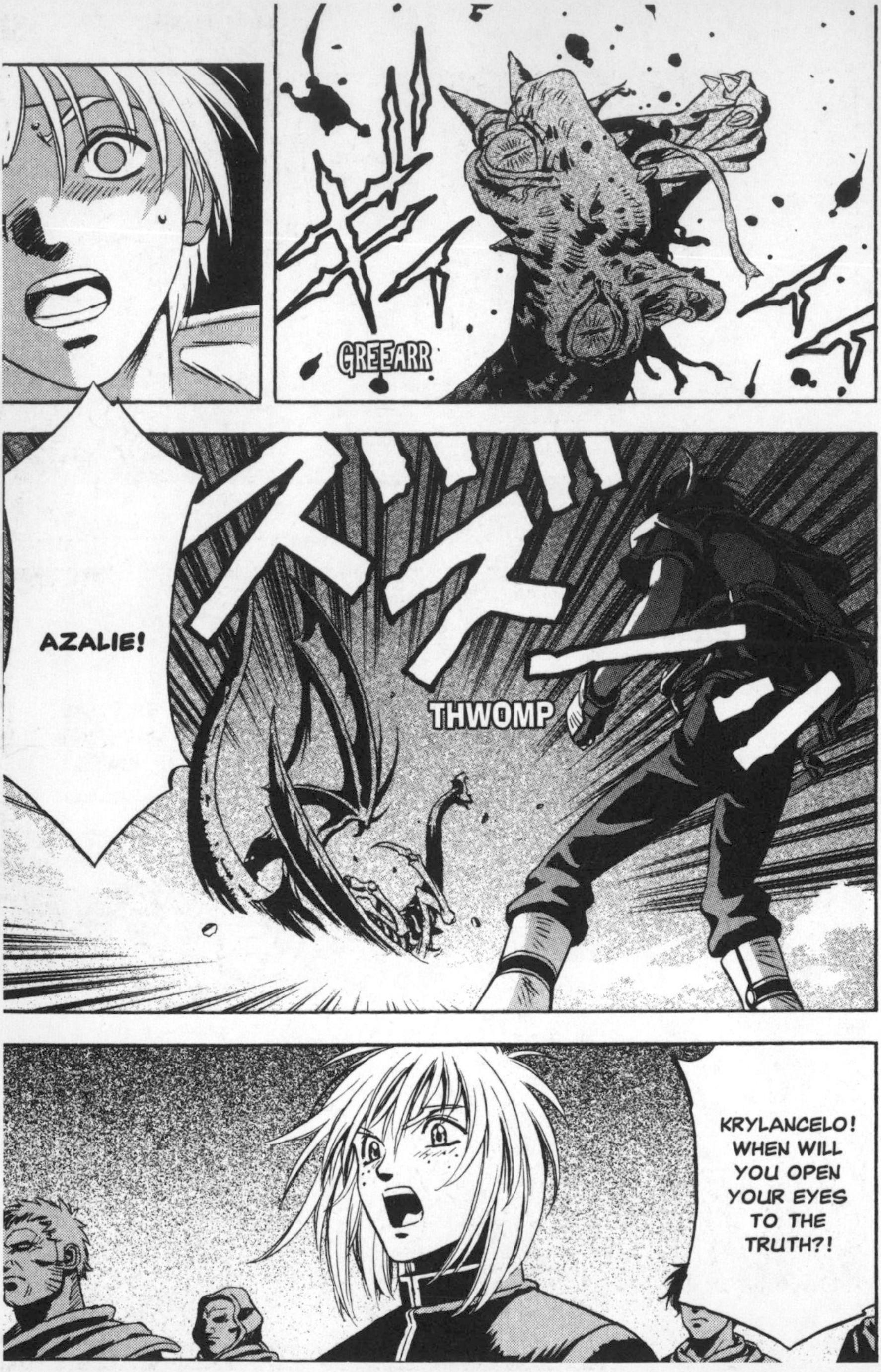
GREEARR
AZALIE!
THWOMP
KRYLANCELO! WHEN WILL YOU OPEN YOUR EYES TO THE TRUTH?!

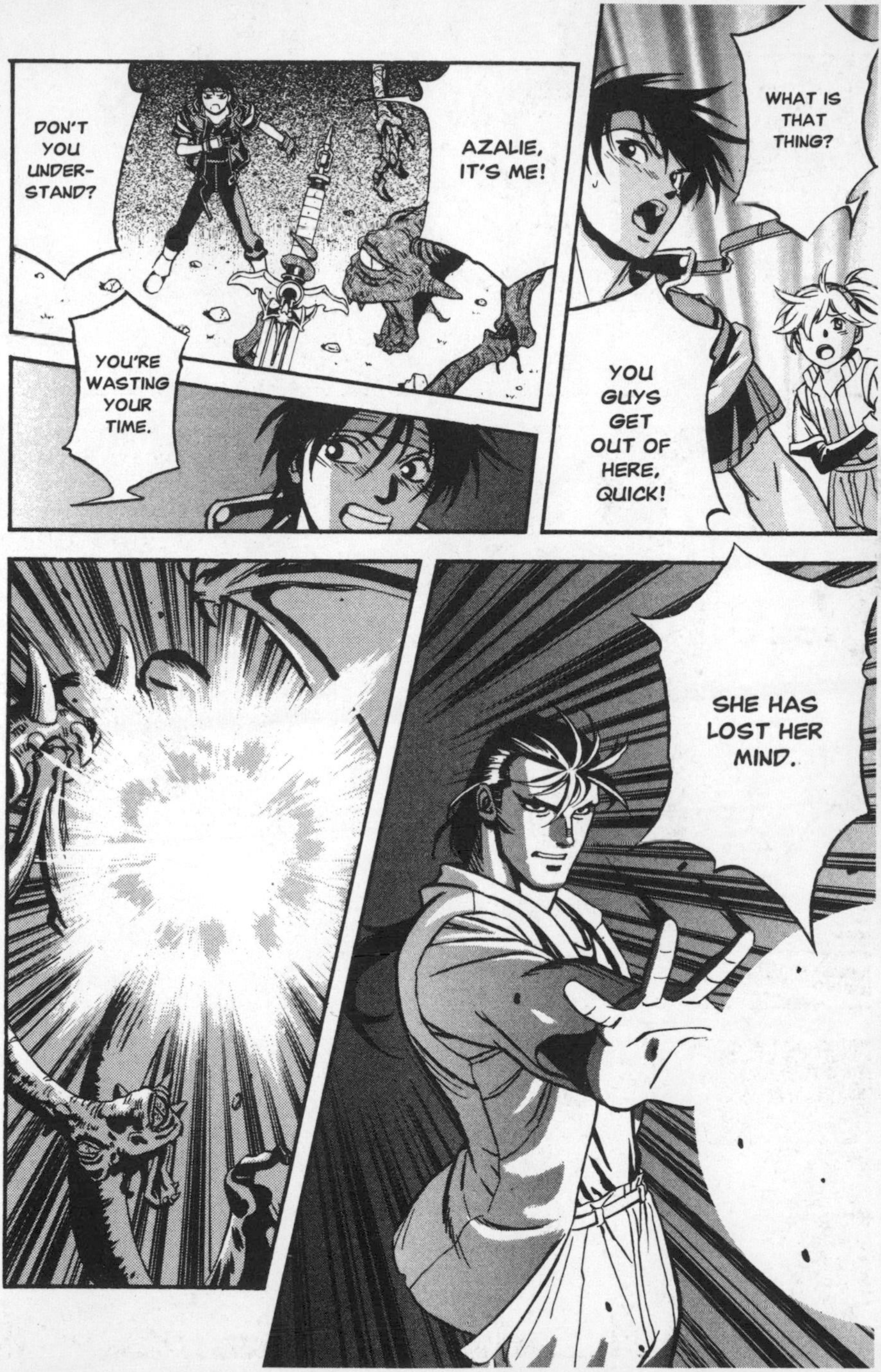
AZALIE, IT'S ME!
DON'T YOU UNDER-STAND?
YOU'RE WASTING YOUR TIME.
WHAT IS THAT THING?
YOU GUYS GET OUT OF HERE, QUICK!
SHE HAS LOST HER MIND.

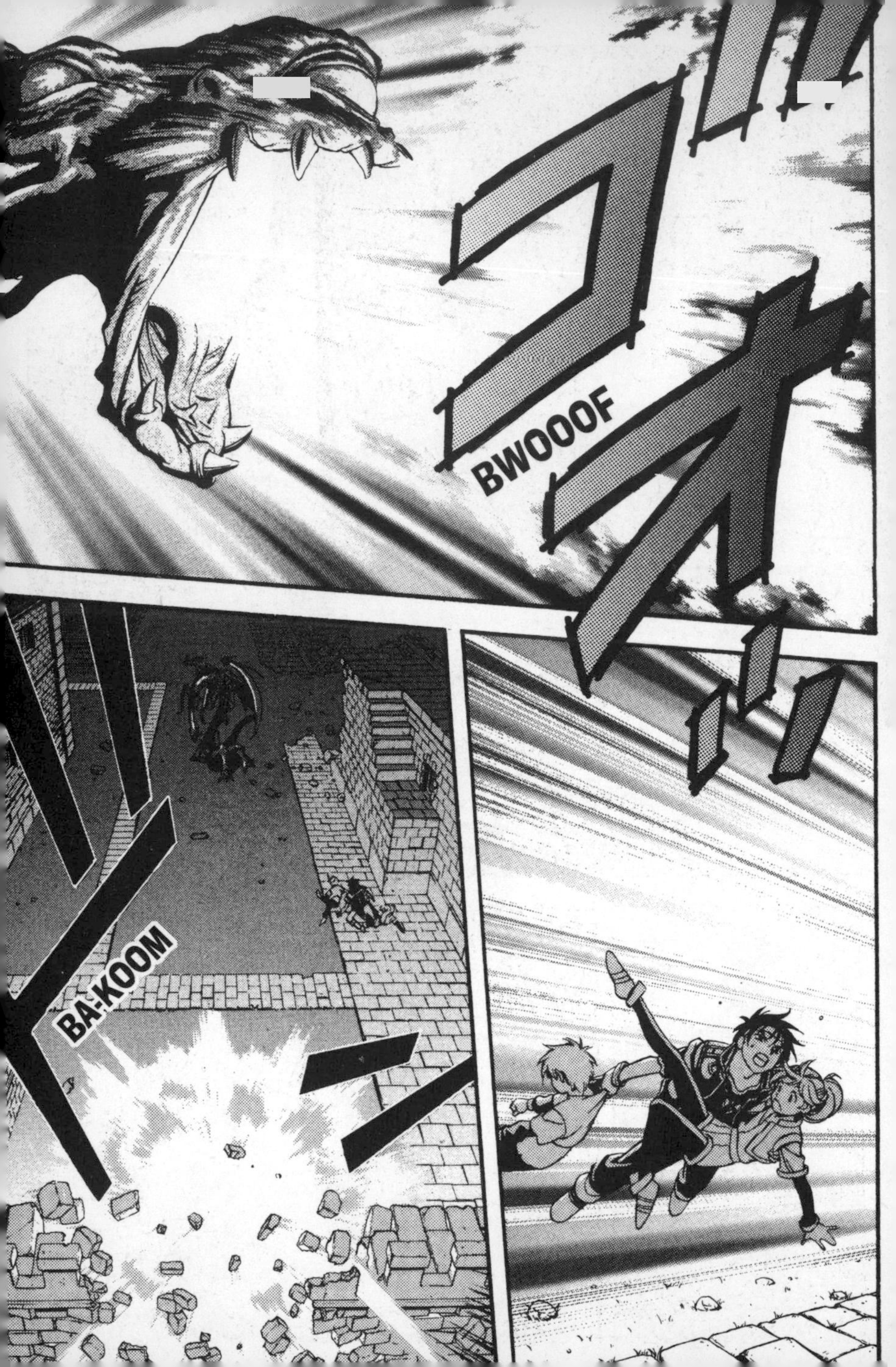
BWOOOF
BA-KOOM

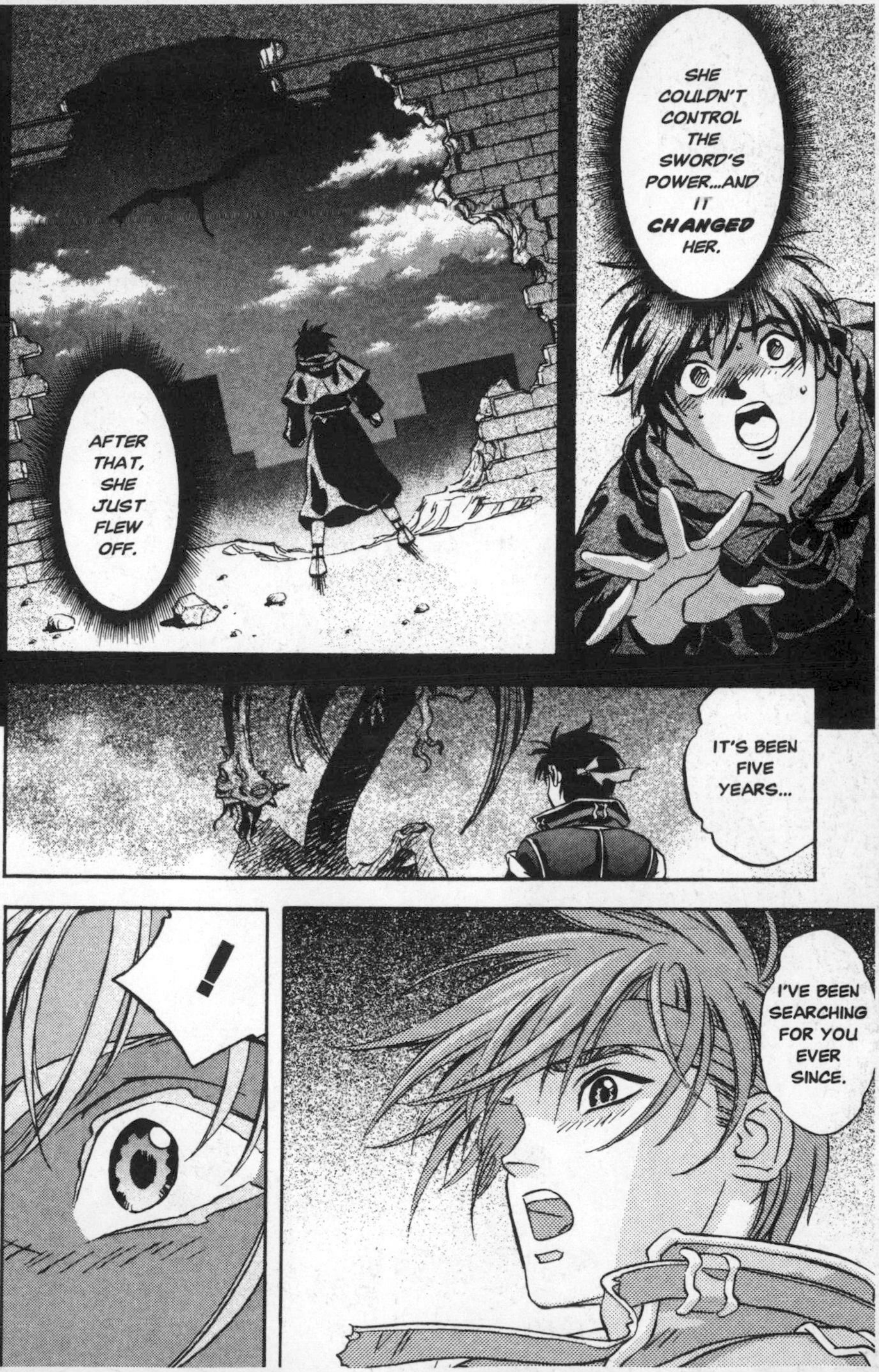
SHE COULDN'T CONTROL THE SWORD'S POWER...AND IT CHANGED HER.
AFTER THAT, SHE JUST FLEW OFF.
IT'S BEEN FIVE YEARS...
!
I'VE BEEN SEARCHING FOR YOU EVER SINCE.

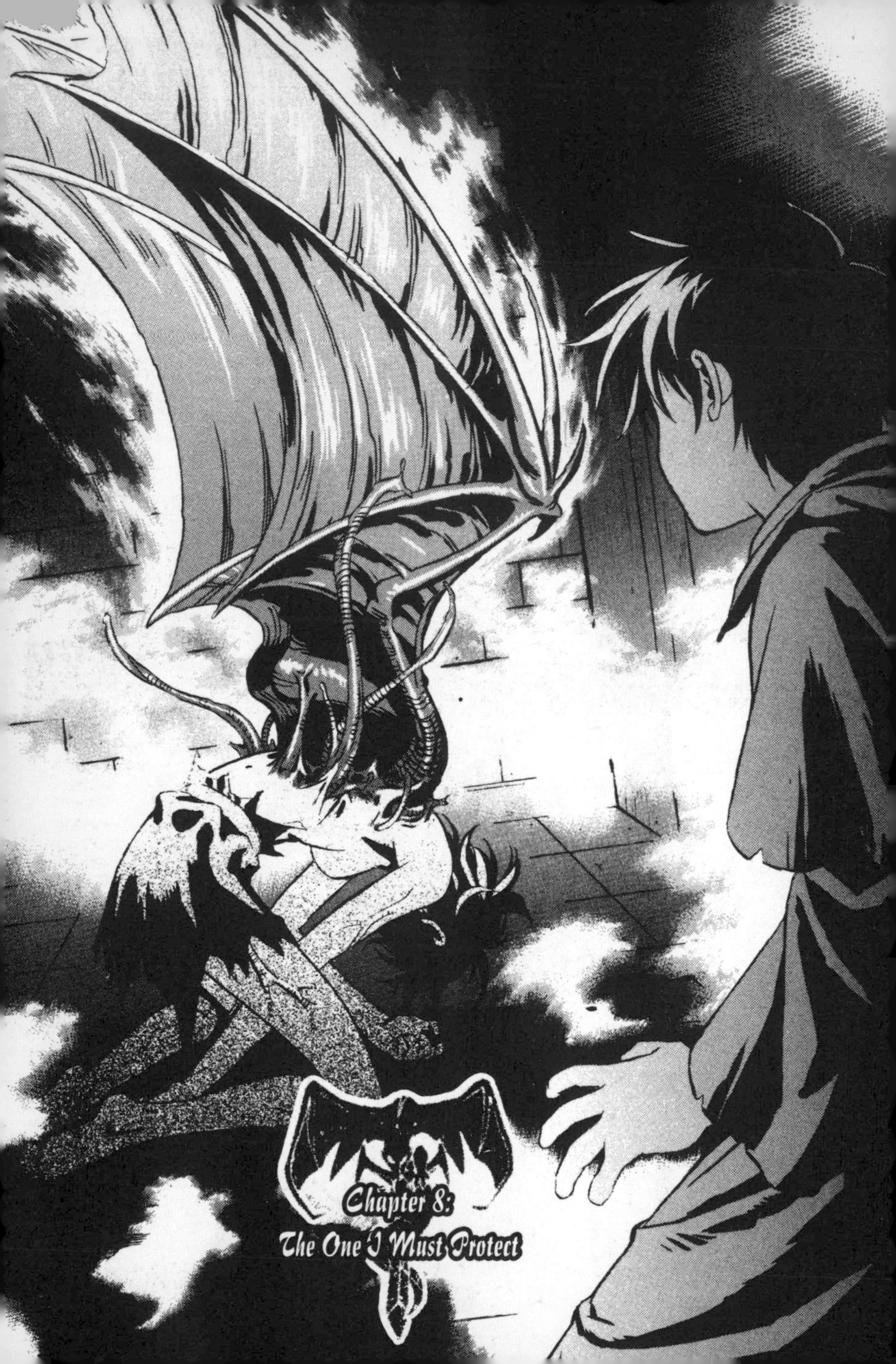
Chapter 8:
The One I Must Protect

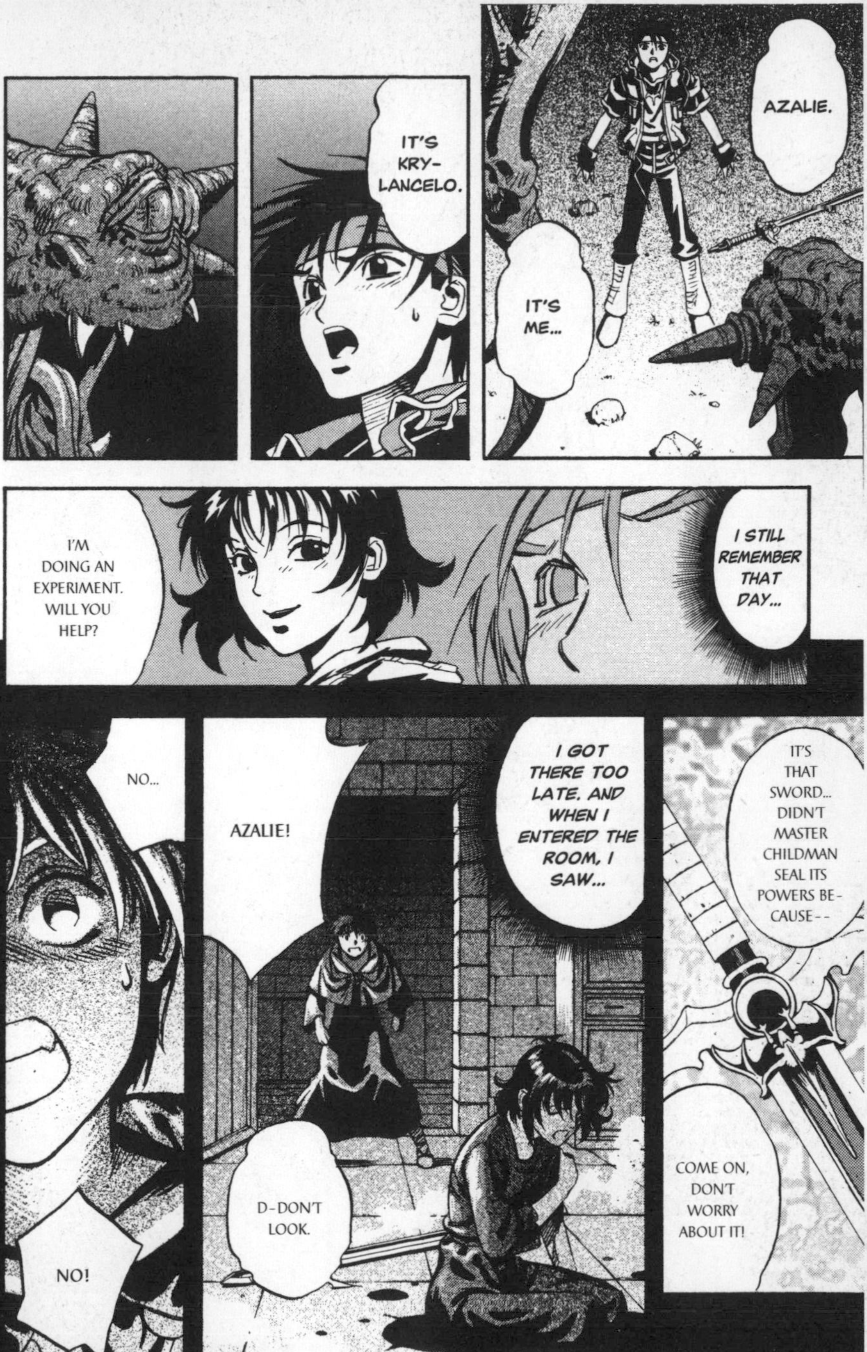

AZALIE.
IT'S ME...
IT'S KRY-LANCELO.
I STILL REMEMBER THAT DAY...
I'M DOING AN EXPERIMENT. WILL YOU HELP?
IT'S THAT SWORD... DIDN'T MASTER CHILDMAN SEAL ITS POWERS BE-CAUSE--
COME ON, DON'T WORRY ABOUT IT!
I GOT THERE TOO LATE. AND WHEN I ENTERED THE ROOM, I SAW...
AZALIE!
D-DON'T LOOK.
NO...
NO!

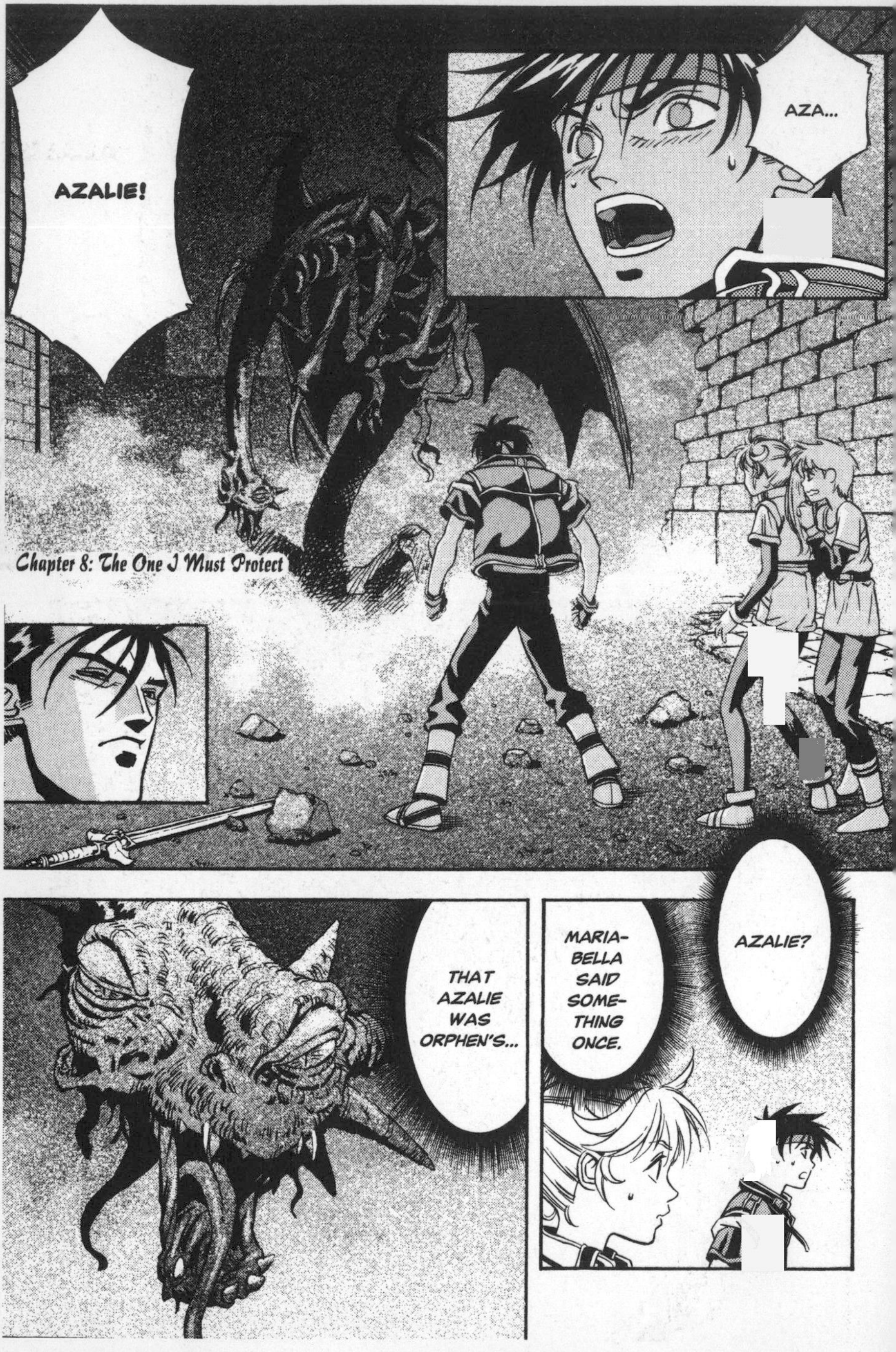
AZA...
AZALIE!
Chapter 8: The One I Must Protect
AZALIE?
MARIA-BELLA SAID SOMETHING ONCE.
THAT AZALIE WAS ORPHEN'S...

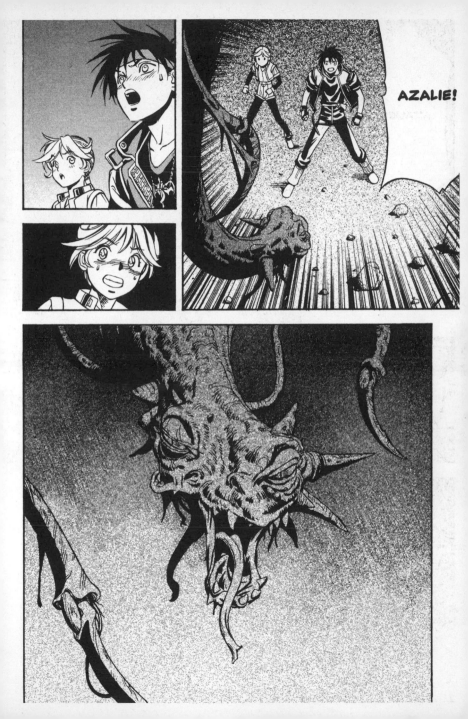

AZALIE!

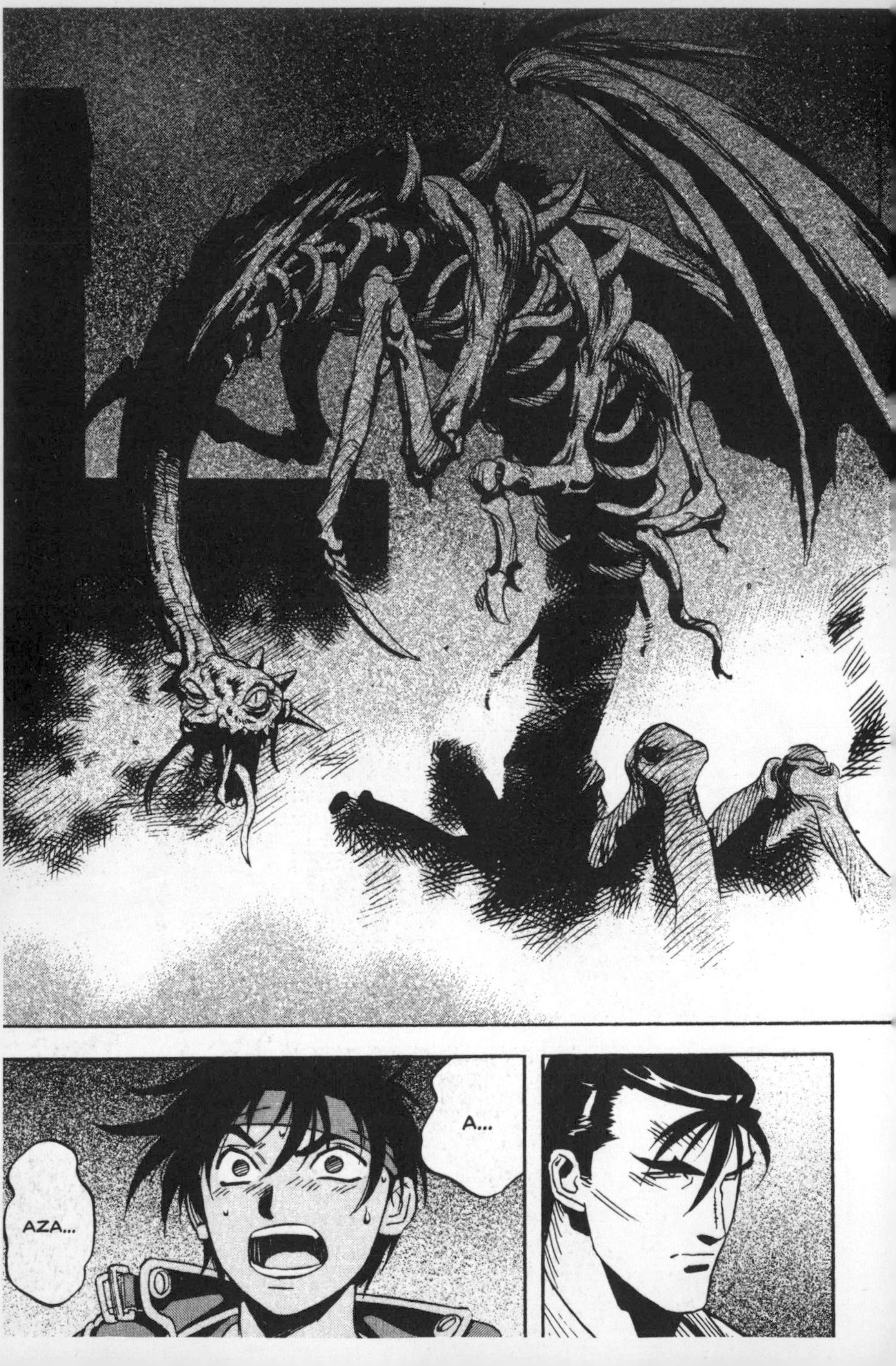
A...
AZA...

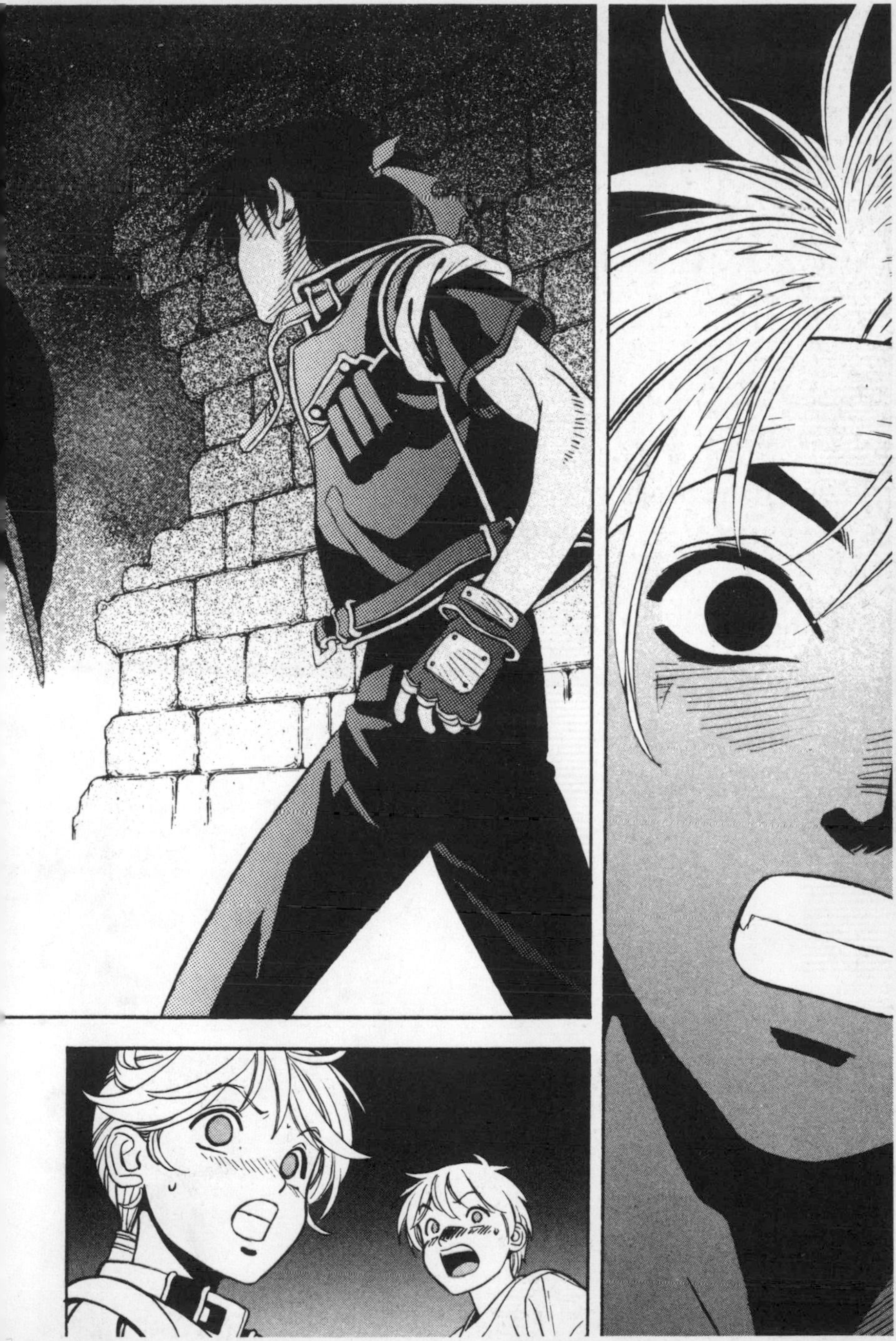

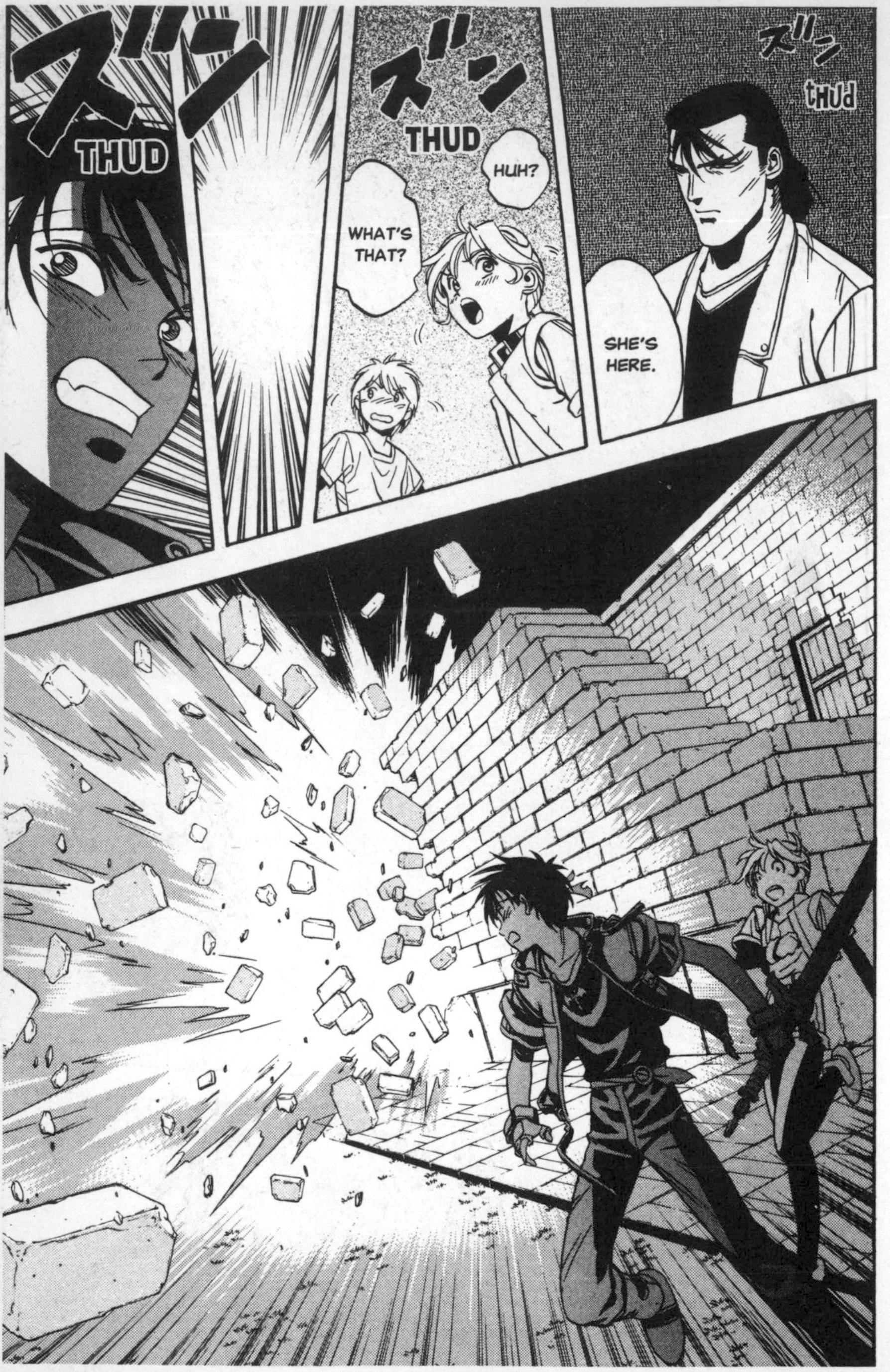
ズン
THUD
SHE'S HERE.
ズン
THUD
HUH?
WHAT'S THAT?
ズン
THUD

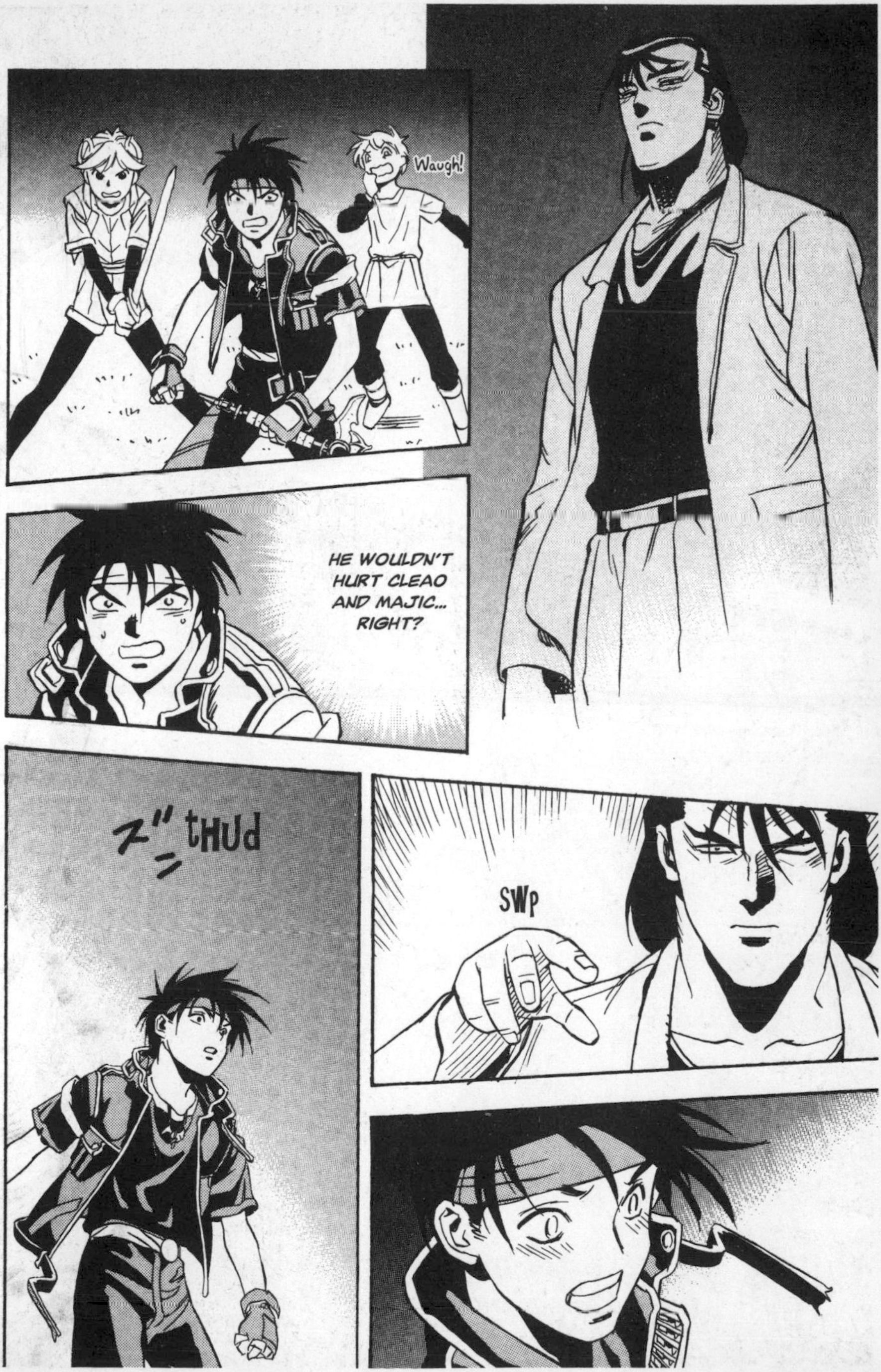
Waugh!
HE WOULDN'T HURT CLEAO AND MAJIC... RIGHT?
SWP
ズ" thUd

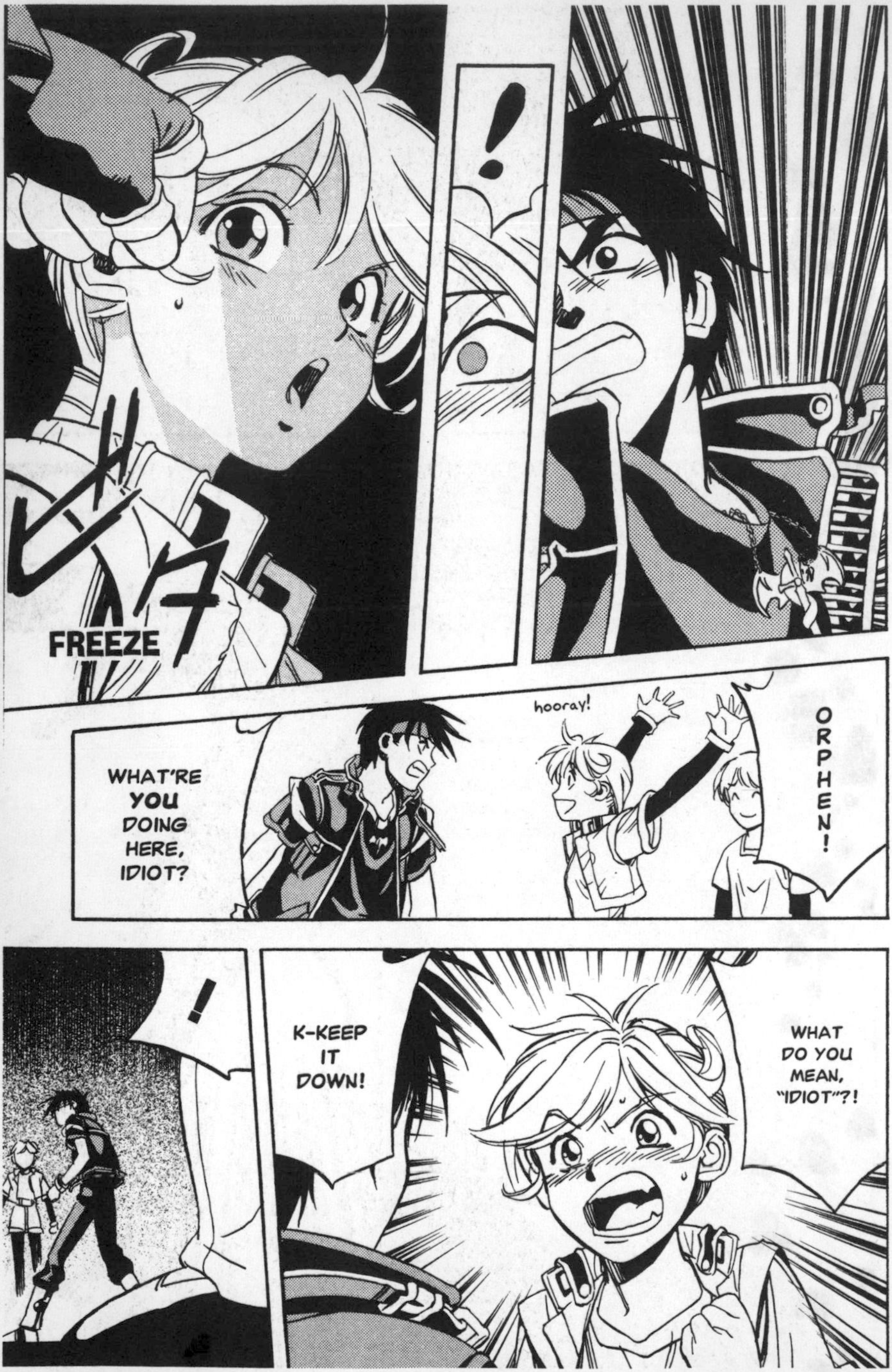
!
FREEZE
ORPHEN!
hooray!
WHAT'RE YOU DOING HERE, IDIOT?
WHAT DO YOU MEAN, "IDIOT"?!
K-KEEP IT DOWN!
!

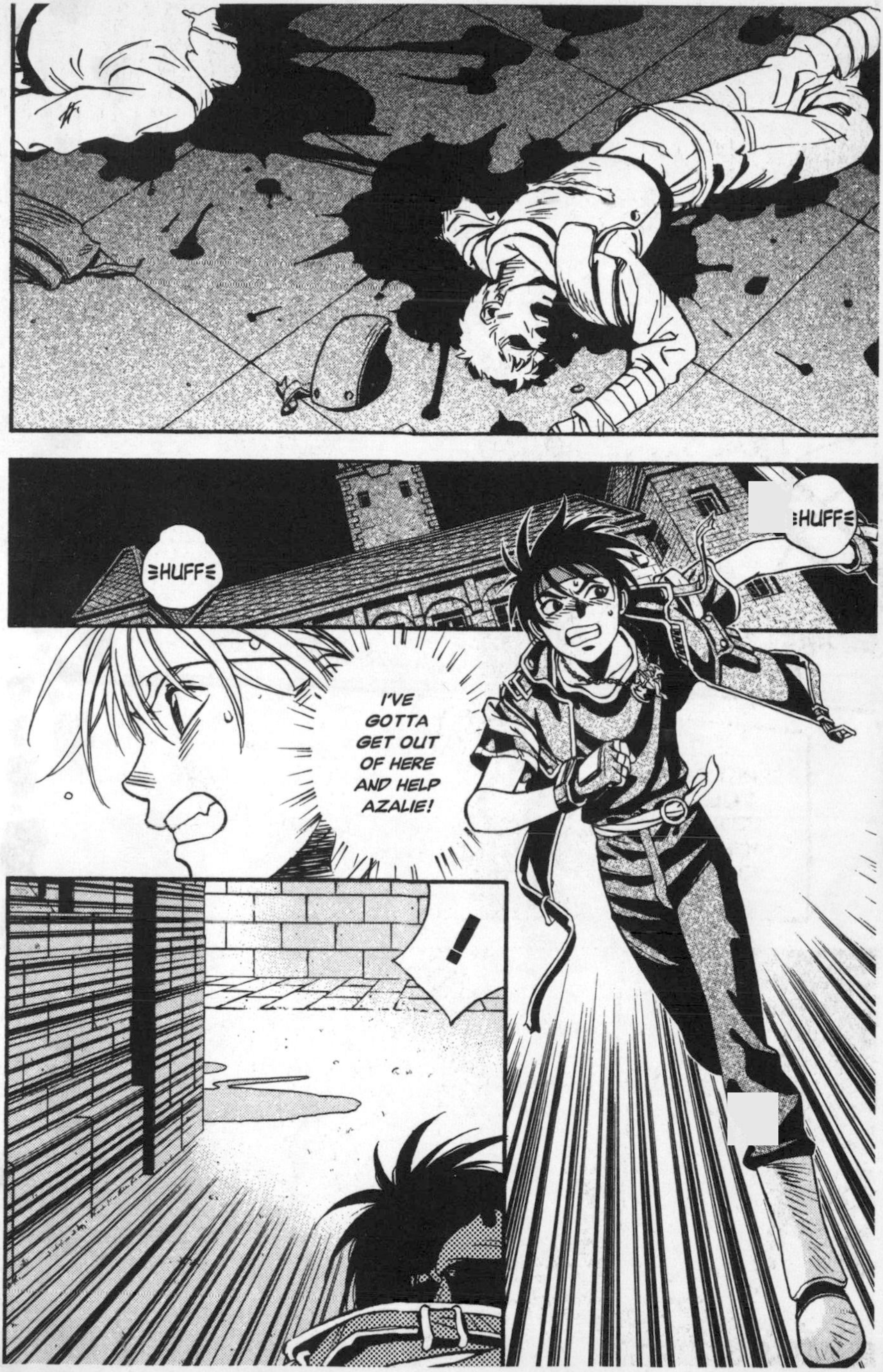
HUFF
HUFF
I'VE GOTTA GET OUT OF HERE AND HELP AZALIE!
!

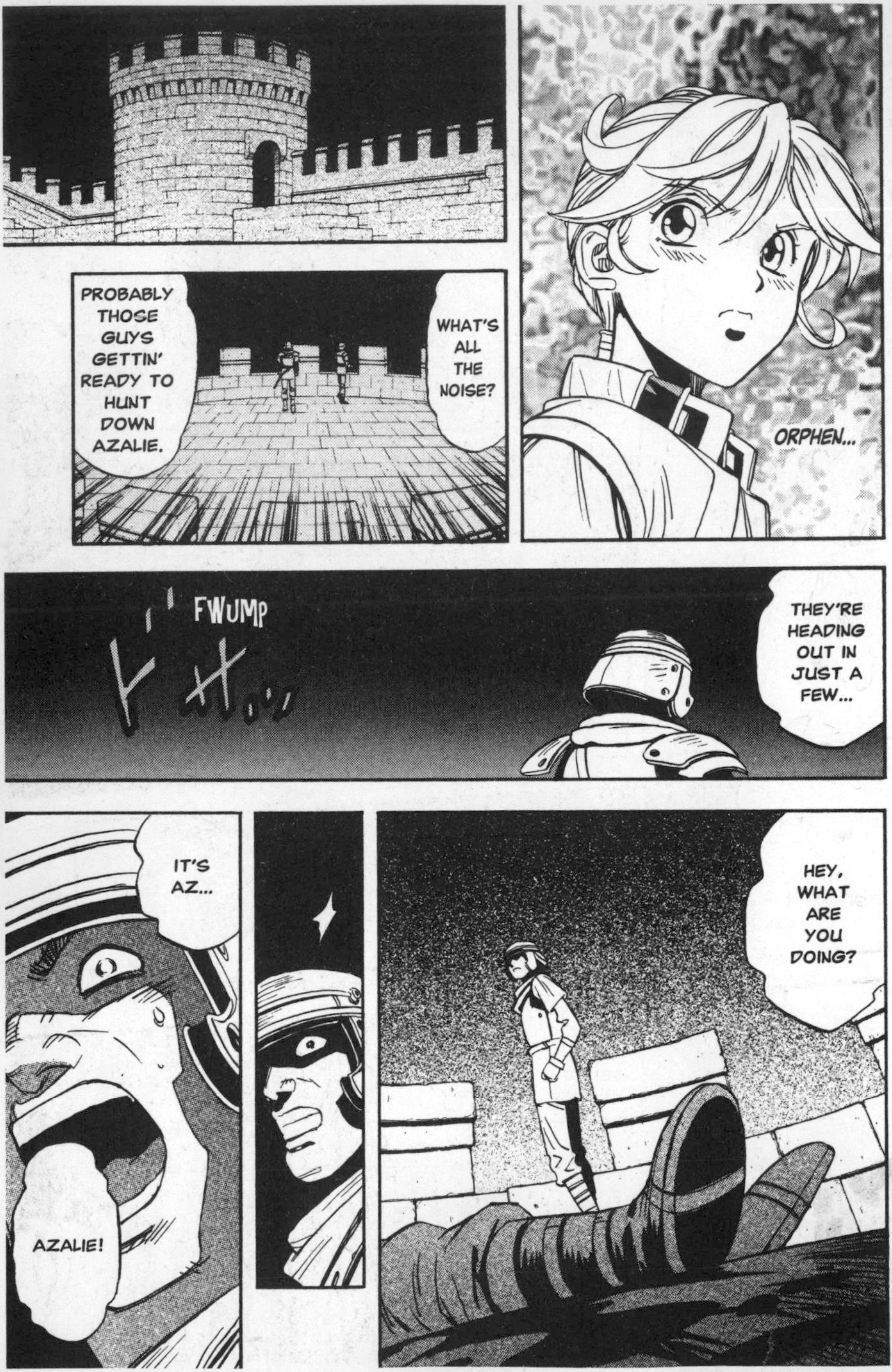
ORPHEN...
WHAT'S ALL THE NOISE?
PROBABLY THOSE GUYS GETTIN' READY TO HUNT DOWN AZALIE.
THEY'RE HEADING OUT IN JUST A FEW...
FWUMP
ドサッ
HEY, WHAT ARE YOU DOING?
IT'S AZ...
AZALIE!

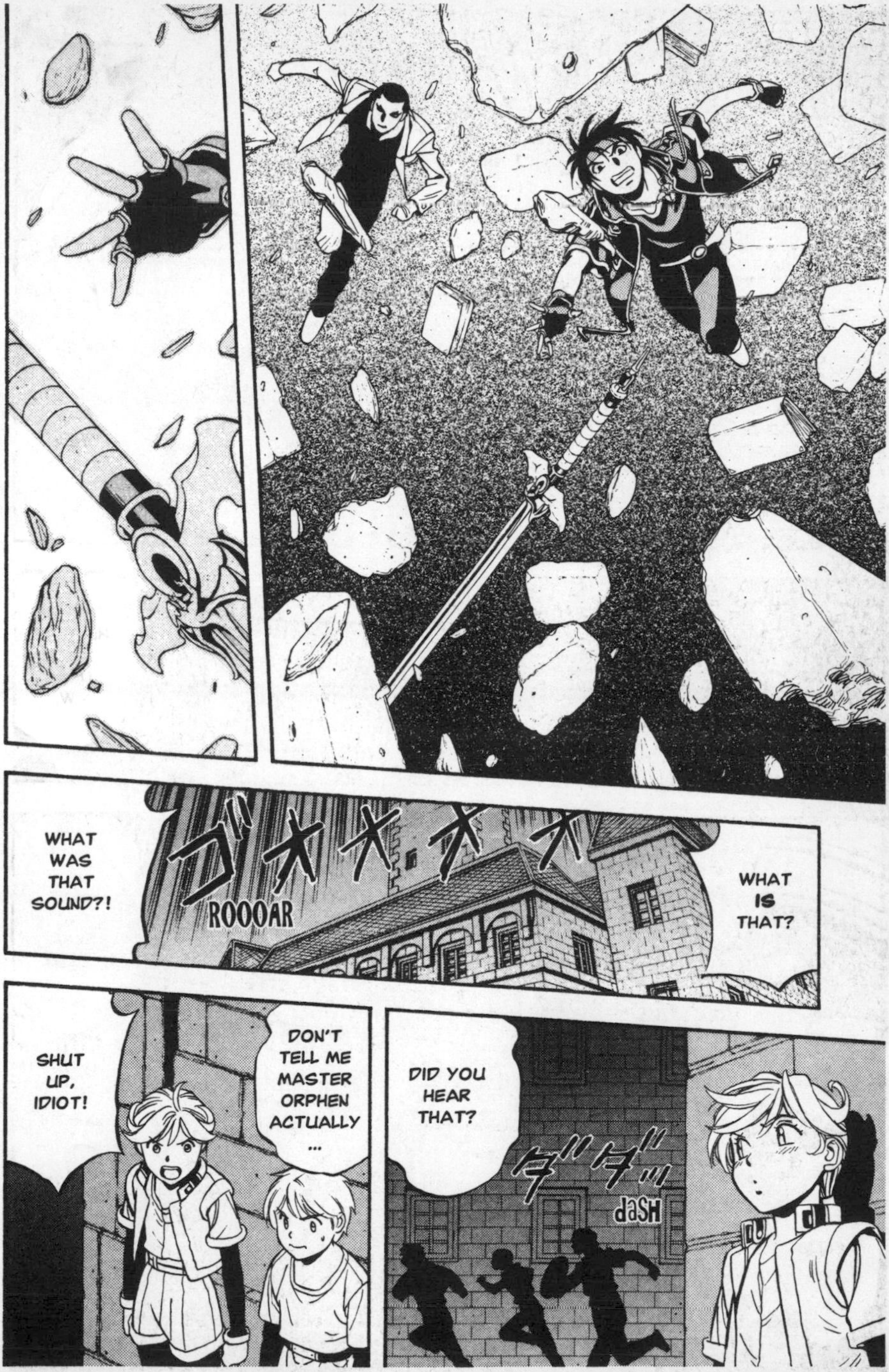
WHAT IS THAT?
ゴオオオオ
ROOOAR
WHAT WAS THAT SOUND?!
DID YOU HEAR THAT?
ダッダッ
dash
DON'T TELL ME MASTER ORPHEN ACTUALLY ...
SHUT UP, IDIOT!

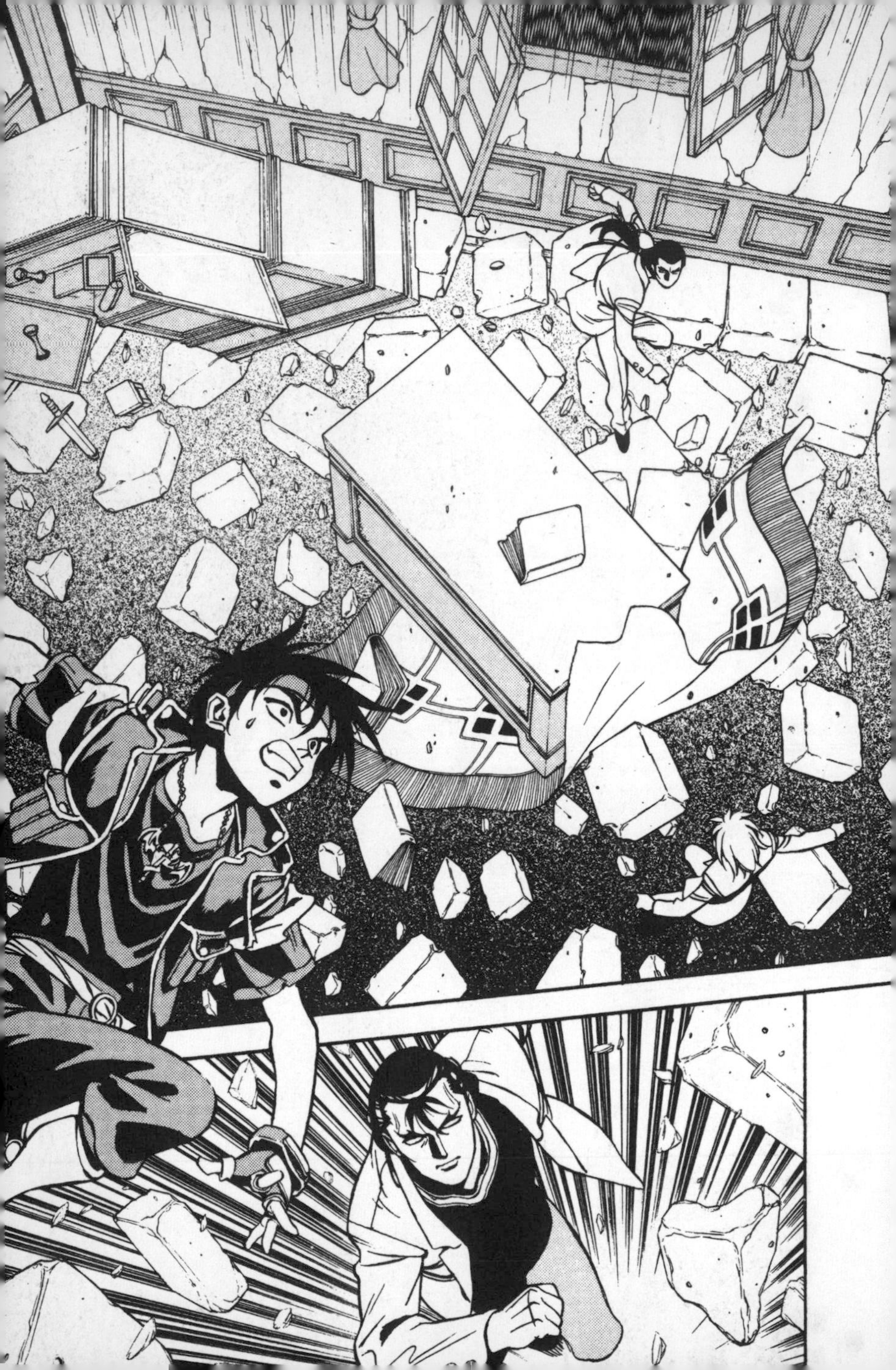

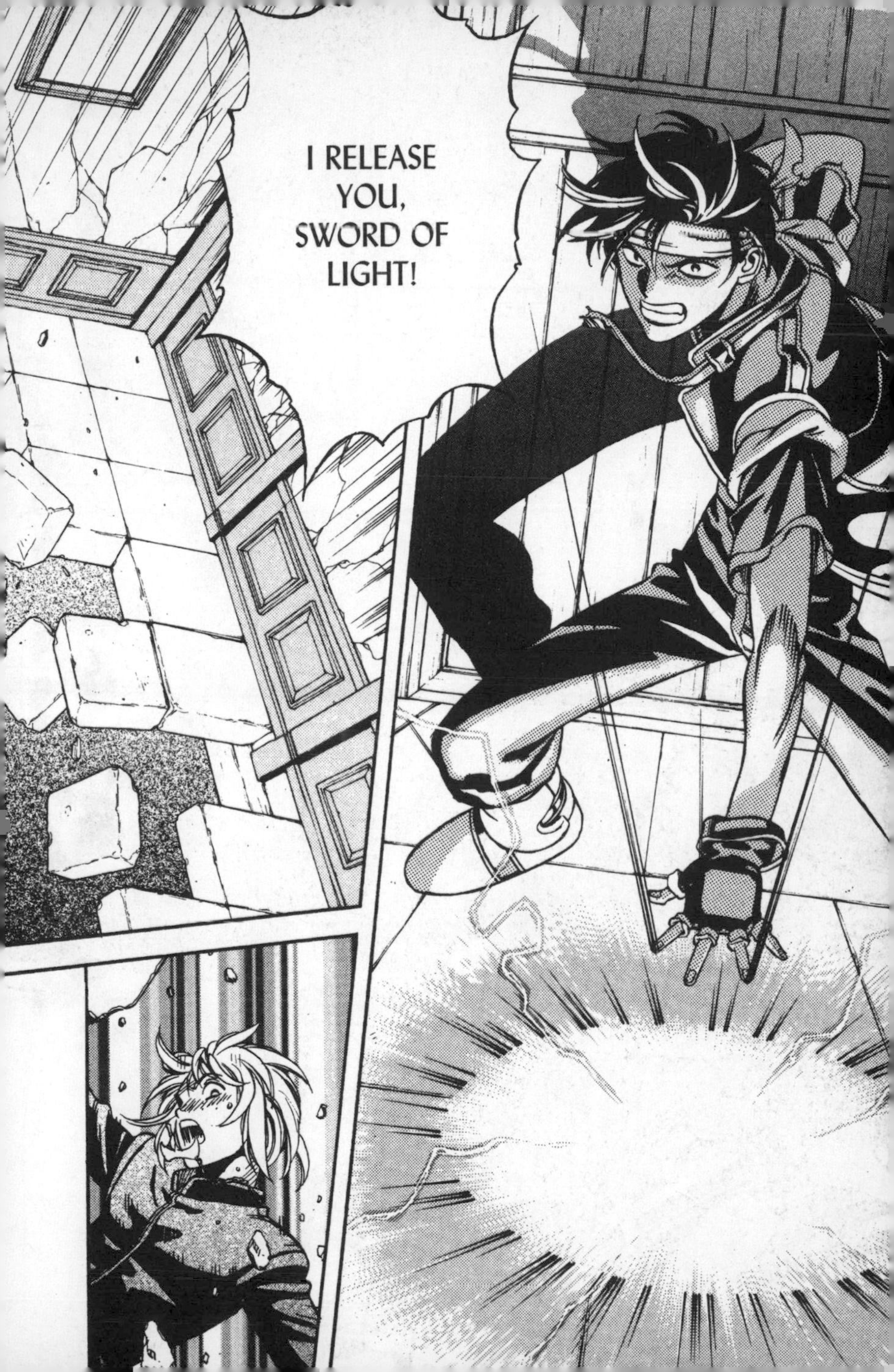
I RELEASE YOU, SWORD OF LIGHT!

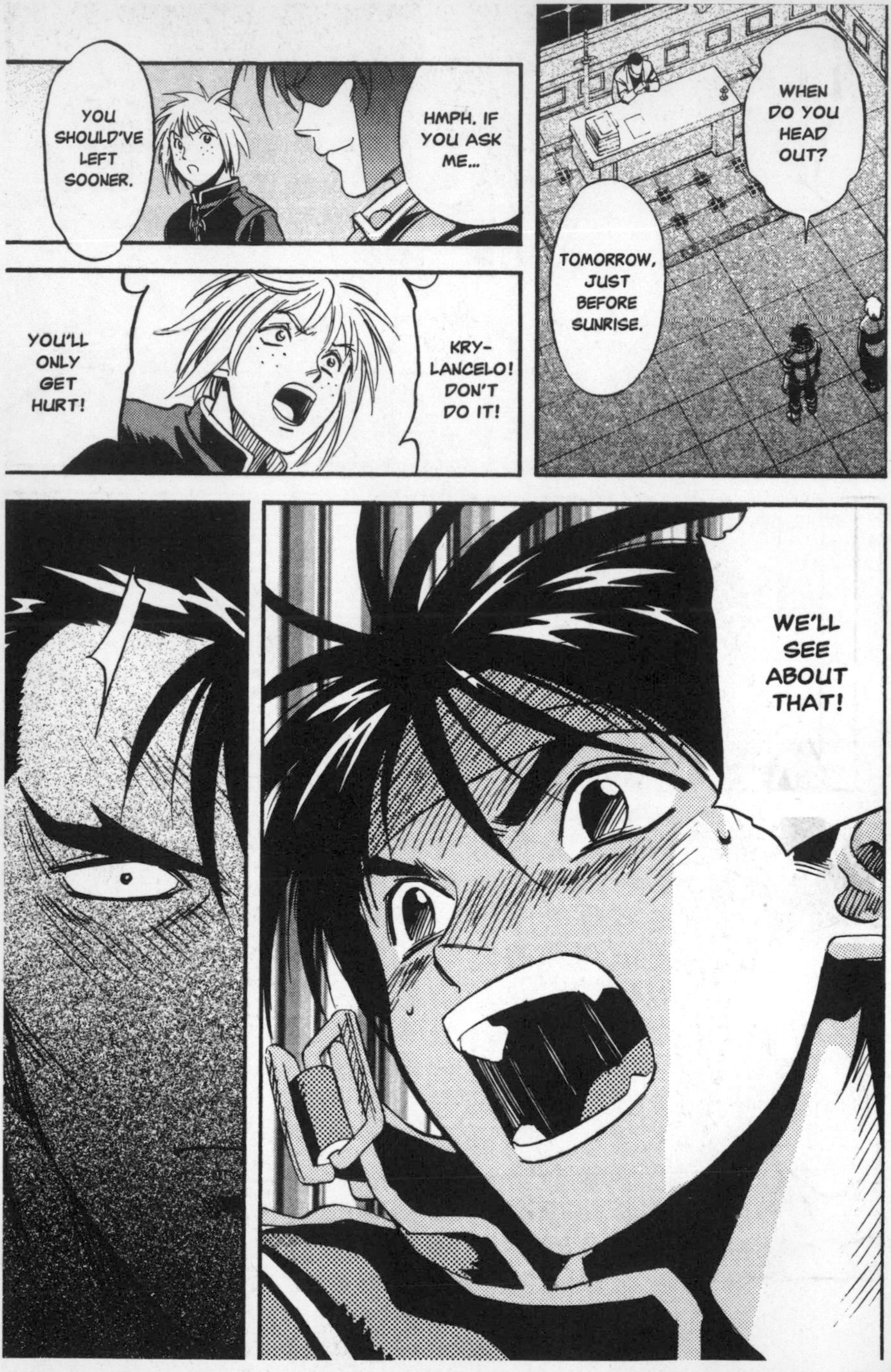
WHEN DO YOU HEAD OUT?
TOMORROW, JUST BEFORE SUNRISE.
HMPH. IF YOU ASK ME...
YOU SHOULD'VE LEFT SOONER.
KRY-LANCELO! DON'T DO IT!
YOU'LL ONLY GET HURT!
WE'LL SEE ABOUT THAT!

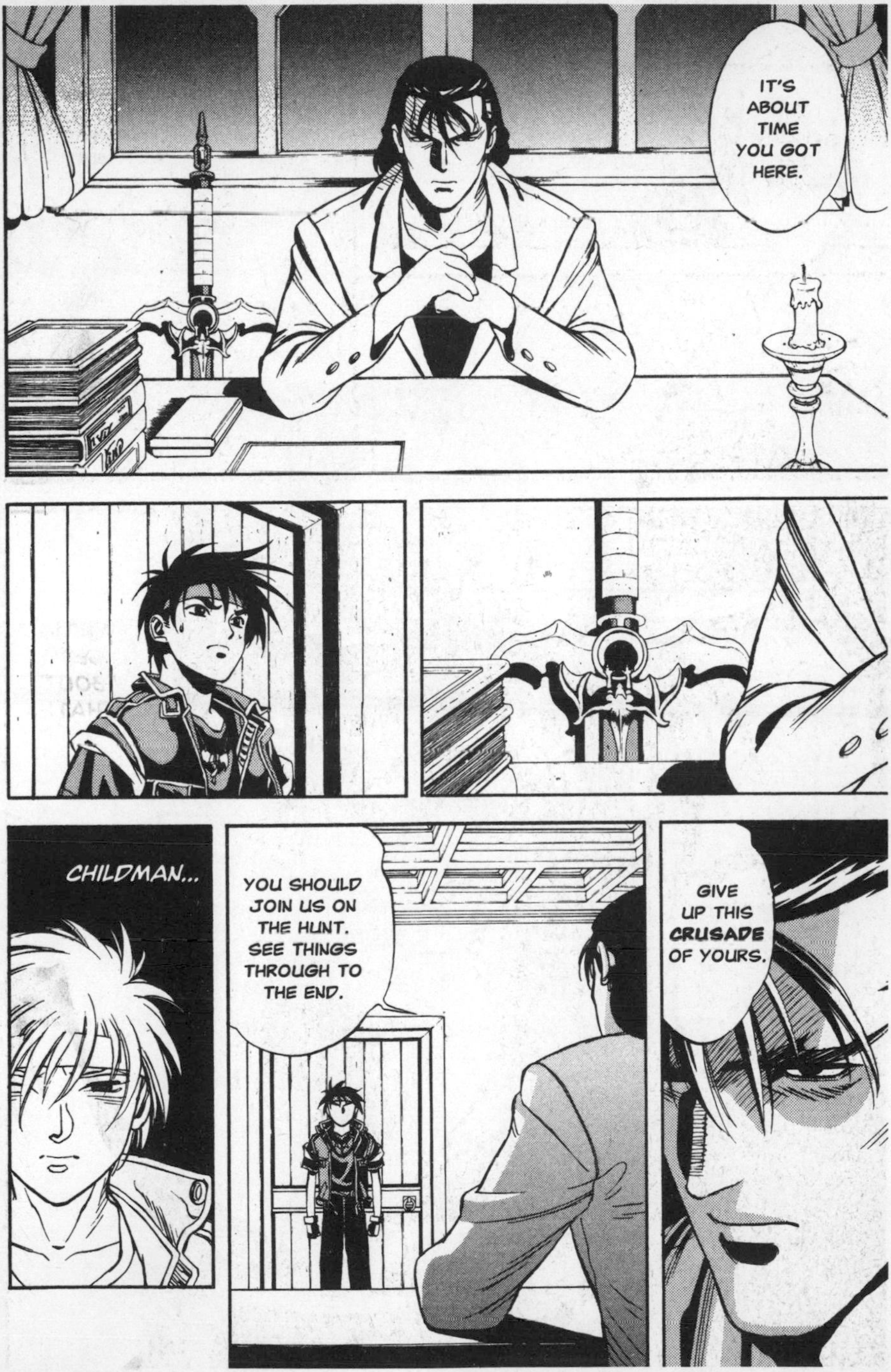

IT'S ABOUT TIME YOU GOT HERE.
CHILDMAN...
YOU SHOULD JOIN US ON THE HUNT. SEE THINGS THROUGH TO THE END.
GIVE UP THIS CRUSADE OF YOURS.

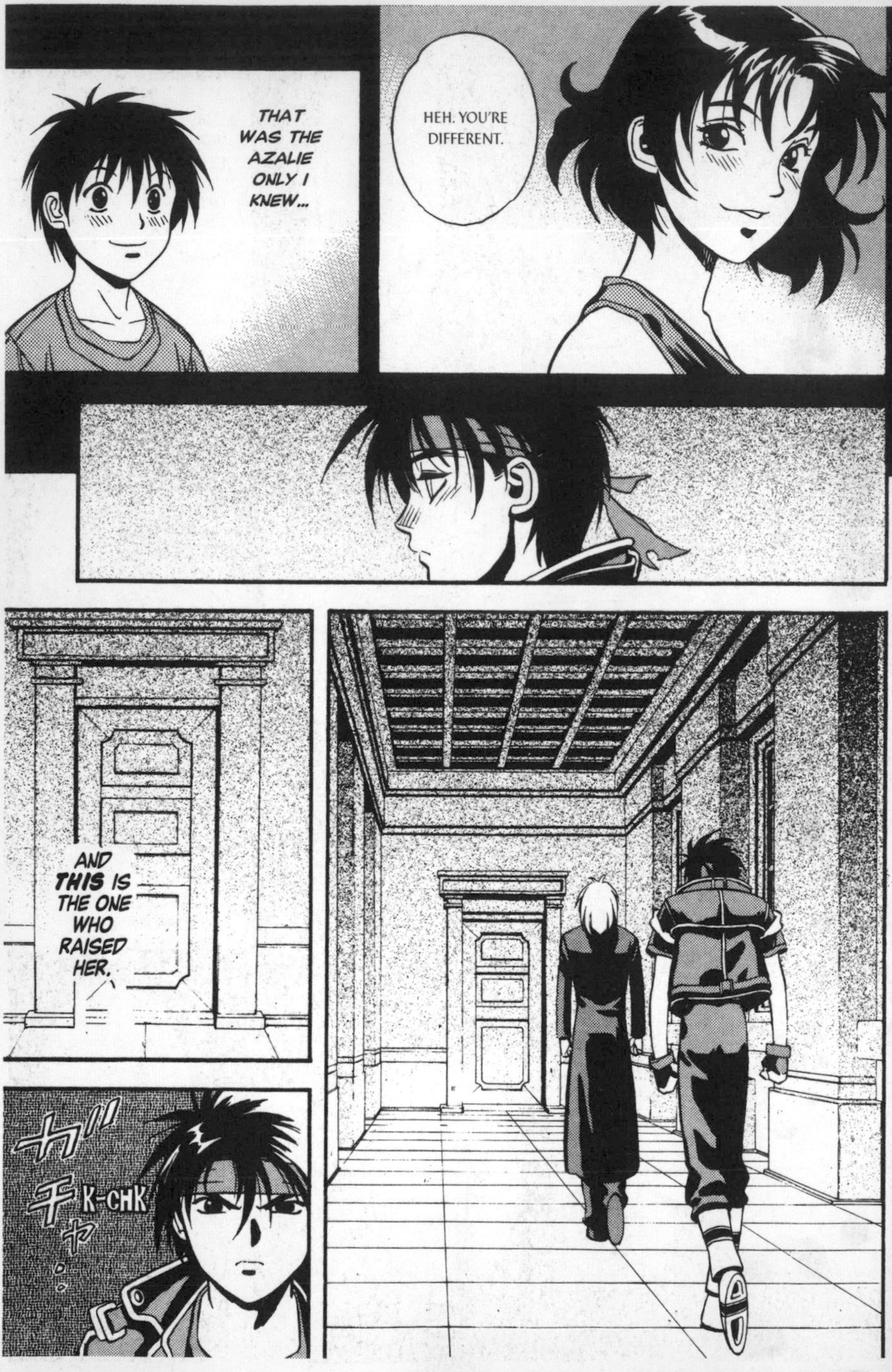
HEH. YOU'RE DIFFERENT.
THAT WAS THE AZALIE ONLY I KNEW...
AND THIS IS THE ONE WHO RAISED HER.
カチャ
K-CHK

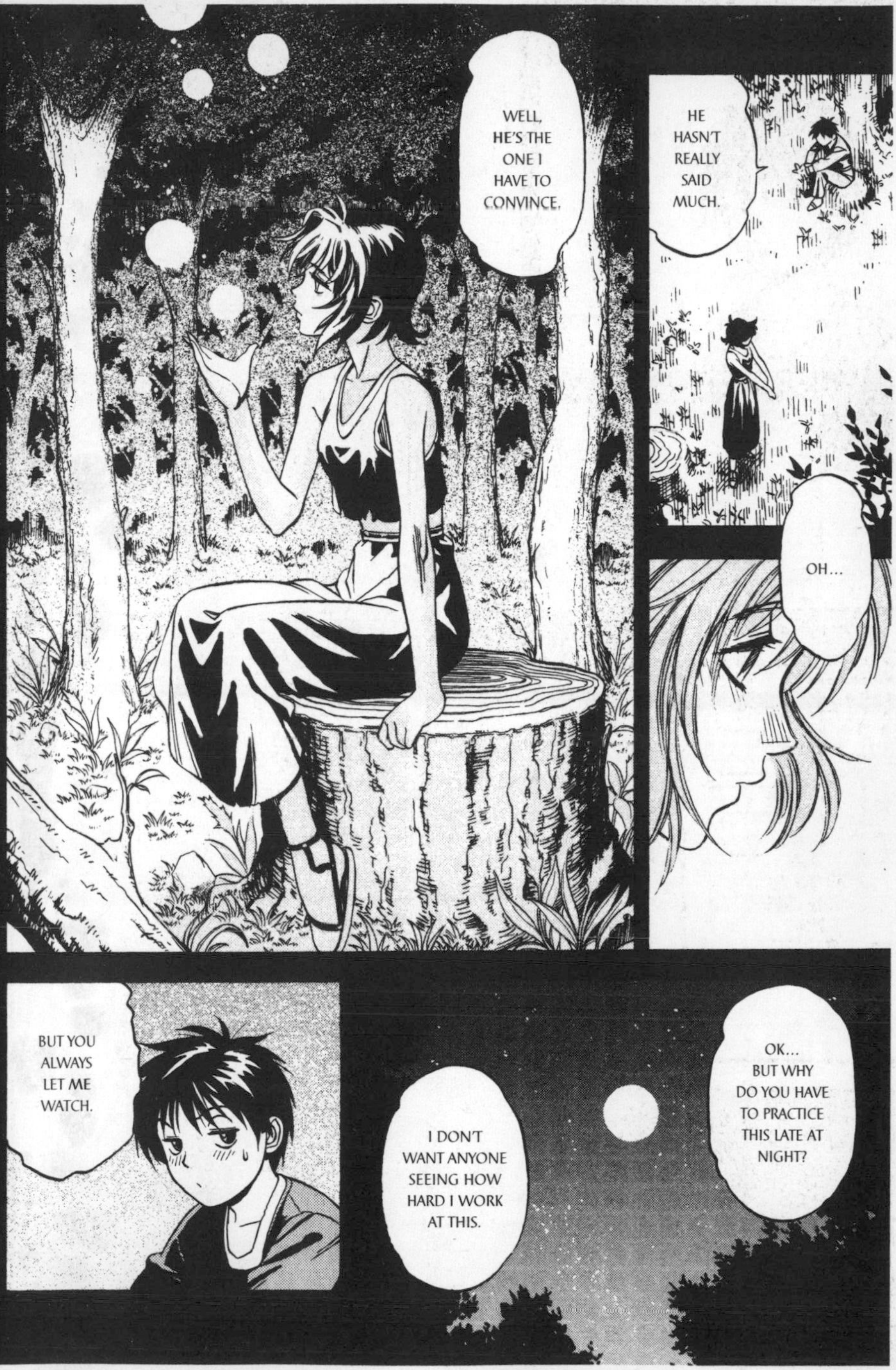
HE HASN'T REALLY SAID MUCH.
WELL, HE'S THE ONE I HAVE TO CONVINCE.
OH...
OK... BUT WHY DO YOU HAVE TO PRACTICE THIS LATE AT NIGHT?
I DON'T WANT ANYONE SEEING HOW HARD I WORK AT THIS.
BUT YOU ALWAYS LET ME WATCH.

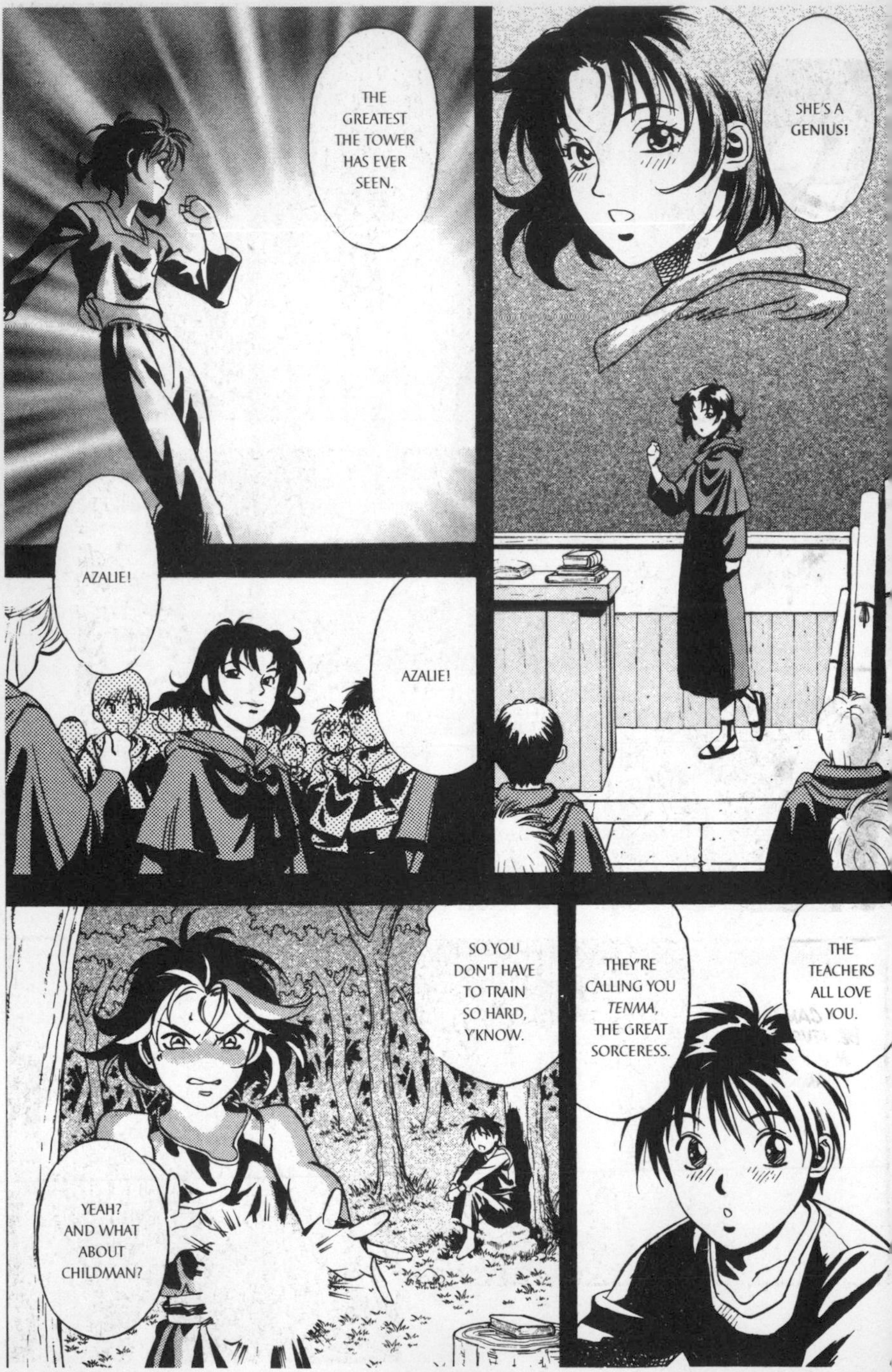
SHE'S A GENIUS!
THE GREATEST THE TOWER HAS EVER SEEN.
AZALIE!
AZALIE!
THE TEACHERS ALL LOVE YOU.
THEY'RE CALLING YOU *TENMA*, THE GREAT SORCERESS.
SO YOU DON'T HAVE TO TRAIN SO HARD, Y'KNOW.
YEAH? AND WHAT ABOUT CHILDMAN?

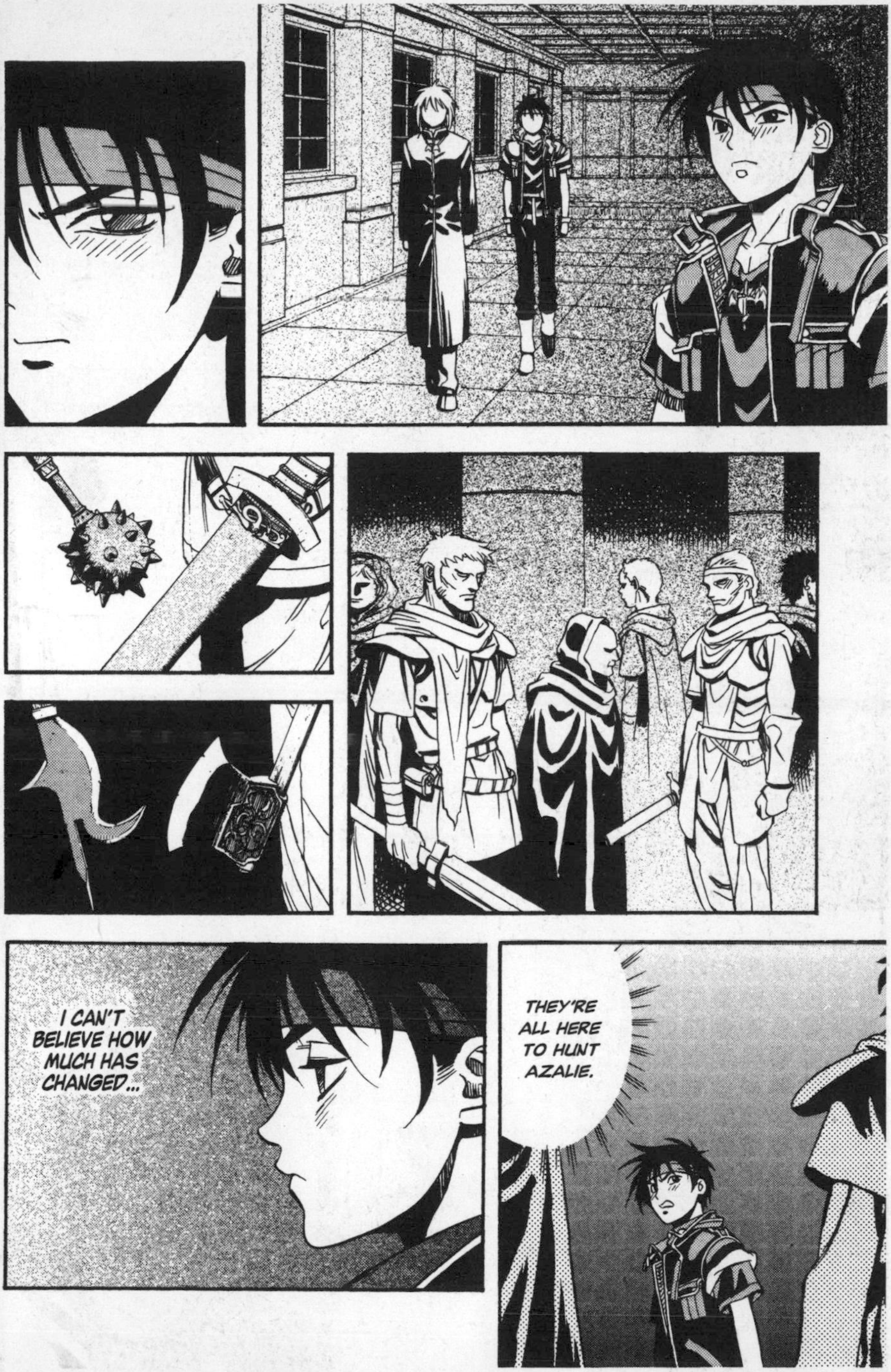
THEY'RE ALL HERE TO HUNT AZALIE.
I CAN'T BELIEVE HOW MUCH HAS CHANGED...

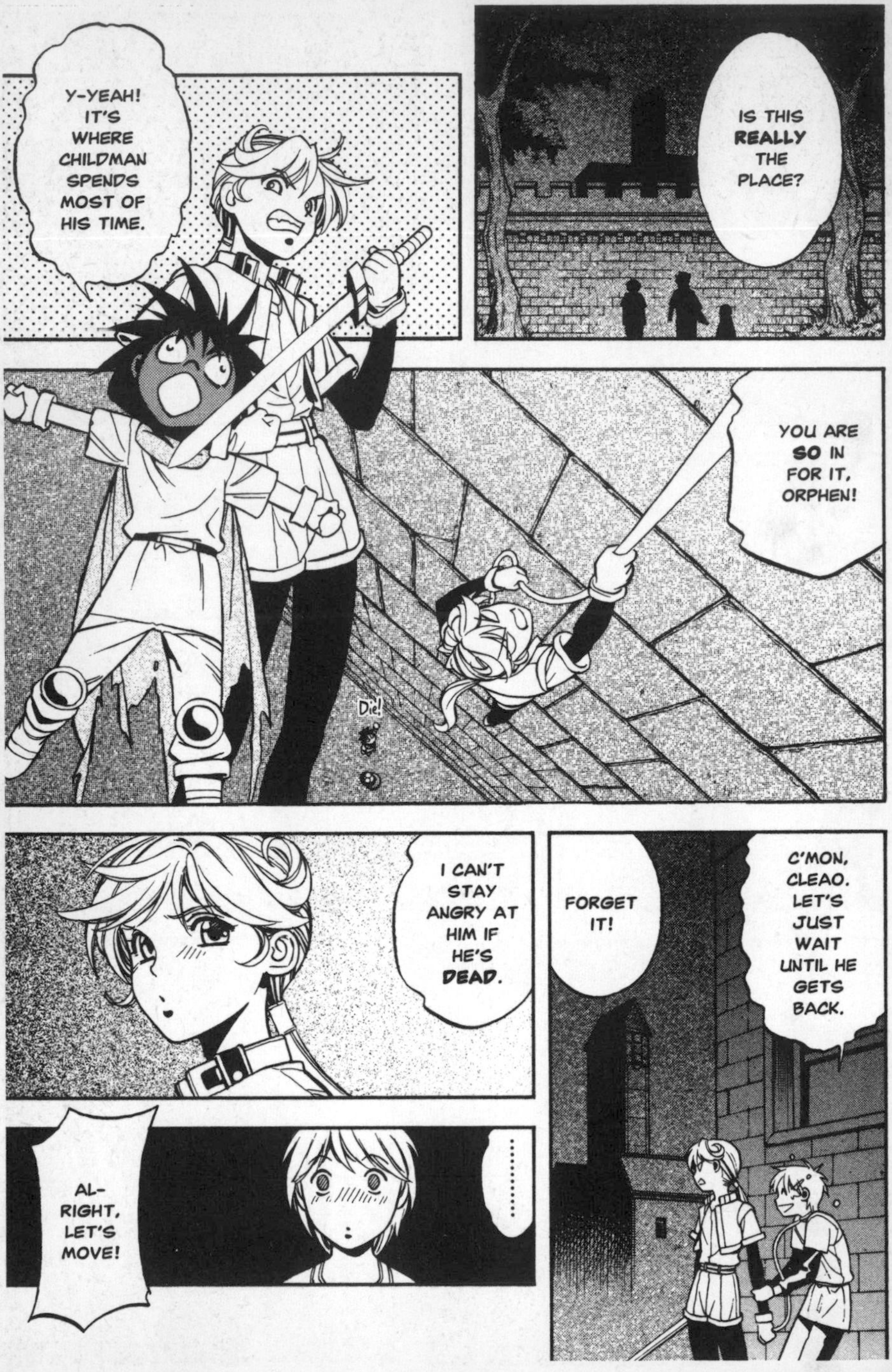
IS THIS REALLY THE PLACE?
Y-YEAH! IT'S WHERE CHILDMAN SPENDS MOST OF HIS TIME.
YOU ARE SO IN FOR IT, ORPHEN!
Die!
FORGET IT!
C'MON, CLEAO. LET'S JUST WAIT UNTIL HE GETS BACK.
I CAN'T STAY ANGRY AT HIM IF HE'S DEAD.
......
AL-RIGHT, LET'S MOVE!

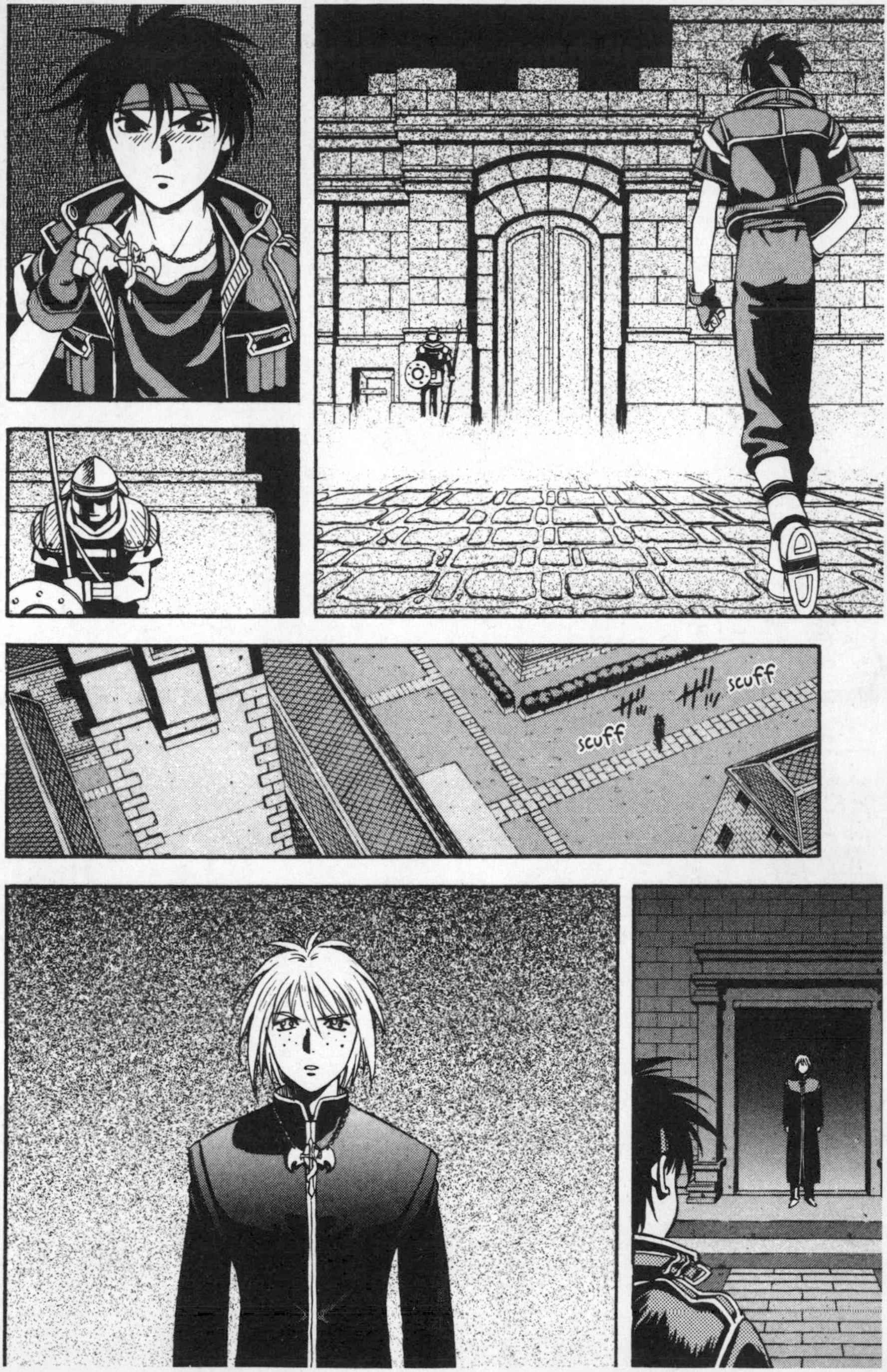
scuff
scuff

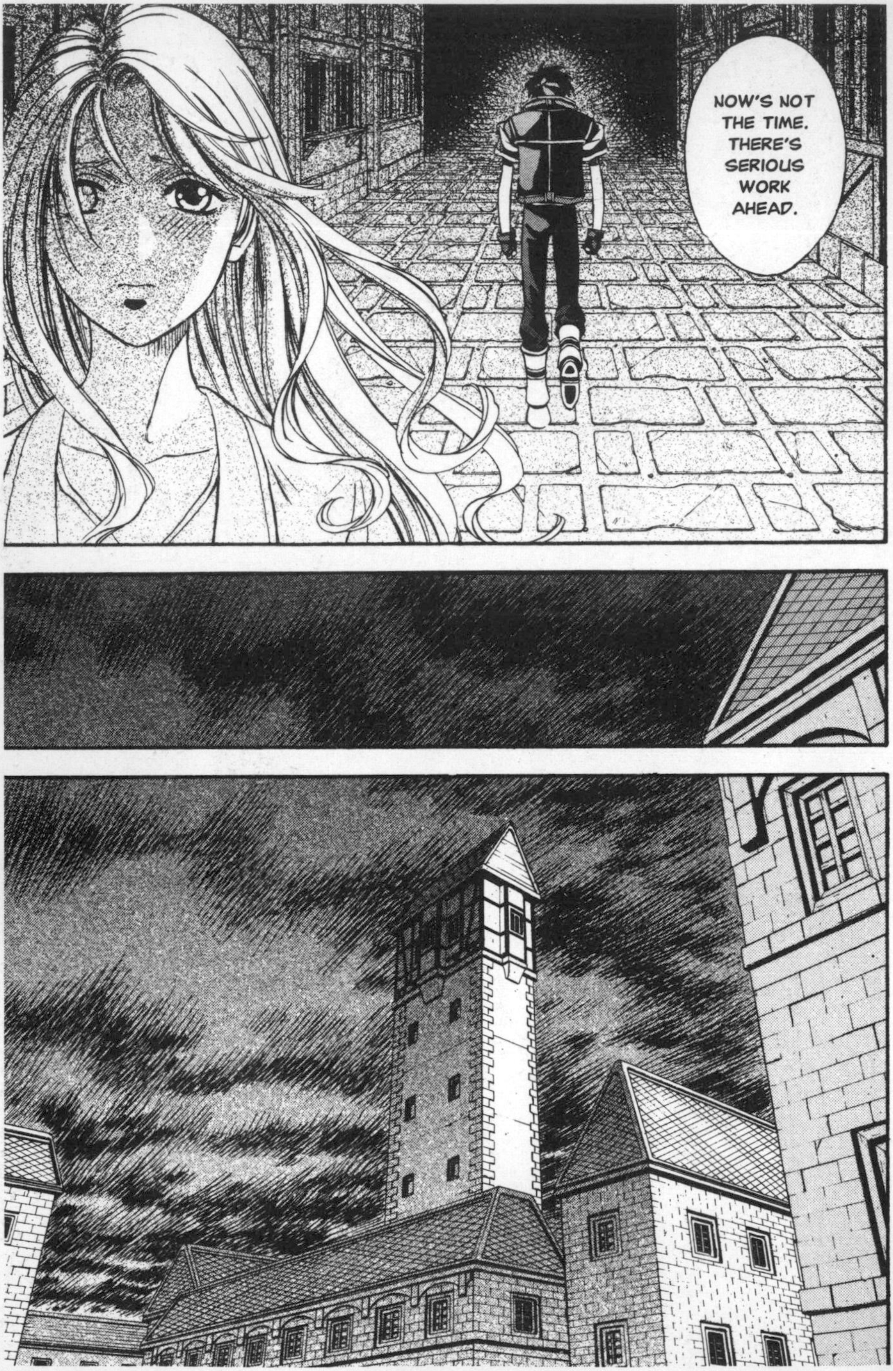
NOW'S NOT THE TIME. THERE'S SERIOUS WORK AHEAD.

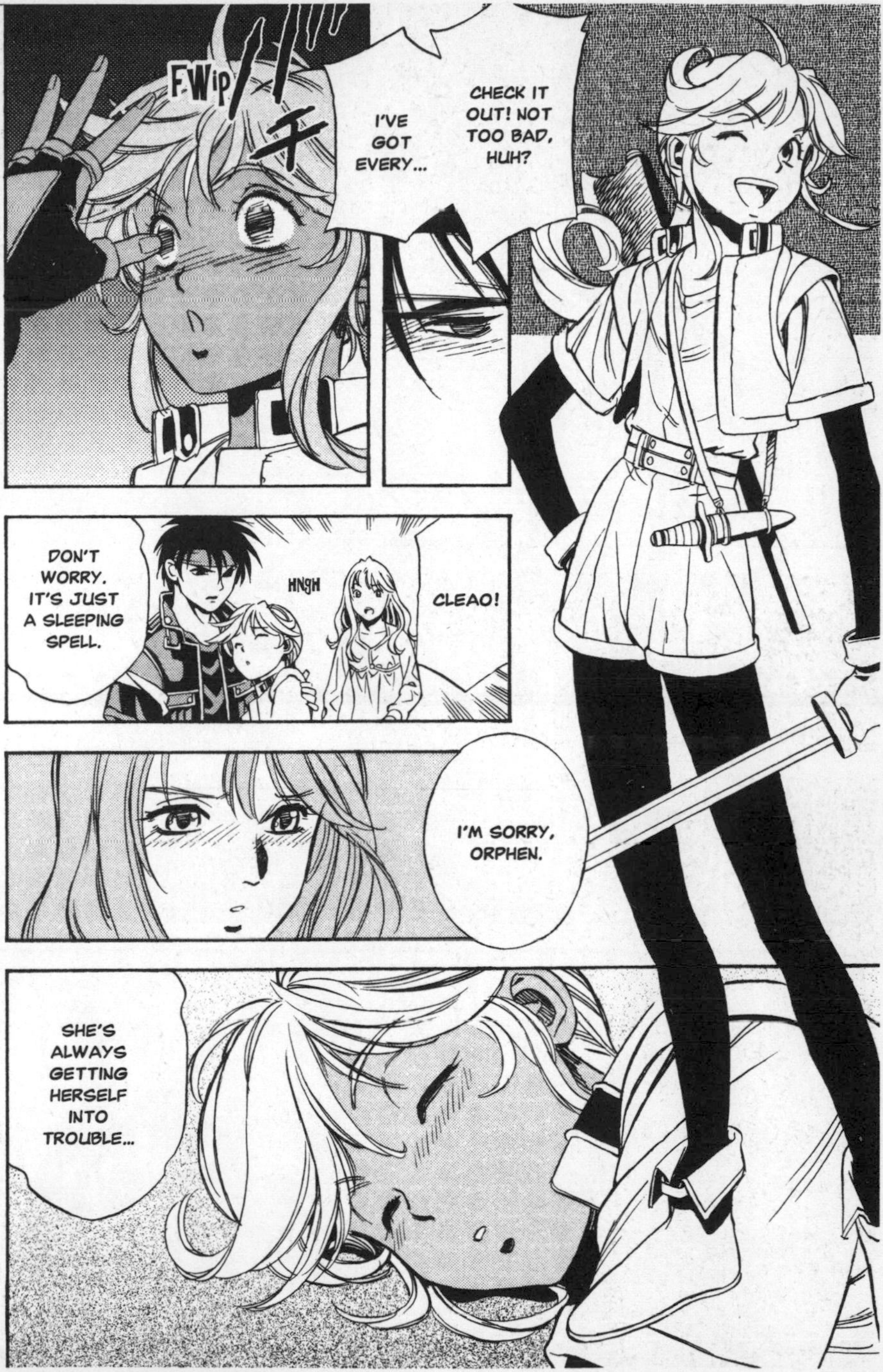
CHECK IT OUT! NOT TOO BAD, HUH?
I'VE GOT EVERY...
FWip
チ
CLEAO!
HNgH
DON'T WORRY. IT'S JUST A SLEEPING SPELL.
I'M SORRY, ORPHEN.
SHE'S ALWAYS GETTING HERSELF INTO TROUBLE...

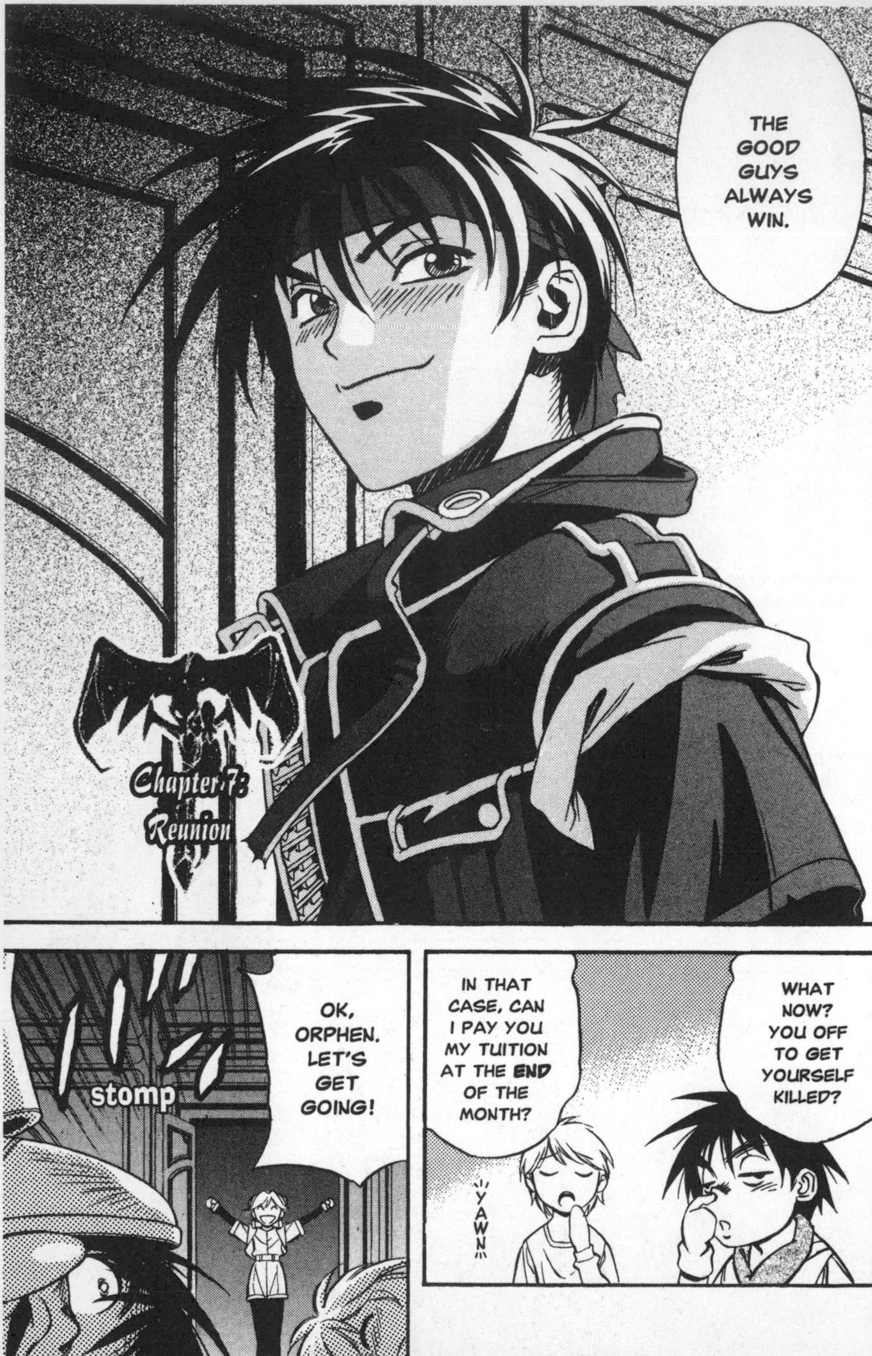
THE GOOD GUYS ALWAYS WIN.
Chapter 7: Reunion
WHAT NOW? YOU OFF TO GET YOURSELF KILLED?
IN THAT CASE, CAN I PAY YOU MY TUITION AT THE END OF THE MONTH?
YAWN
OK, ORPHEN. LET'S GET GOING!
stomp

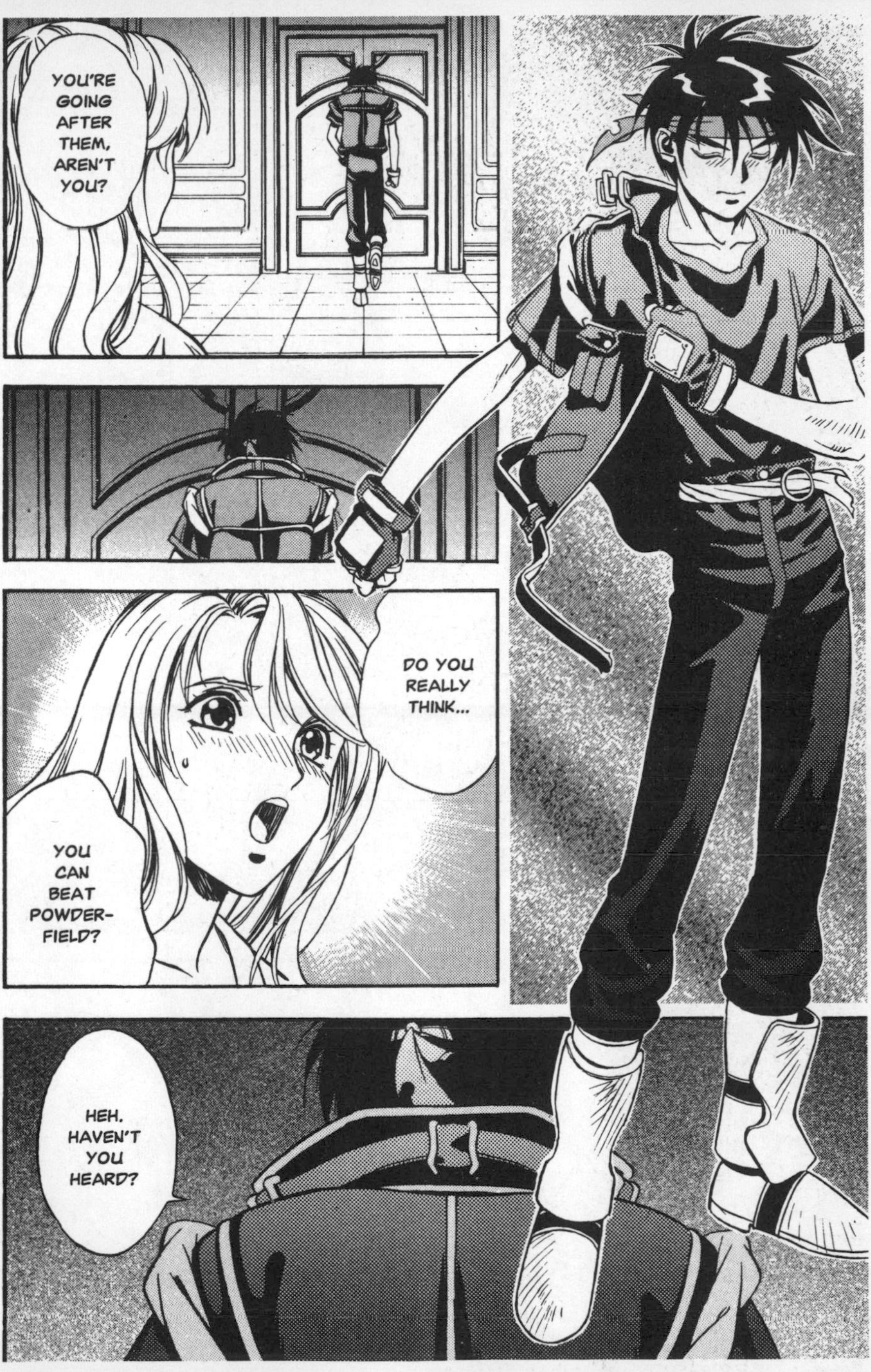
YOU'RE GOING AFTER THEM, AREN'T YOU?
DO YOU REALLY THINK...
YOU CAN BEAT POWDER-FIELD?
HEH. HAVEN'T YOU HEARD?

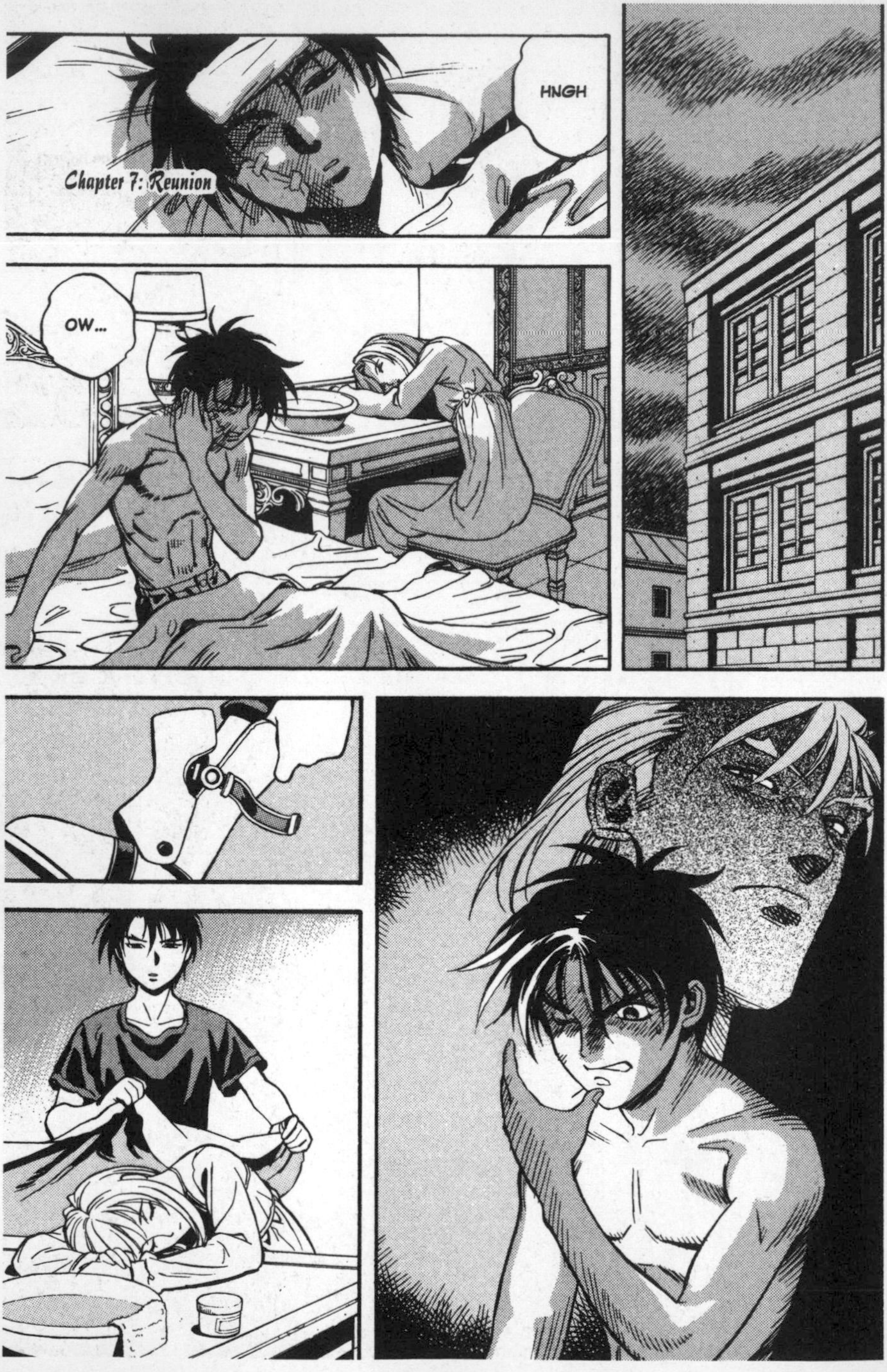
HNGH
Chapter 7: Reunion
OW...

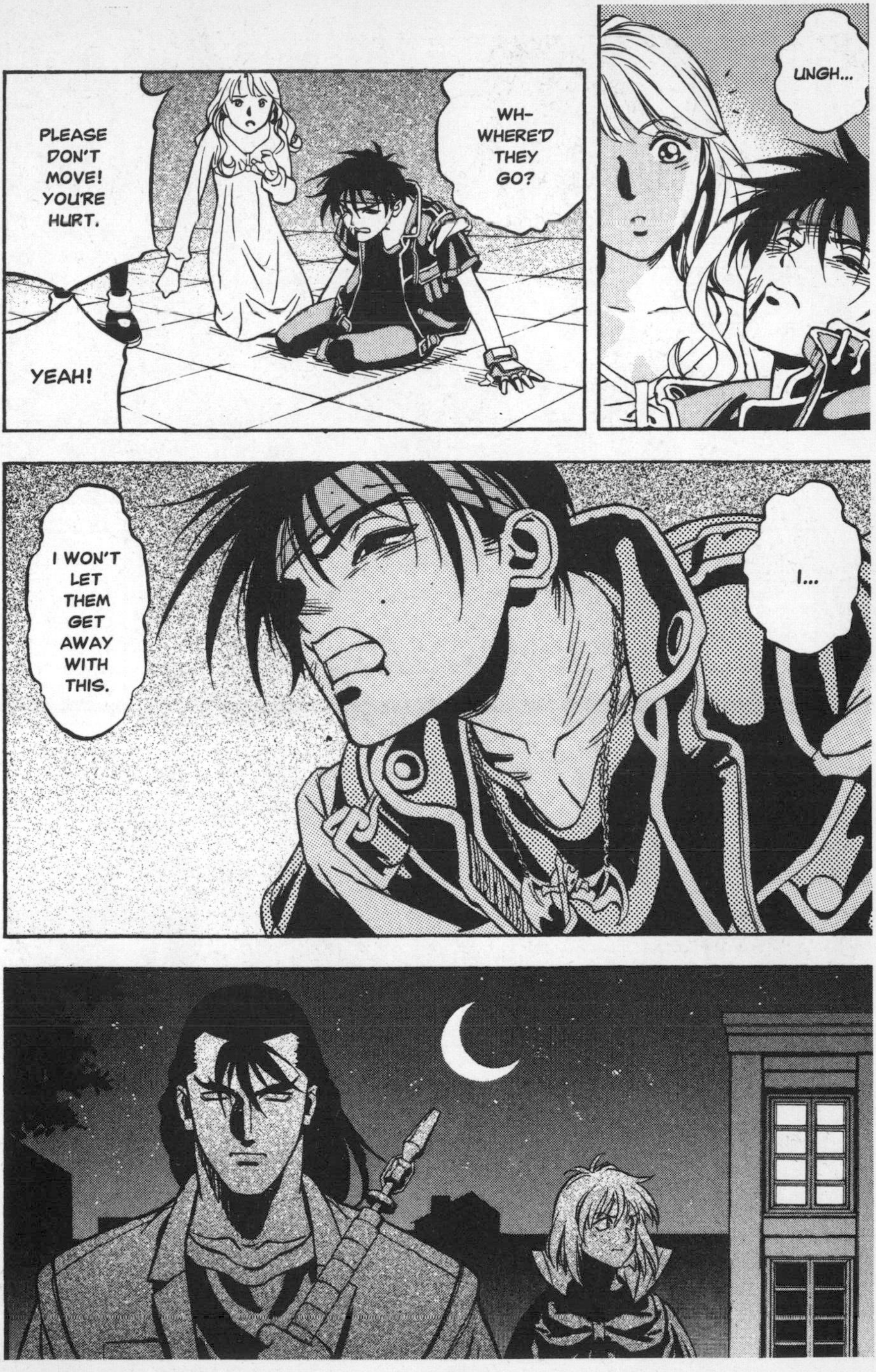
UNGH...
WH-WHERE'D THEY GO?
PLEASE DON'T MOVE! YOU'RE HURT.
YEAH!
I...
I WON'T LET THEM GET AWAY WITH THIS.

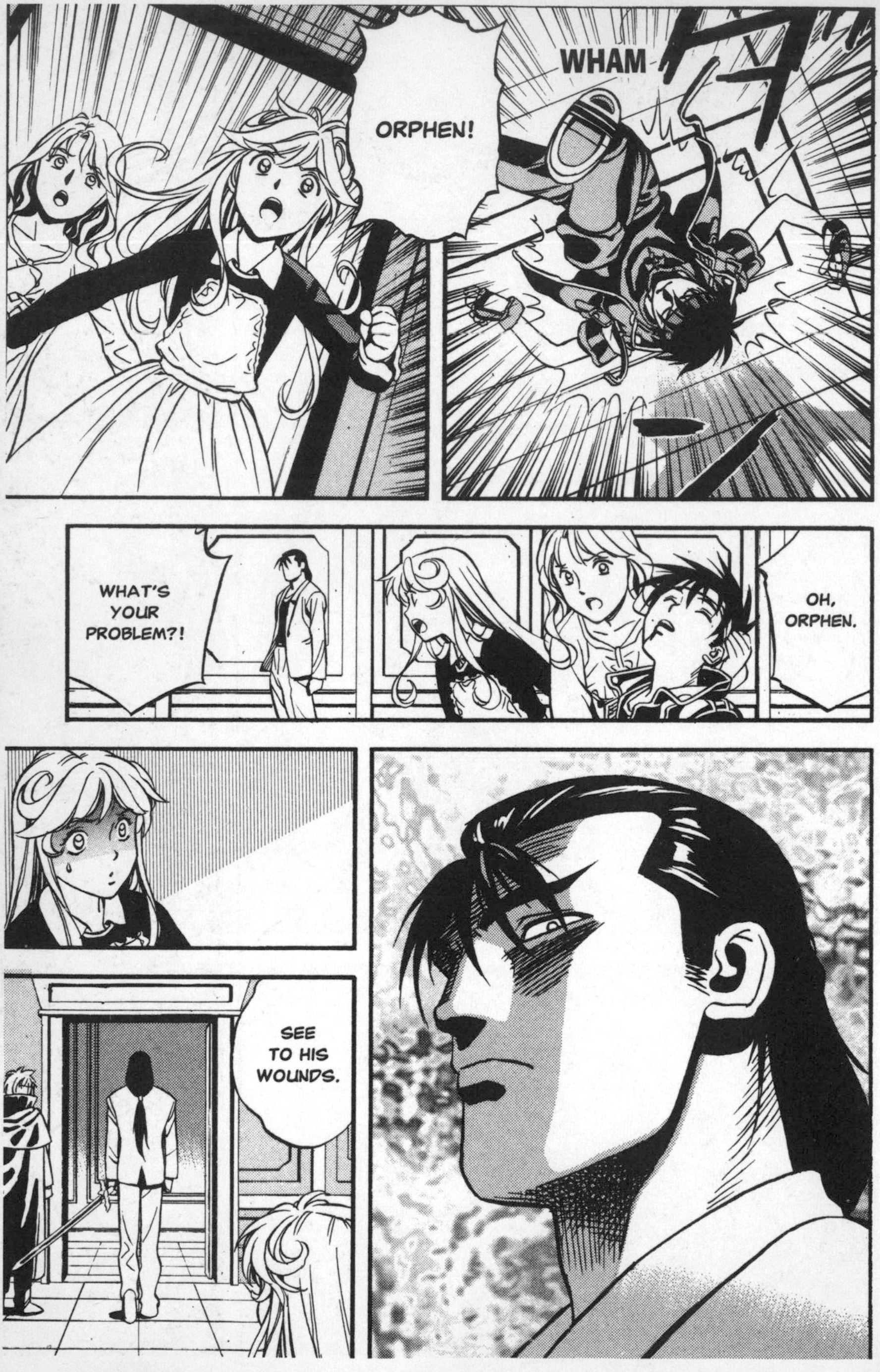
WHAM
ORPHEN!
OH, ORPHEN.
WHAT'S YOUR PROBLEM?!
SEE TO HIS WOUNDS.

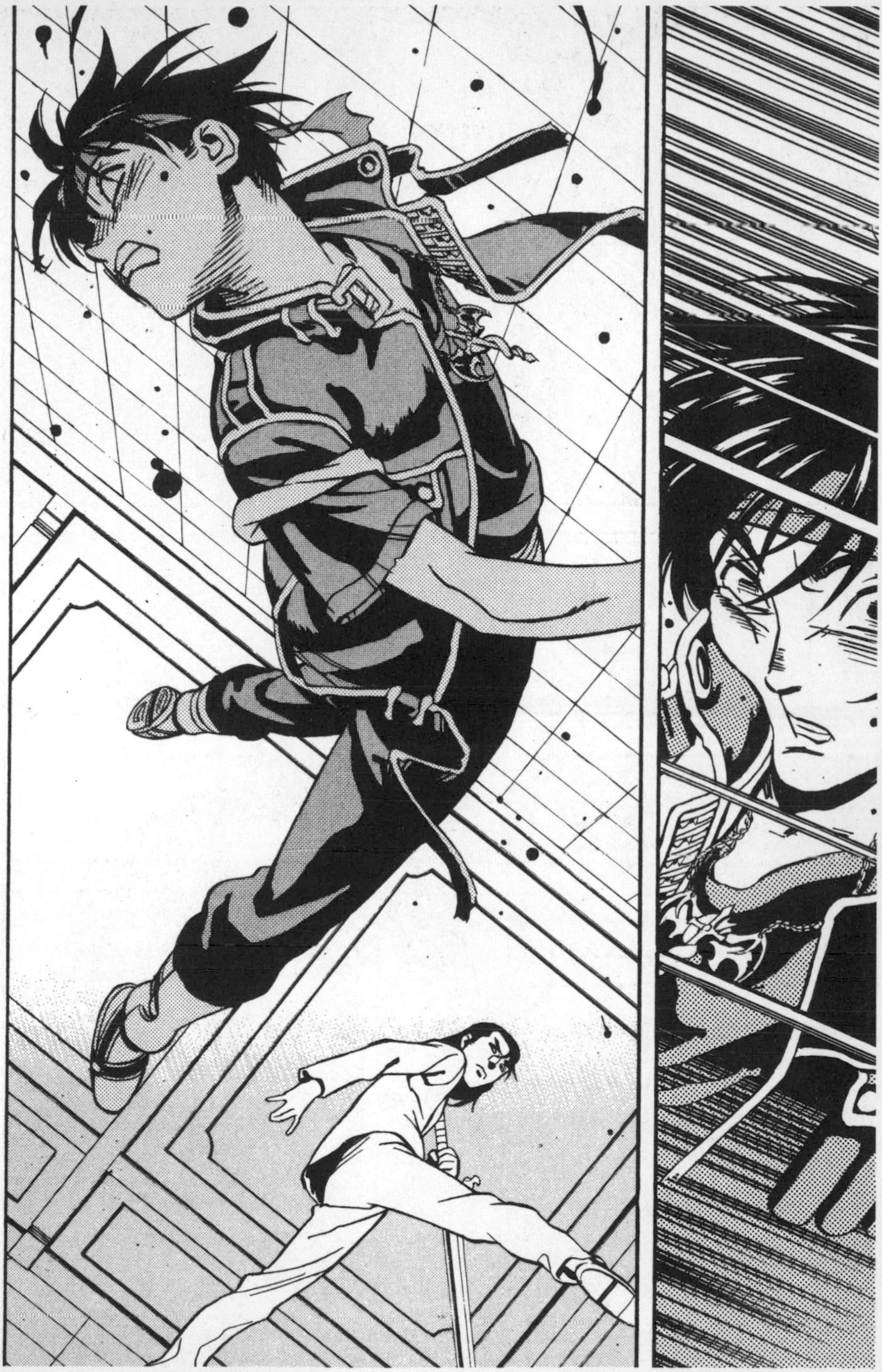

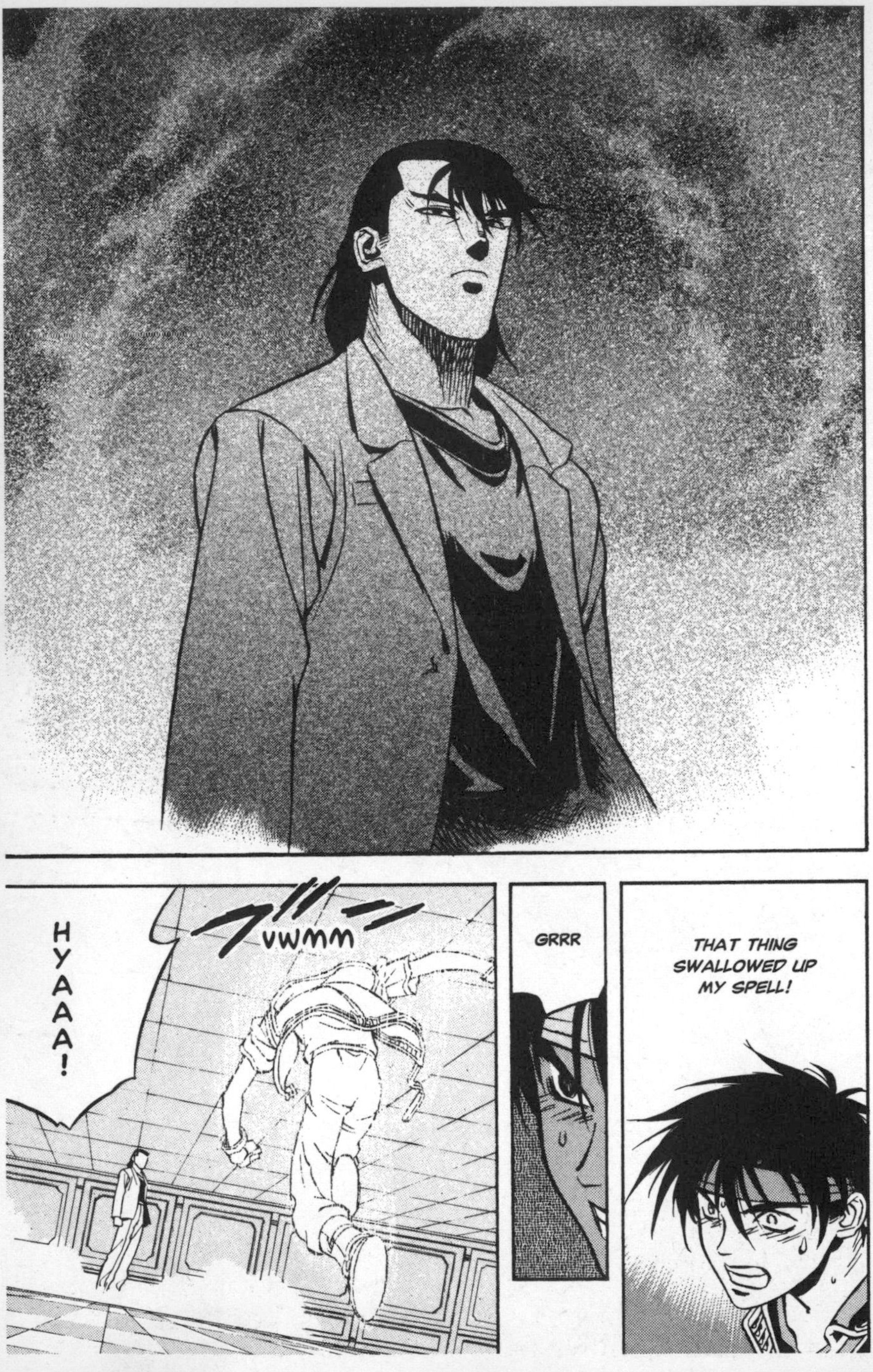
THAT THING SWALLOWED UP MY SPELL!
GRRR
VWMM
HYAAAA!

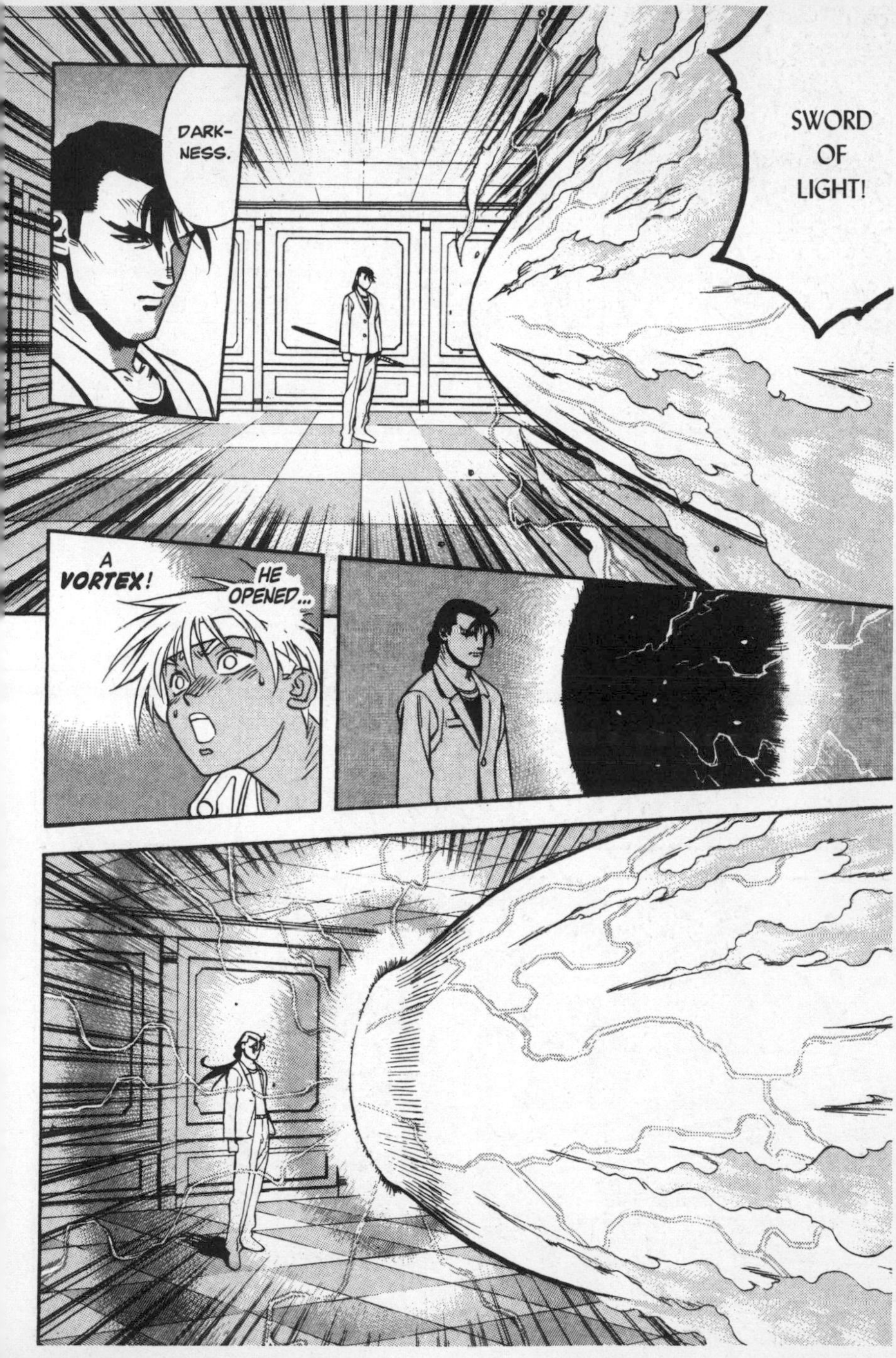
SWORD
OF
LIGHT!
DARK-
NESS.
HE
OPENED...
A
VORTEX!

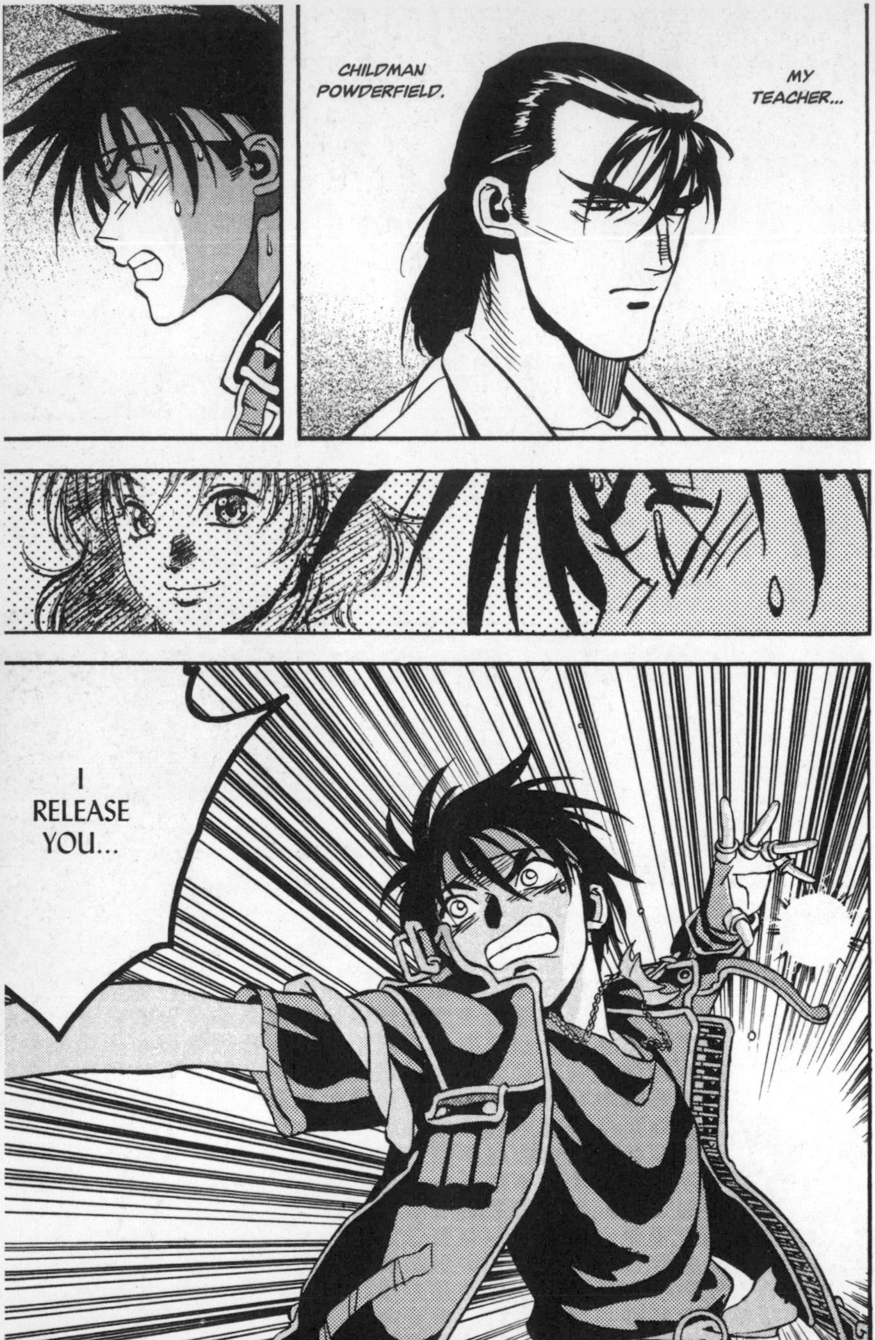

CHILDMAN POWDERFIELD.
MY TEACHER...
I RELEASE YOU...

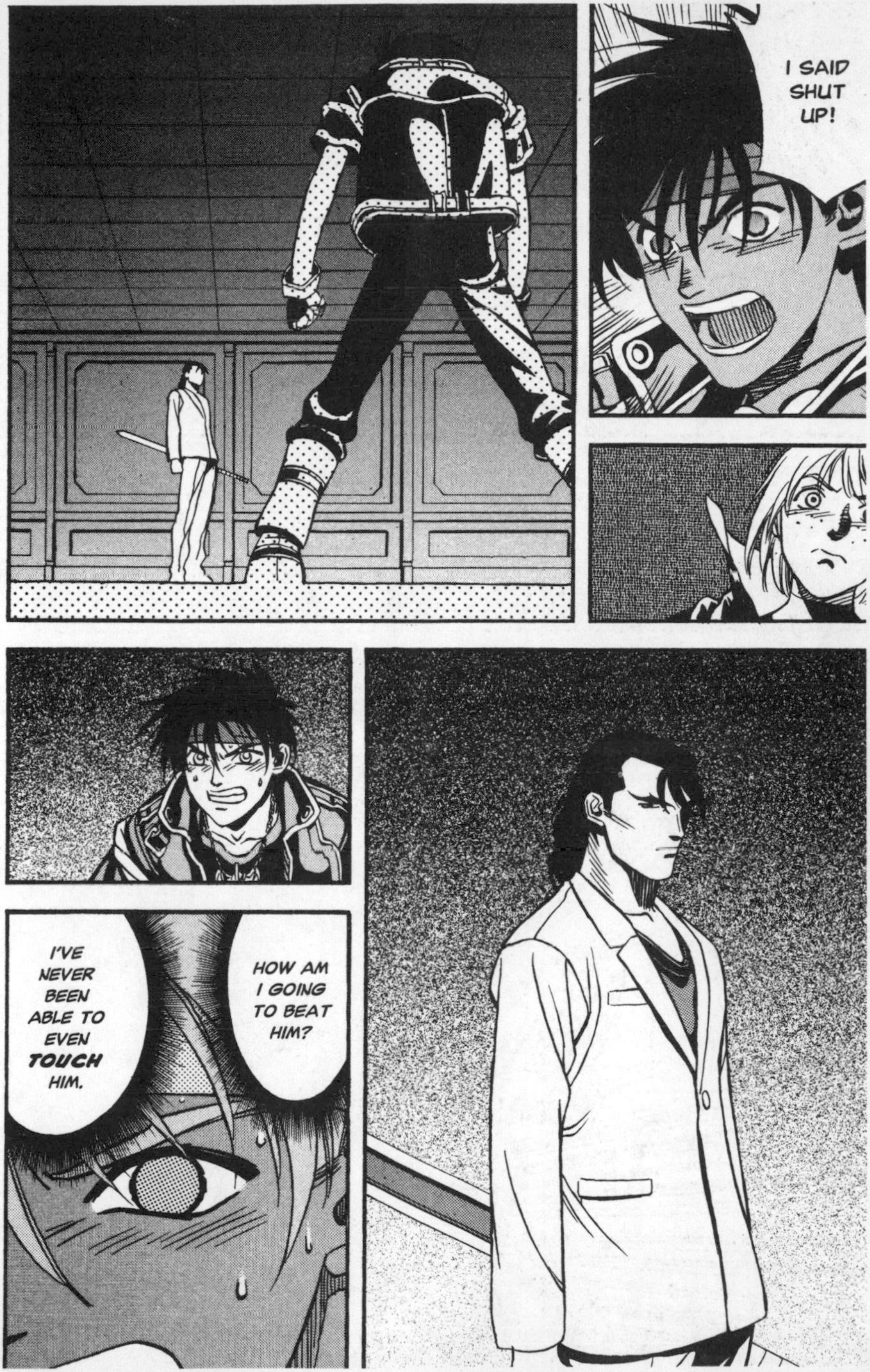
I SAID SHUT UP!
HOW AM I GOING TO BEAT HIM?
I'VE NEVER BEEN ABLE TO EVEN TOUCH HIM.

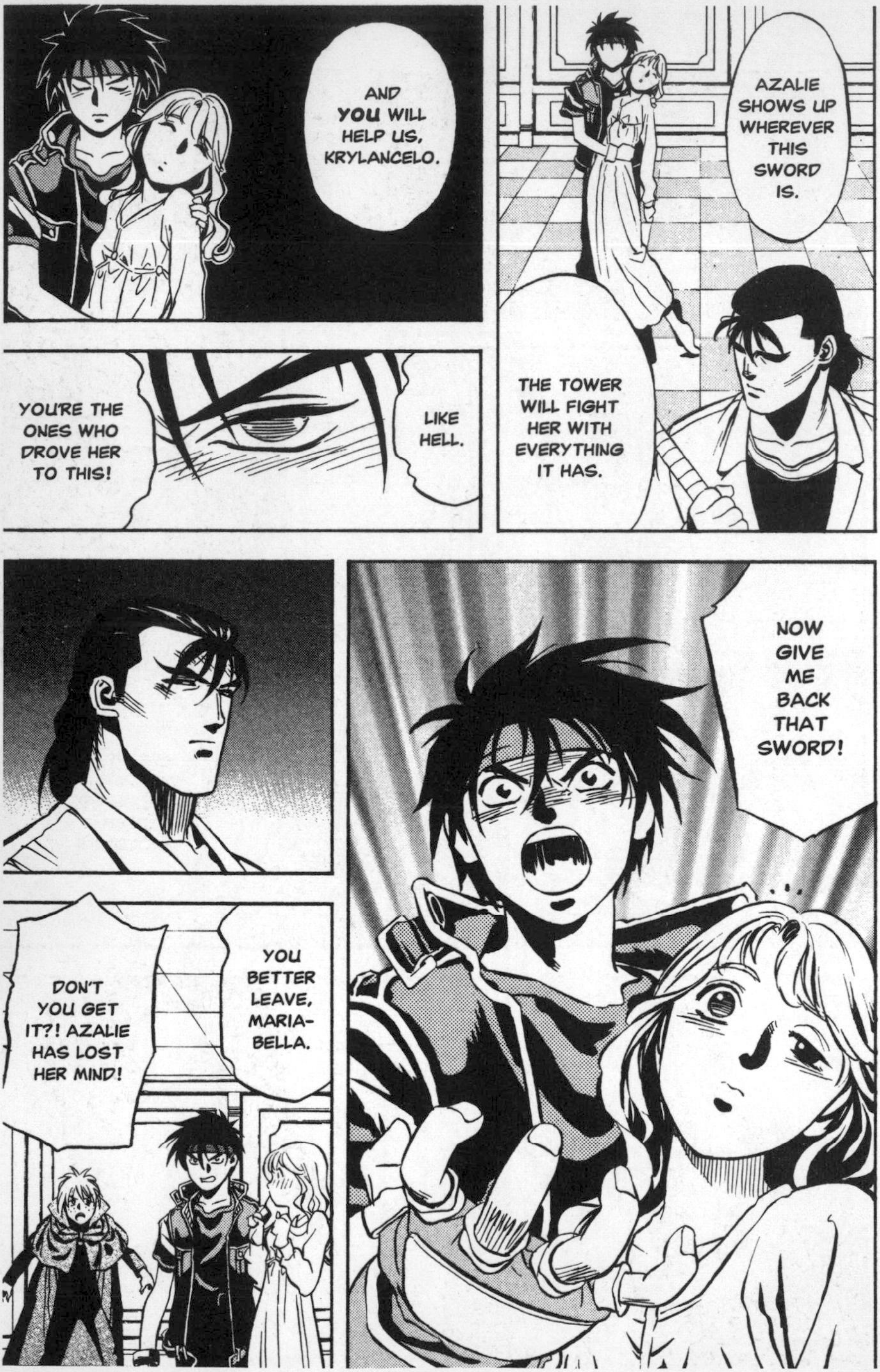
AND YOU WILL HELP US, KRYLANCELO.
AZALIE SHOWS UP WHEREVER THIS SWORD IS.
THE TOWER WILL FIGHT HER WITH EVERYTHING IT HAS.
LIKE HELL.
YOU'RE THE ONES WHO DROVE HER TO THIS!
NOW GIVE ME BACK THAT SWORD!
YOU BETTER LEAVE, MARIA-BELLA.
DON'T YOU GET IT?! AZALIE HAS LOST HER MIND!

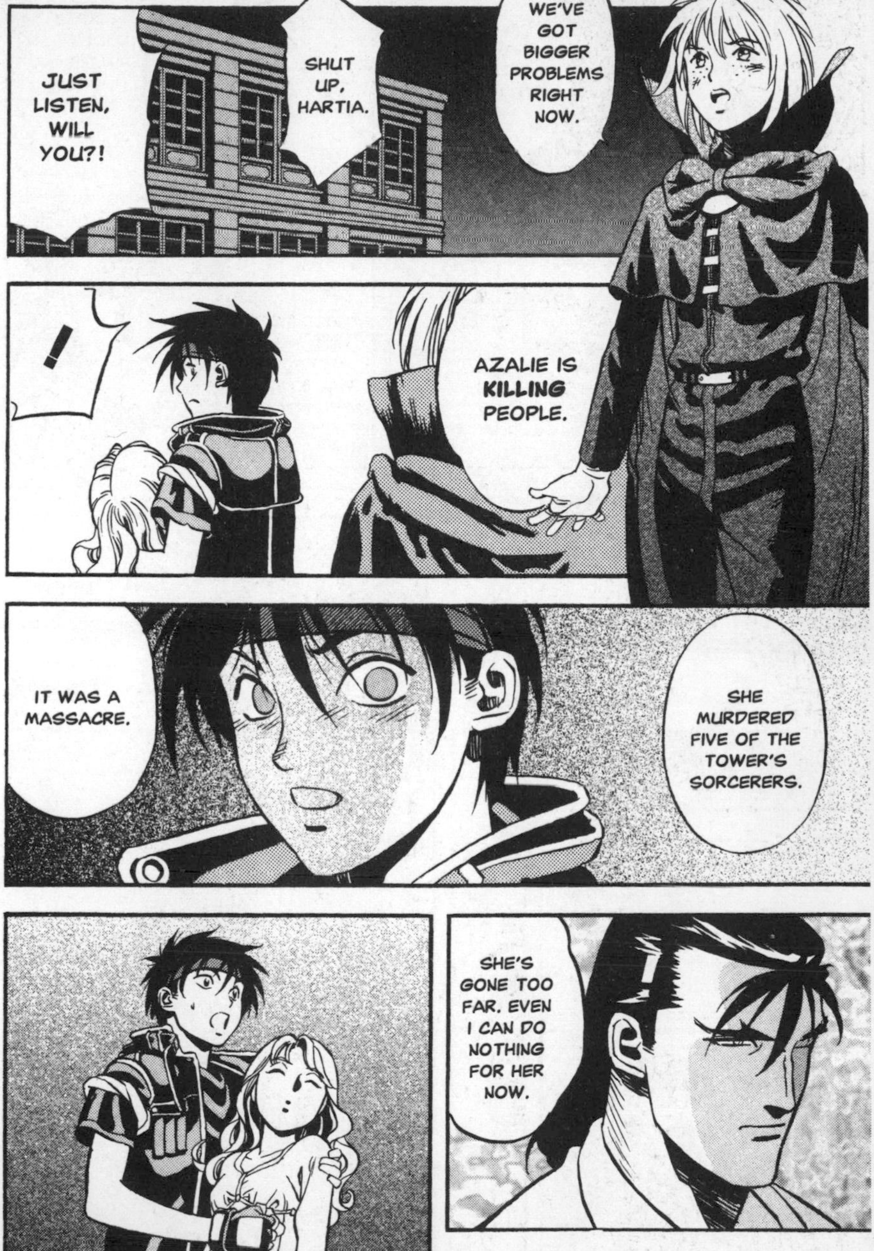
WE'VE GOT BIGGER PROBLEMS RIGHT NOW.
SHUT UP, HARTIA.
JUST LISTEN, WILL YOU?!
AZALIE IS **KILLING** PEOPLE.
!
SHE MURDERED FIVE OF THE TOWER'S SORCERERS.
IT WAS A MASSACRE.
SHE'S GONE TOO FAR. EVEN I CAN DO NOTHING FOR HER NOW.

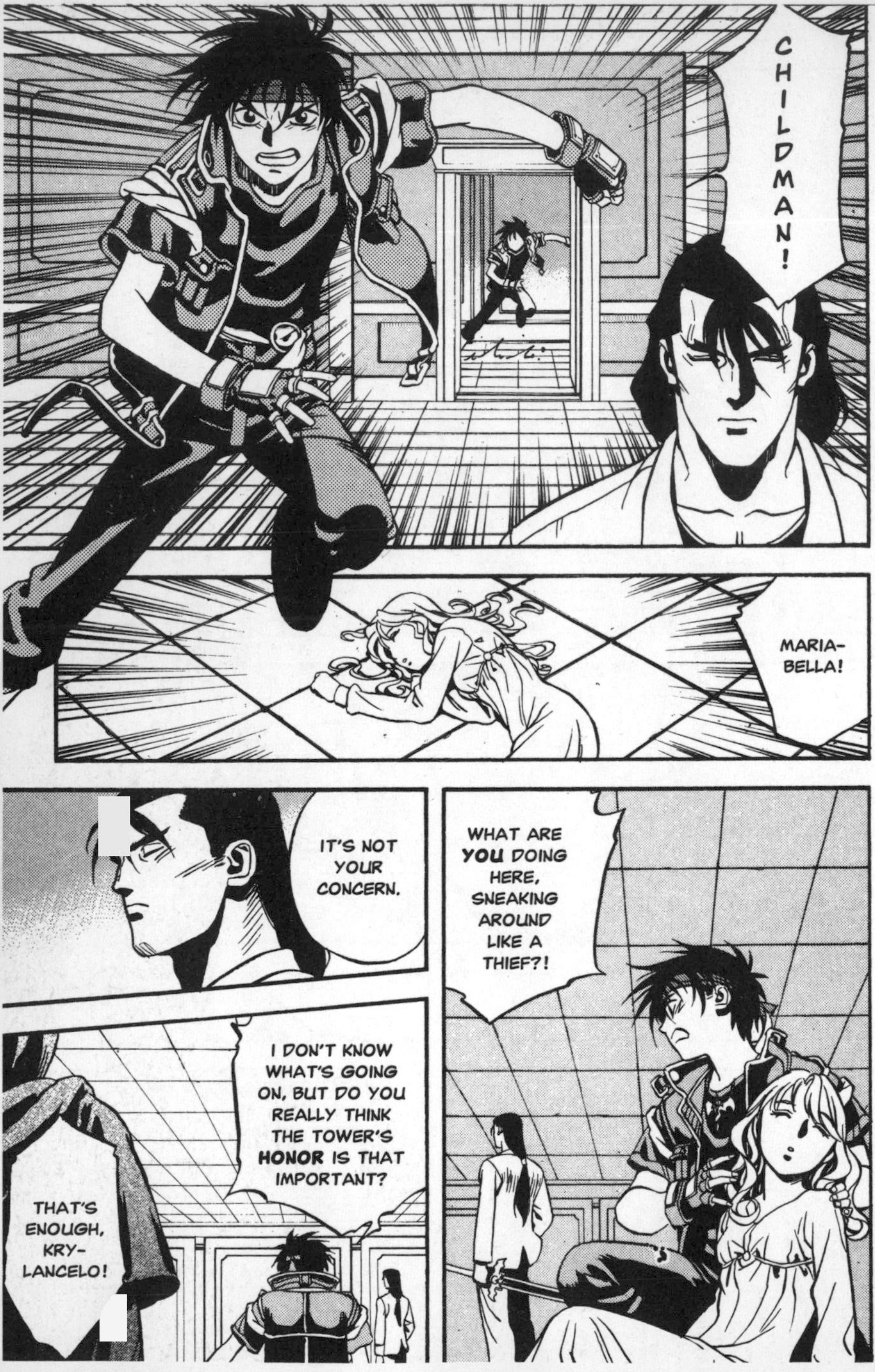
CHILDMAN!
MARIA-BELLA!
WHAT ARE YOU DOING HERE, SNEAKING AROUND LIKE A THIEF?!
IT'S NOT YOUR CONCERN.
I DON'T KNOW WHAT'S GOING ON, BUT DO YOU REALLY THINK THE TOWER'S HONOR IS THAT IMPORTANT?
THAT'S ENOUGH, KRY-LANCELO!

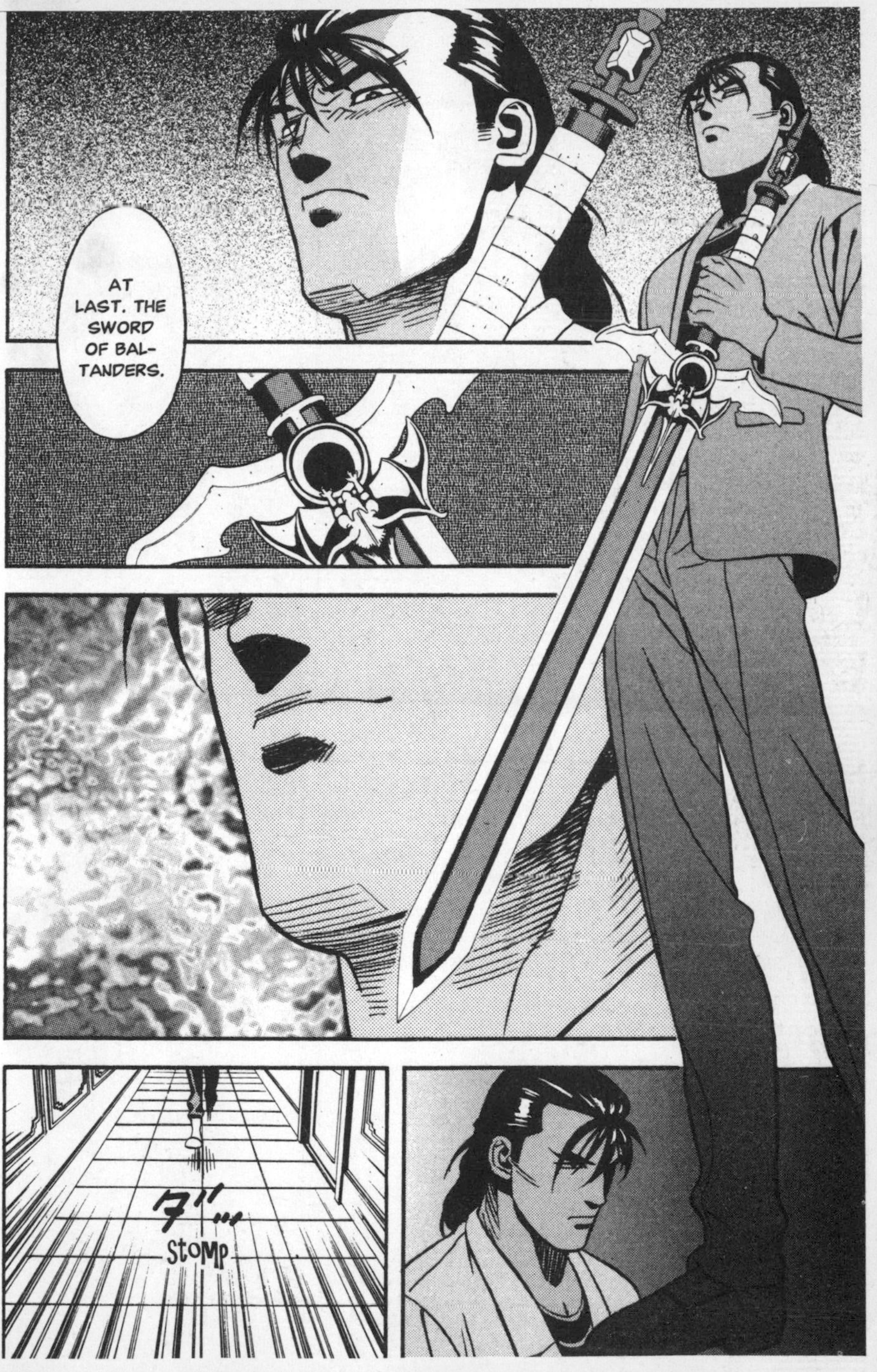
AT LAST. THE SWORD OF BAL-TANDERS.
ド...
STOMP

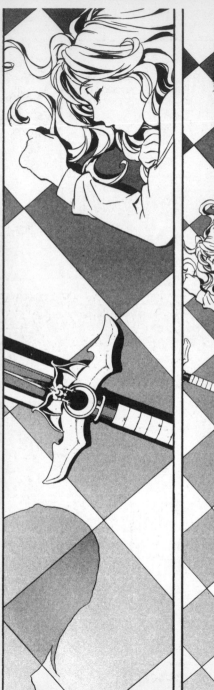

THE ONE WHO'S REALLY BEHIND ALL THIS IS...

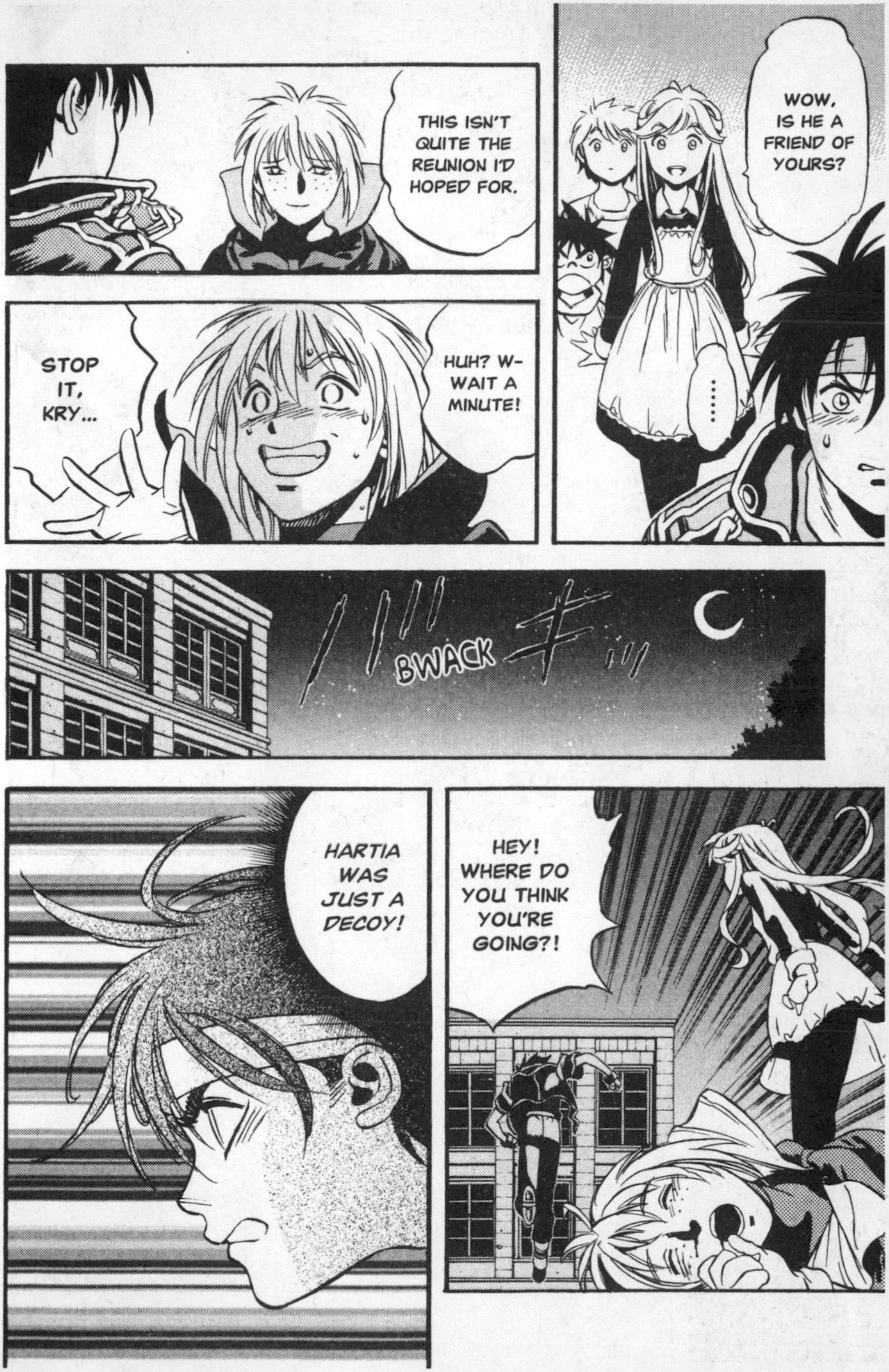
WOW, IS HE A FRIEND OF YOURS?
......
THIS ISN'T QUITE THE REUNION I'D HOPED FOR.
HUH? W-WAIT A MINUTE!
STOP IT, KRY...
BWACK
HEY! WHERE DO YOU THINK YOU'RE GOING?!
HARTIA WAS JUST A DECOY!

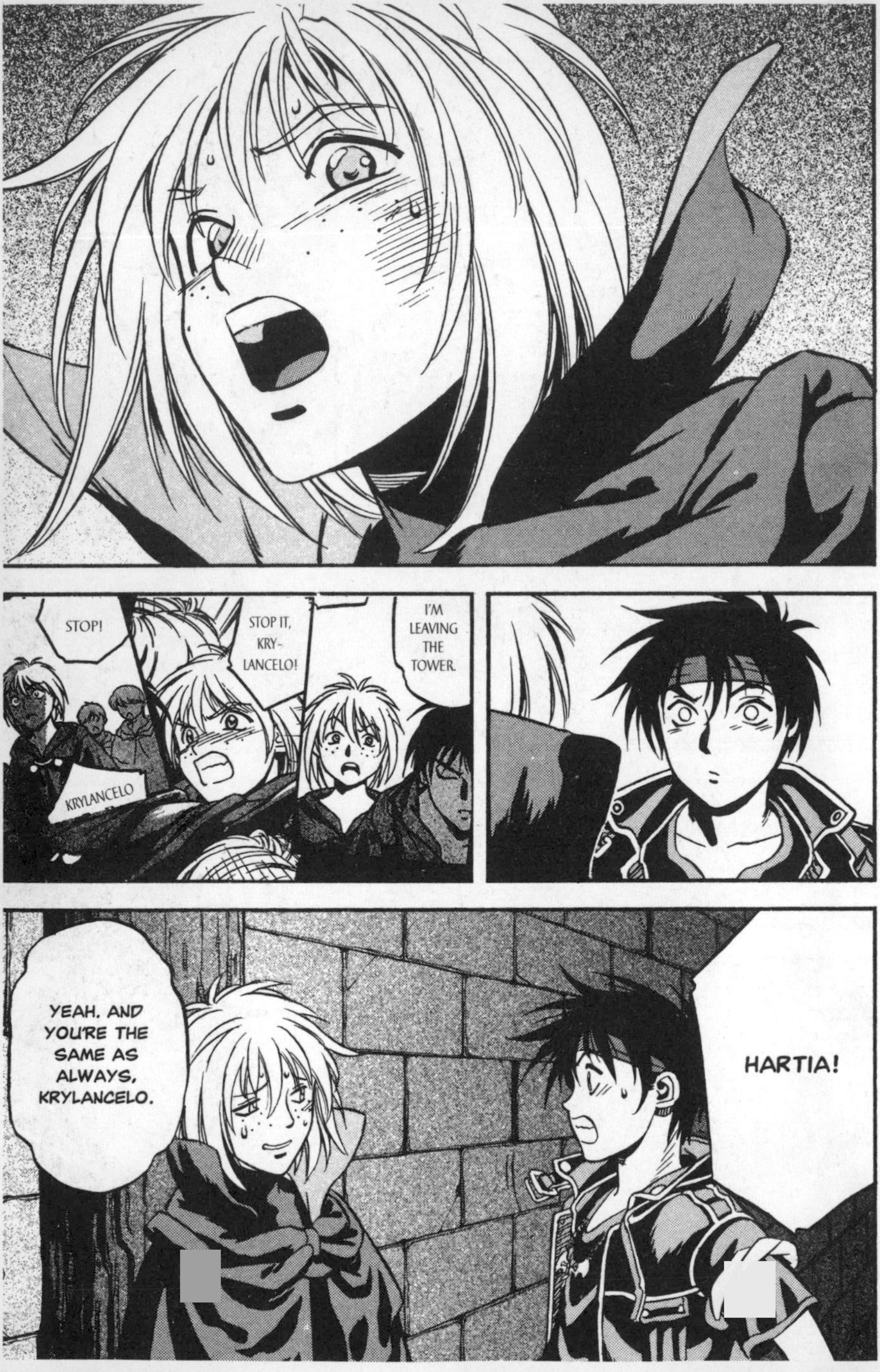
I'M LEAVING THE TOWER.
STOP IT, KRY-LANCELO!
STOP!
KRYLANCELO
HARTIA!
YEAH. AND YOU'RE THE SAME AS ALWAYS, KRYLANCELO.

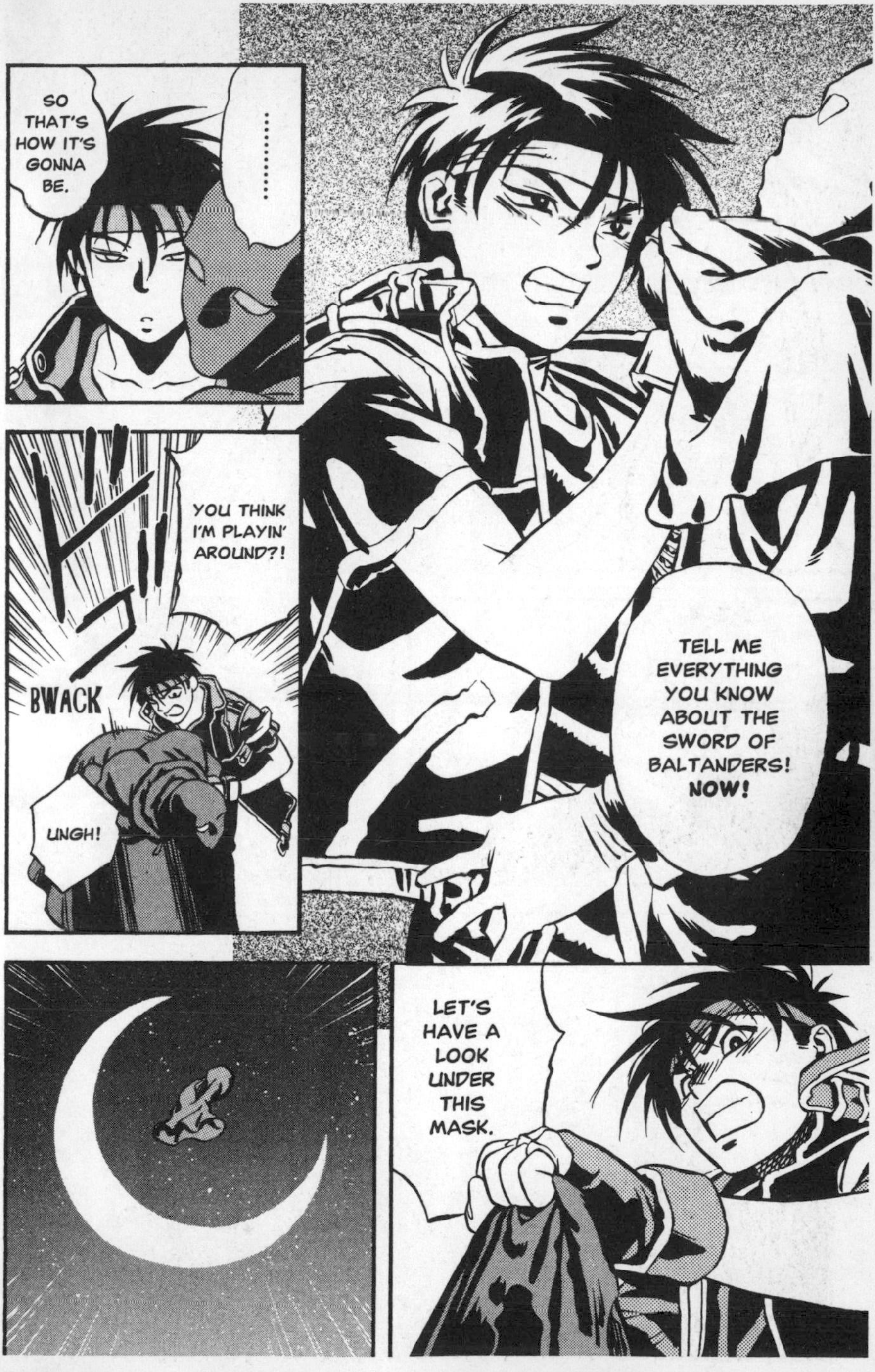

SO THAT'S HOW IT'S GONNA BE.
....
YOU THINK I'M PLAYIN' AROUND?!
BWACK
UNGH!
TELL ME EVERYTHING YOU KNOW ABOUT THE SWORD OF BALTANDERS! NOW!
LET'S HAVE A LOOK UNDER THIS MASK.

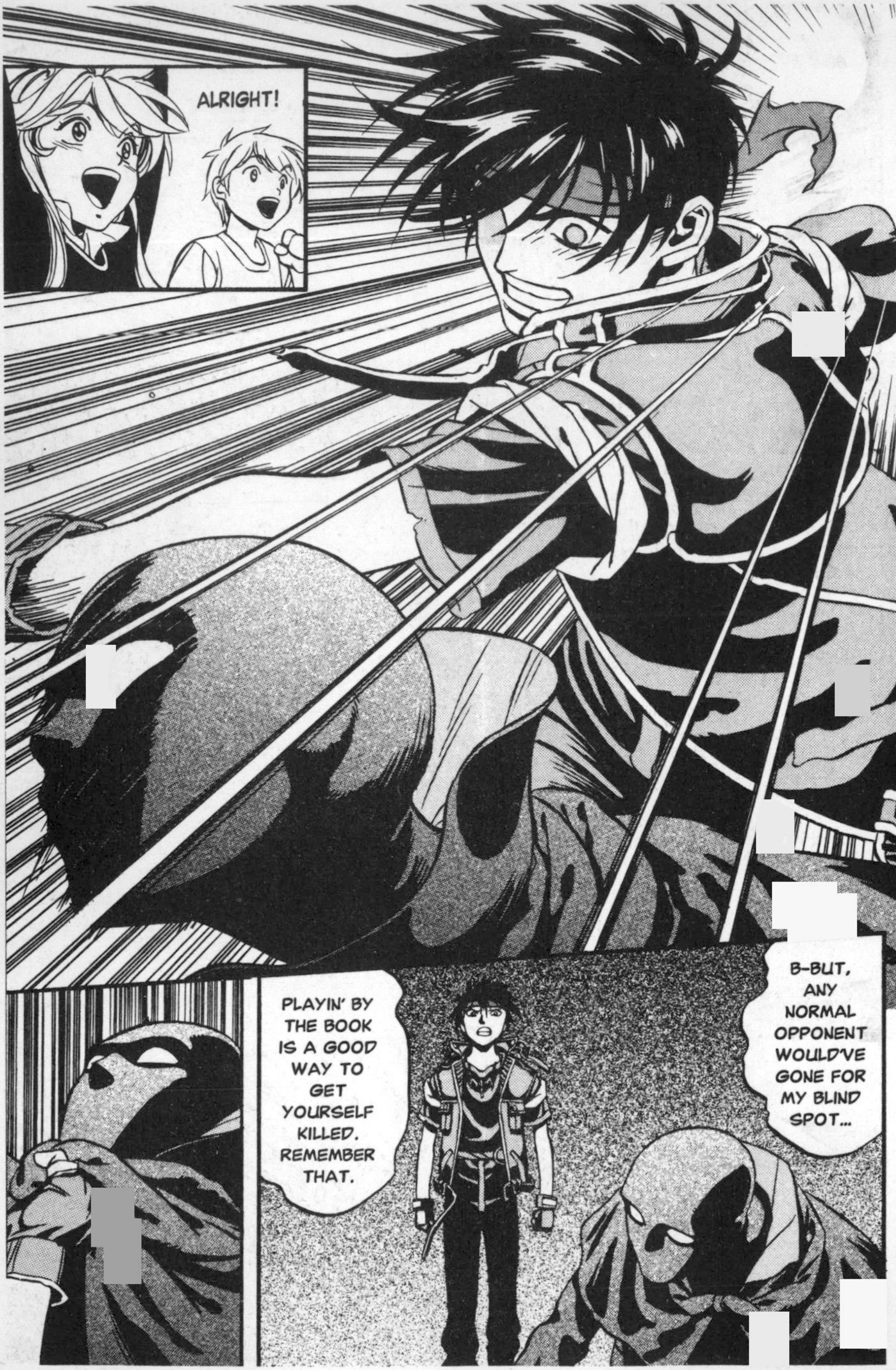
ALRIGHT!
B-BUT, ANY NORMAL OPPONENT WOULD'VE GONE FOR MY BLIND SPOT...
PLAYIN' BY THE BOOK IS A GOOD WAY TO GET YOURSELF KILLED. REMEMBER THAT.

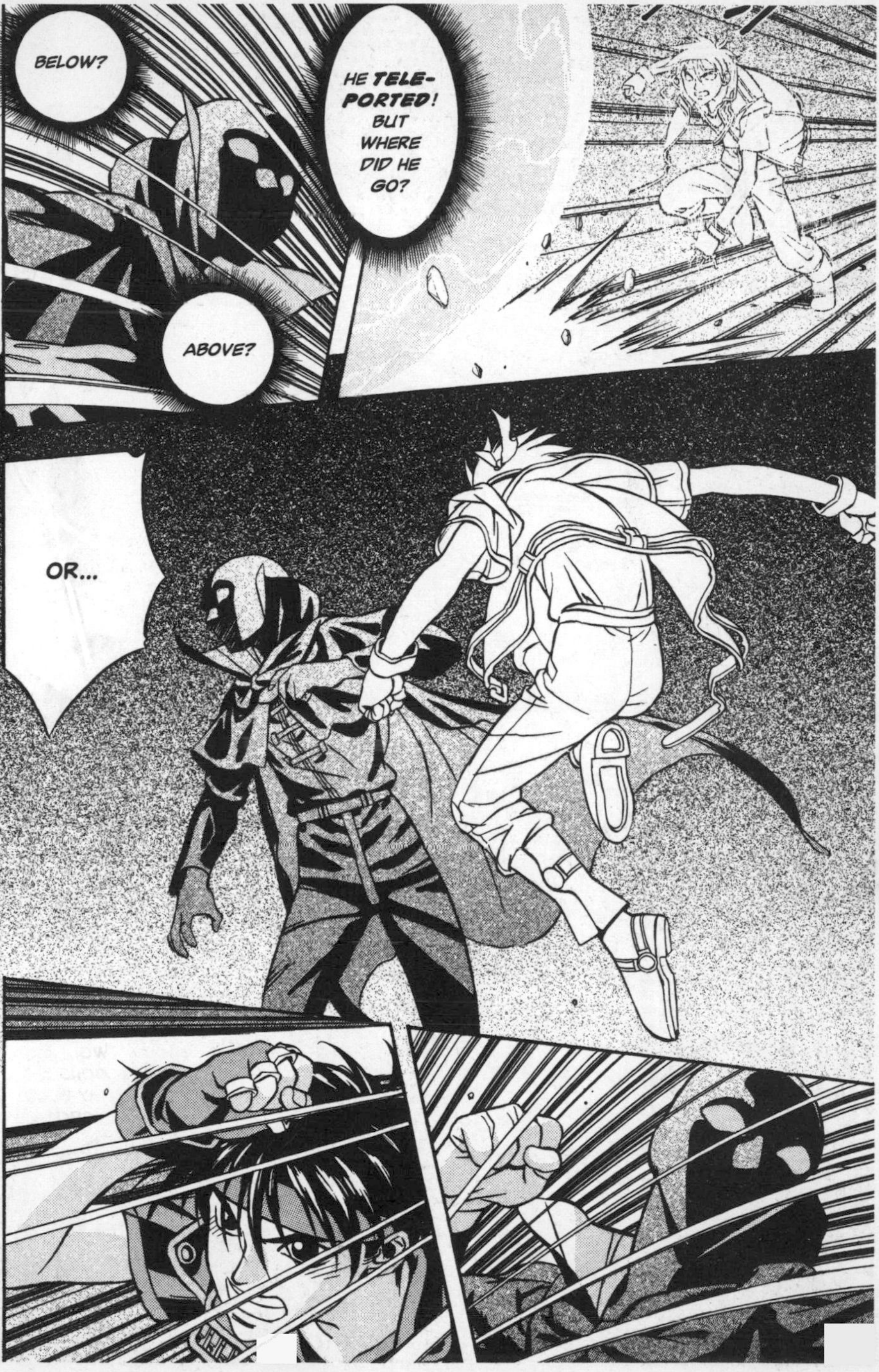
HE TELE-PORTED! BUT WHERE DID HE GO?
BELOW?
ABOVE?
OR...

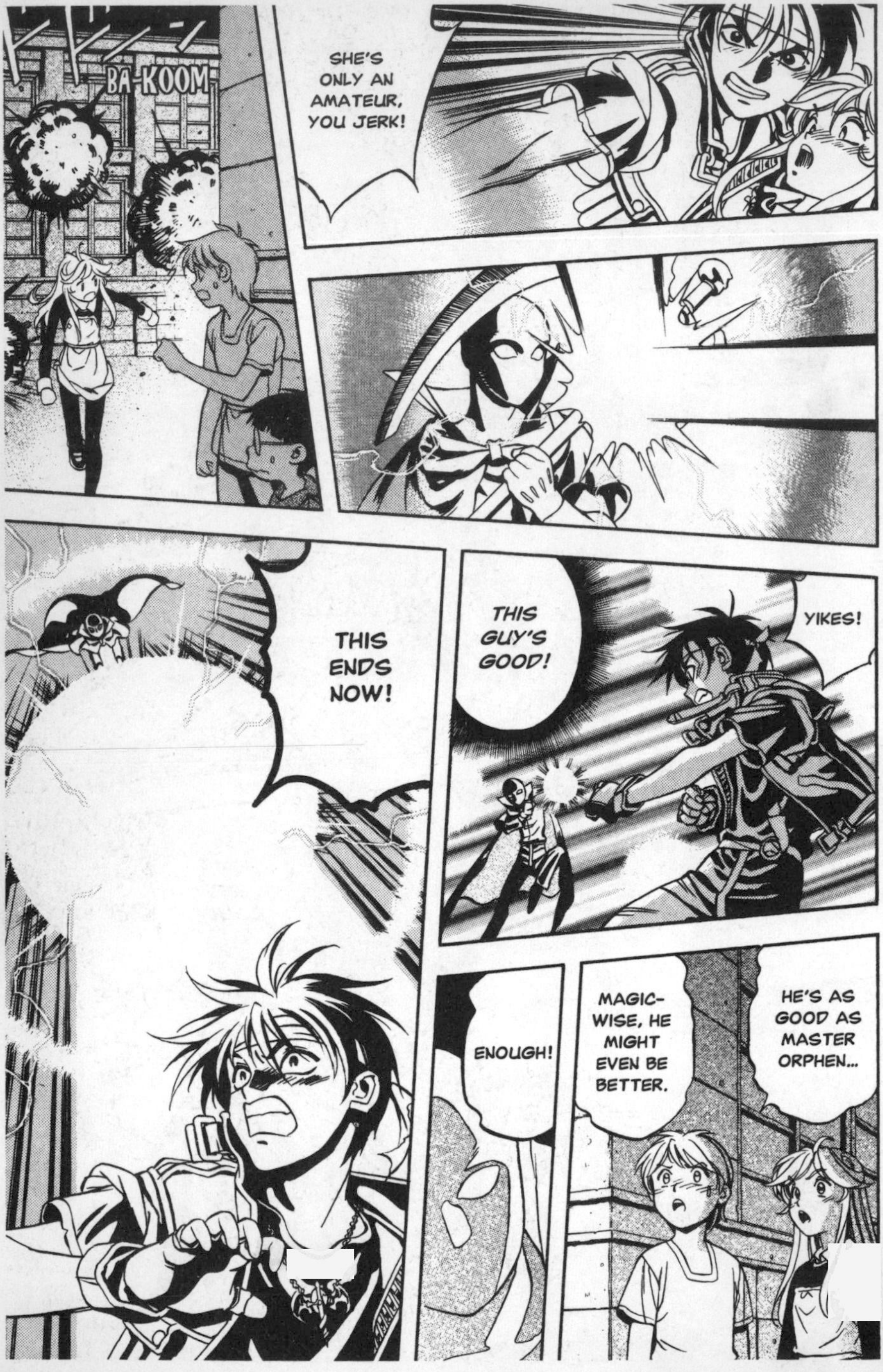

BA-KOOM
SHE'S ONLY AN AMATEUR, YOU JERK!
THIS ENDS NOW!
THIS GUY'S GOOD!
YIKES!
ENOUGH!
MAGIC-WISE, HE MIGHT EVEN BE BETTER.
HE'S AS GOOD AS MASTER ORPHEN...

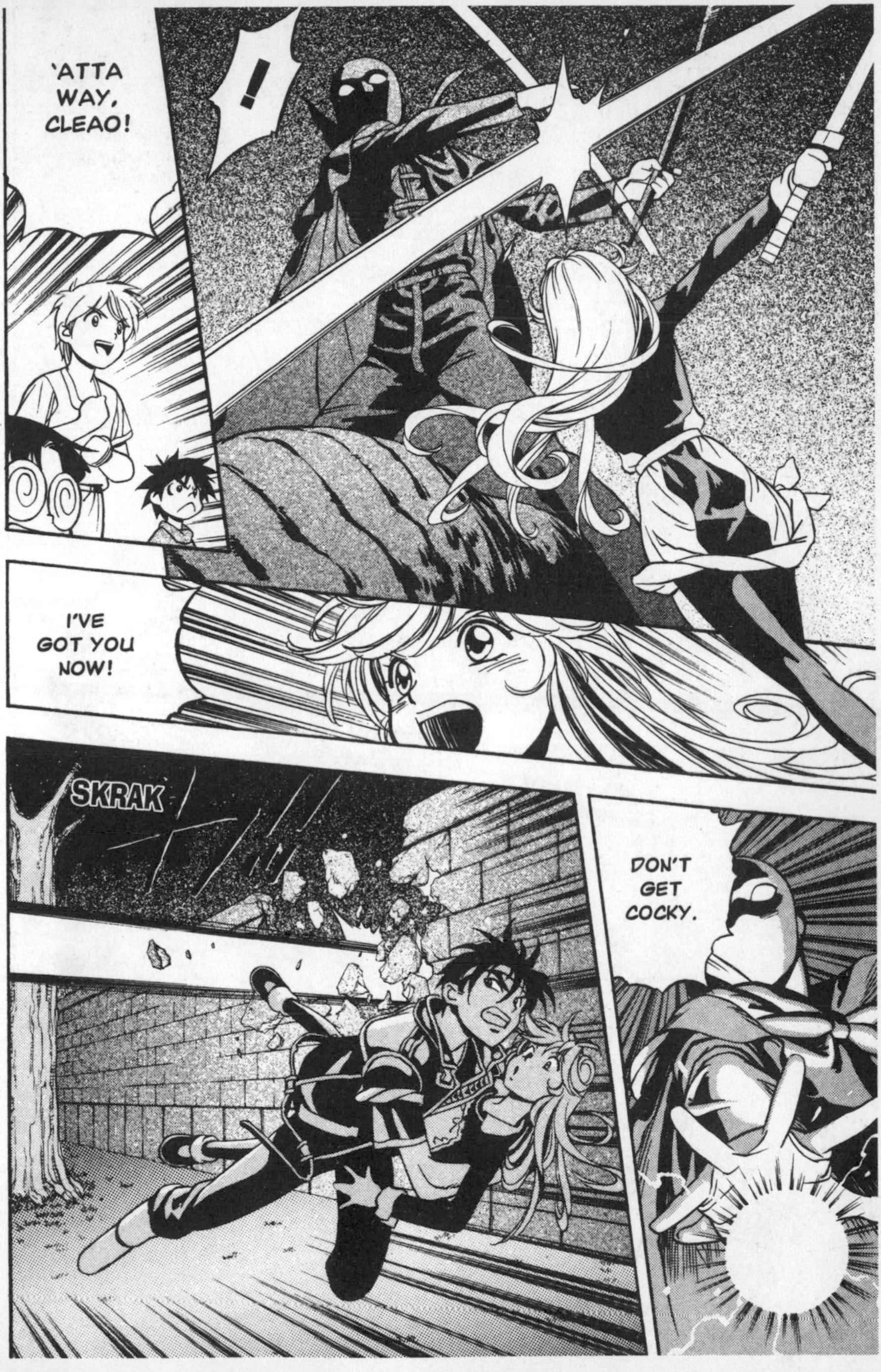
!
'ATTA WAY, CLEAO!
I'VE GOT YOU NOW!
SKRAK
DON'T GET COCKY.

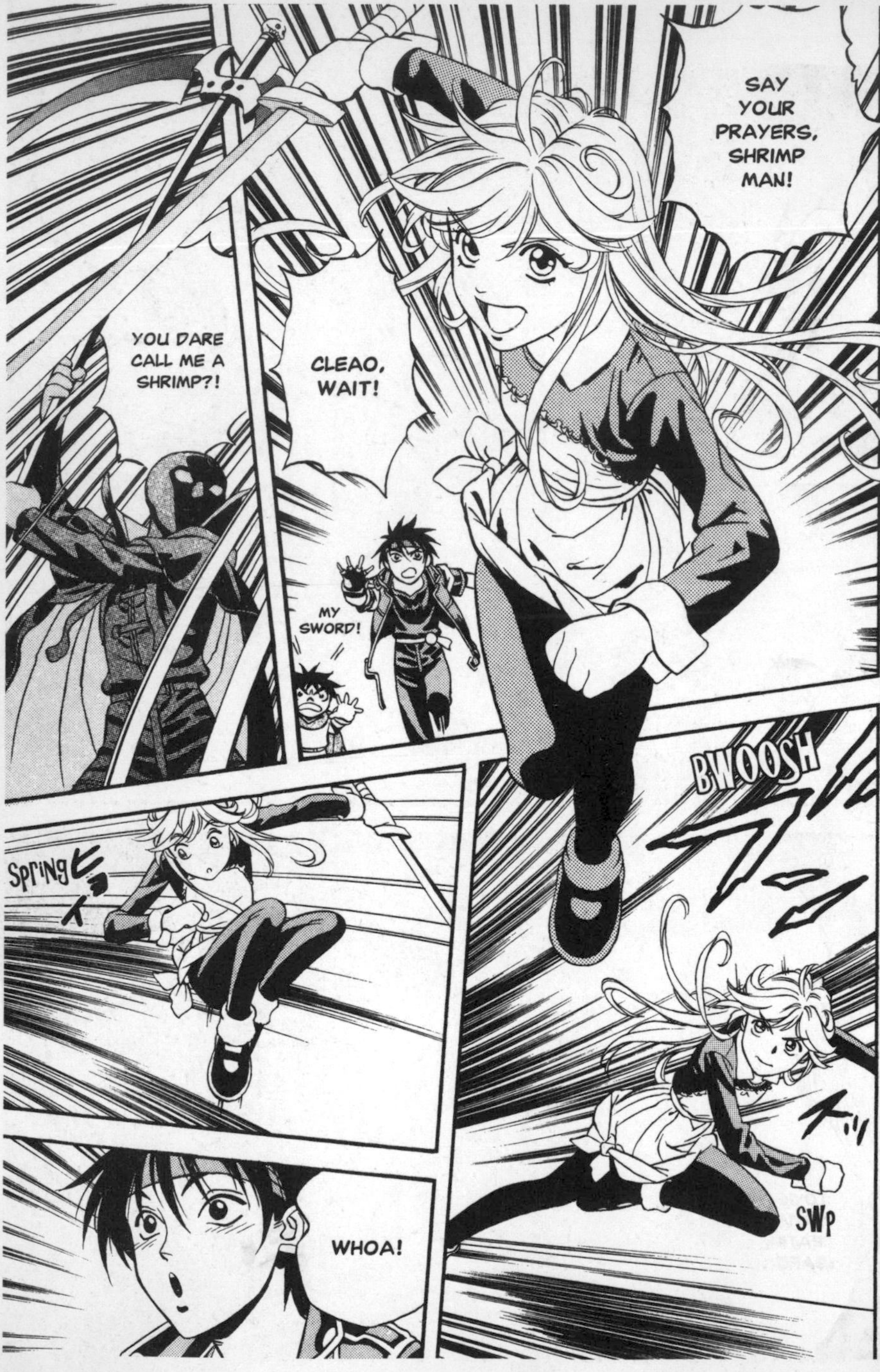
SAY YOUR PRAYERS, SHRIMP MAN!
CLEAO, WAIT!
YOU DARE CALL ME A SHRIMP?!
MY SWORD!
BWOOSH
Spring
SWP
WHOA!

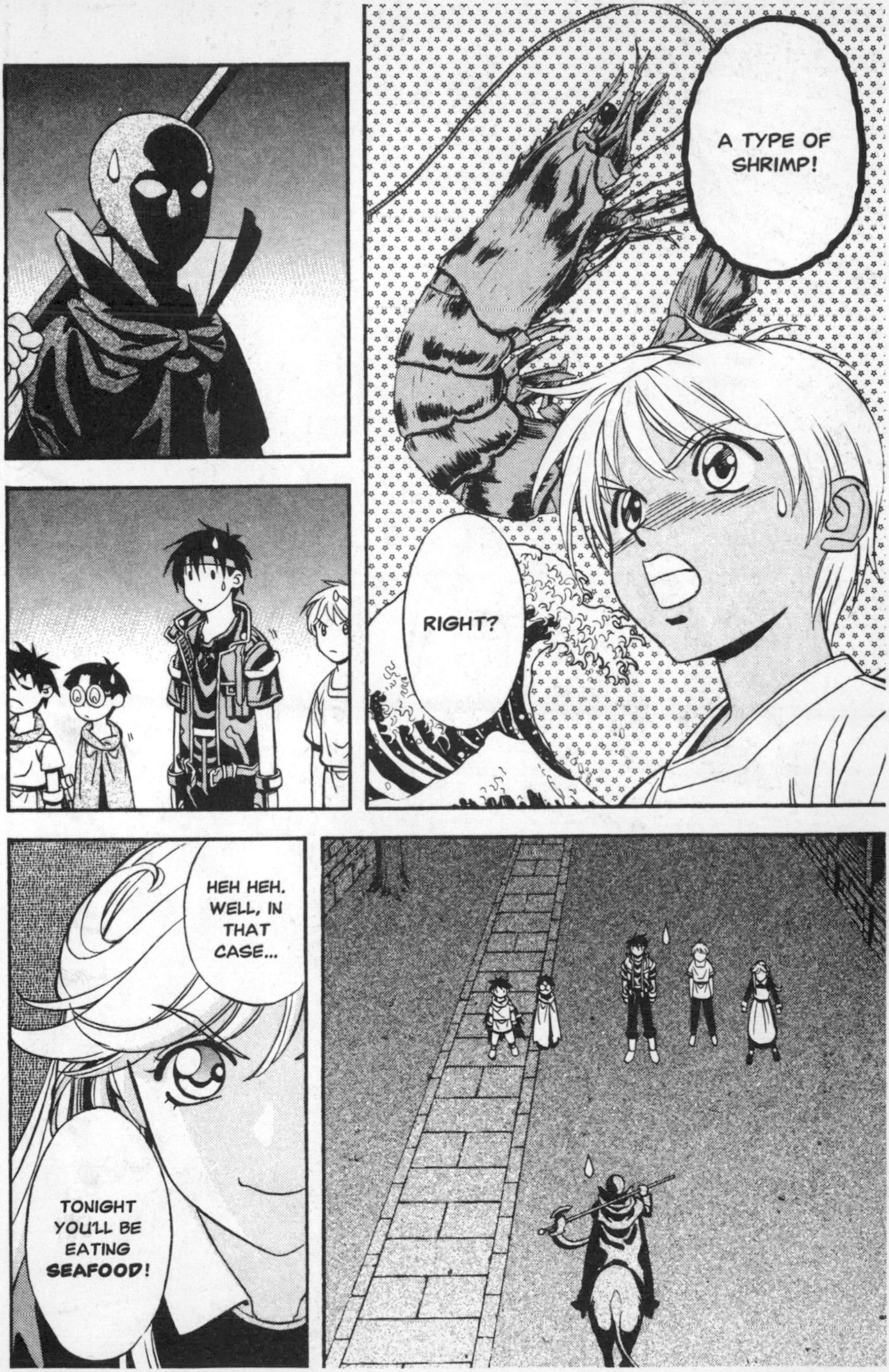
A TYPE OF SHRIMP!
RIGHT?
HEH HEH. WELL, IN THAT CASE...
TONIGHT YOU'LL BE EATING SEAFOOD!

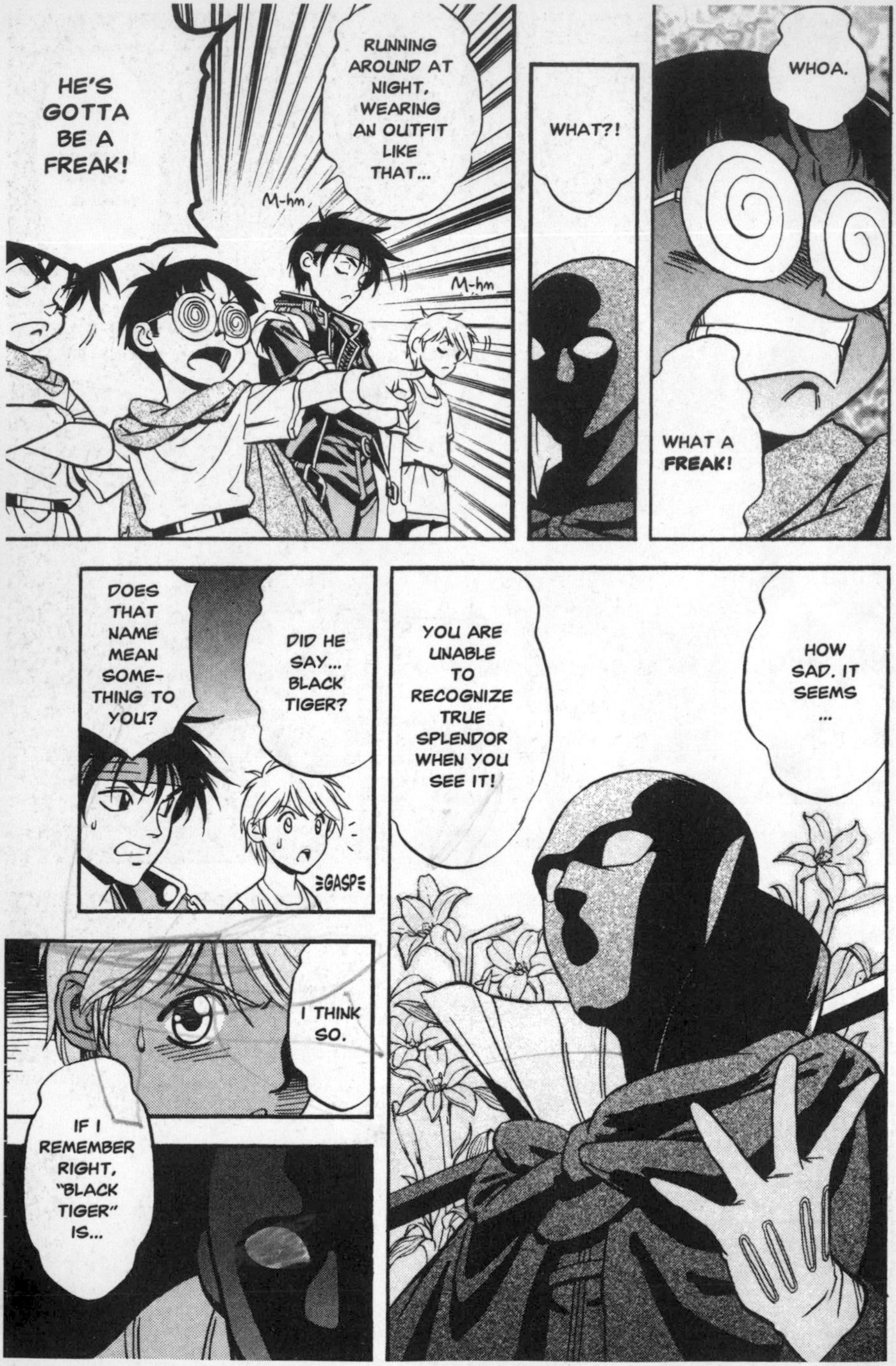
WHOA.
WHAT A FREAK!
WHAT?!
RUNNING AROUND AT NIGHT, WEARING AN OUTFIT LIKE THAT...
HE'S GOTTA BE A FREAK!
M-hm
M-hm
HOW SAD. IT SEEMS ...
YOU ARE UNABLE TO RECOGNIZE TRUE SPLENDOR WHEN YOU SEE IT!
DID HE SAY... BLACK TIGER?
DOES THAT NAME MEAN SOME-THING TO YOU?
GASP
I THINK SO.
IF I REMEMBER RIGHT, "BLACK TIGER" IS...

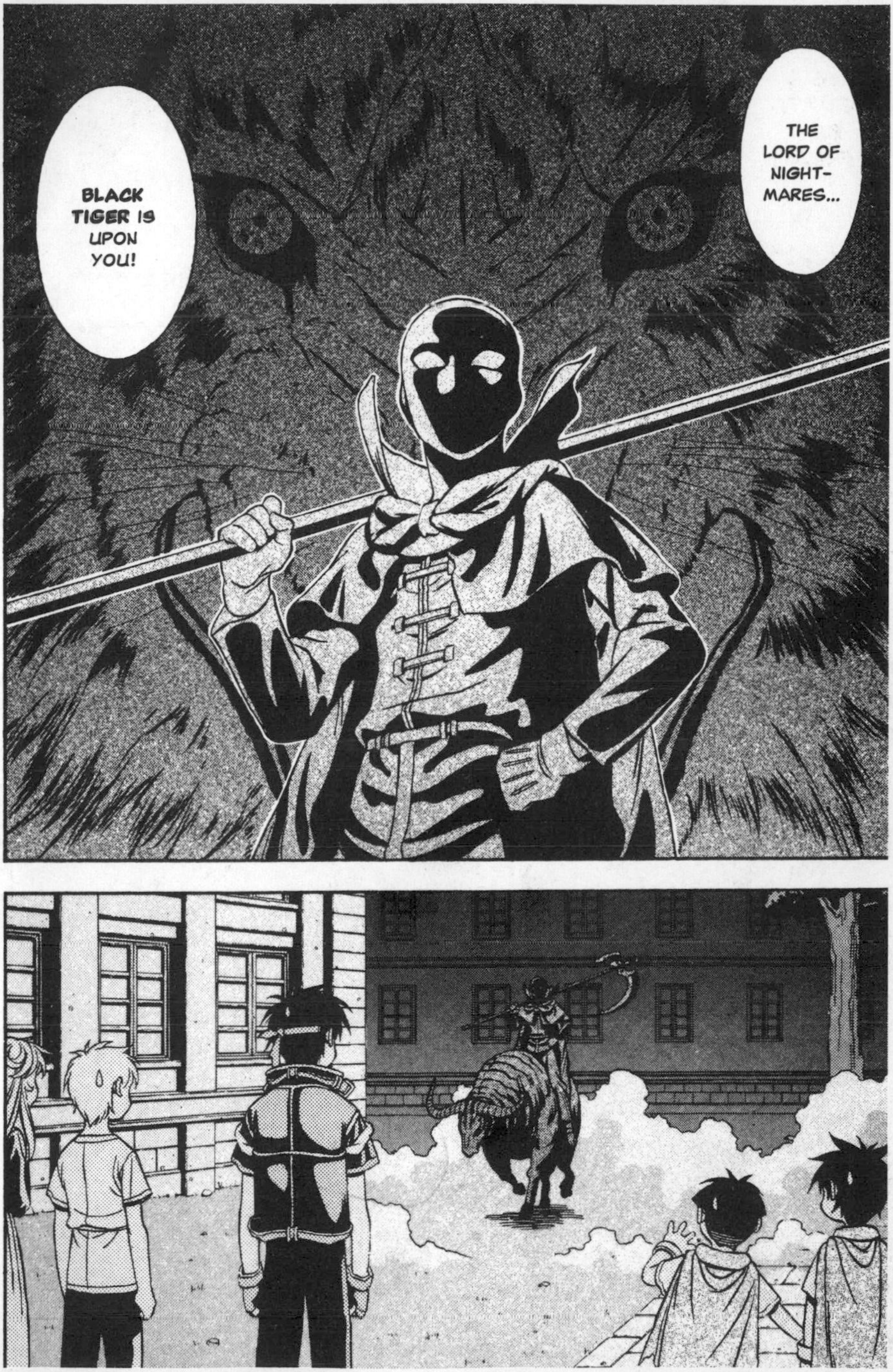
THE LORD OF NIGHT-MARES...
BLACK TIGER IS UPON YOU!

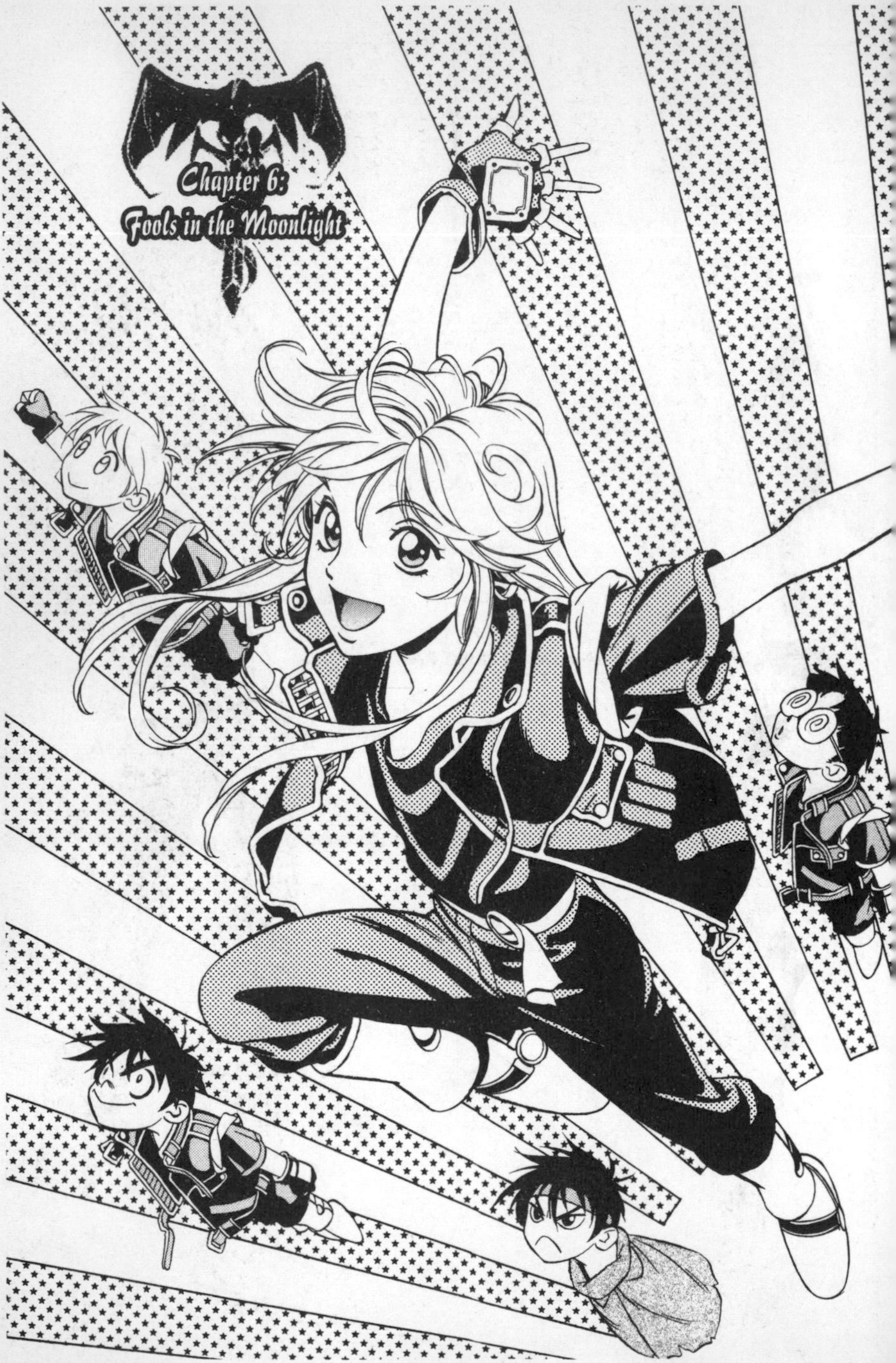
Chapter 6:
Fools in the Moonlight

ORPHEN

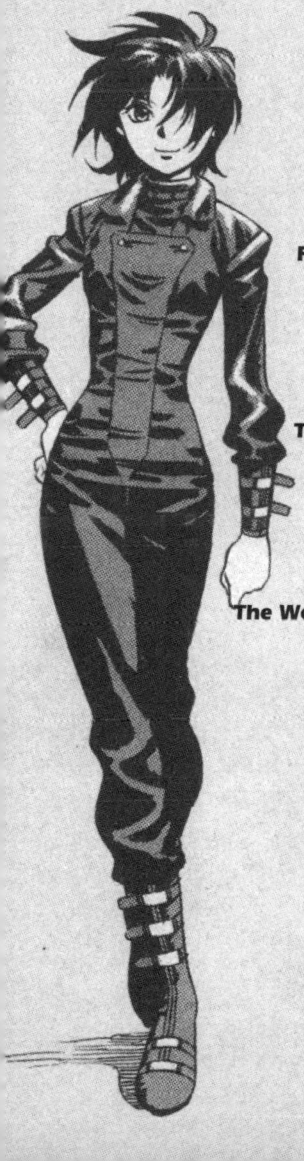

CONTENTS

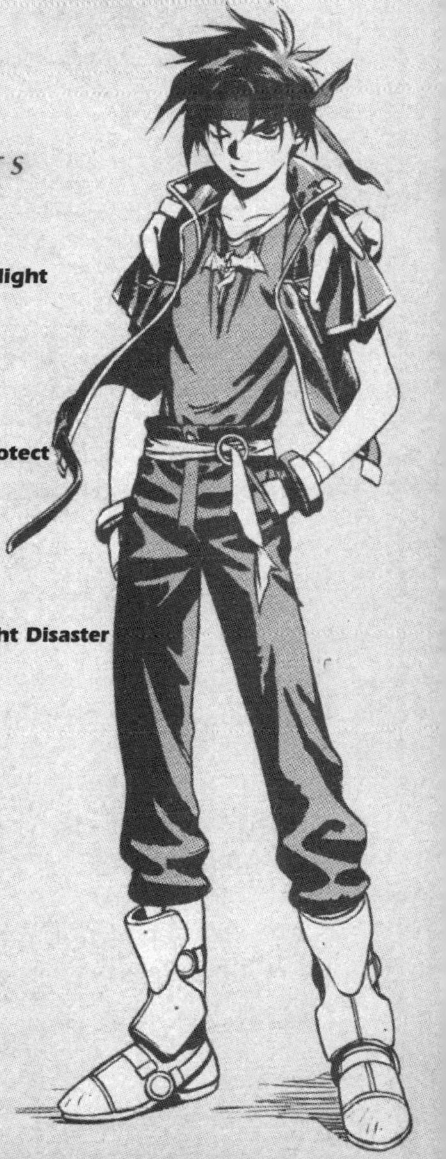

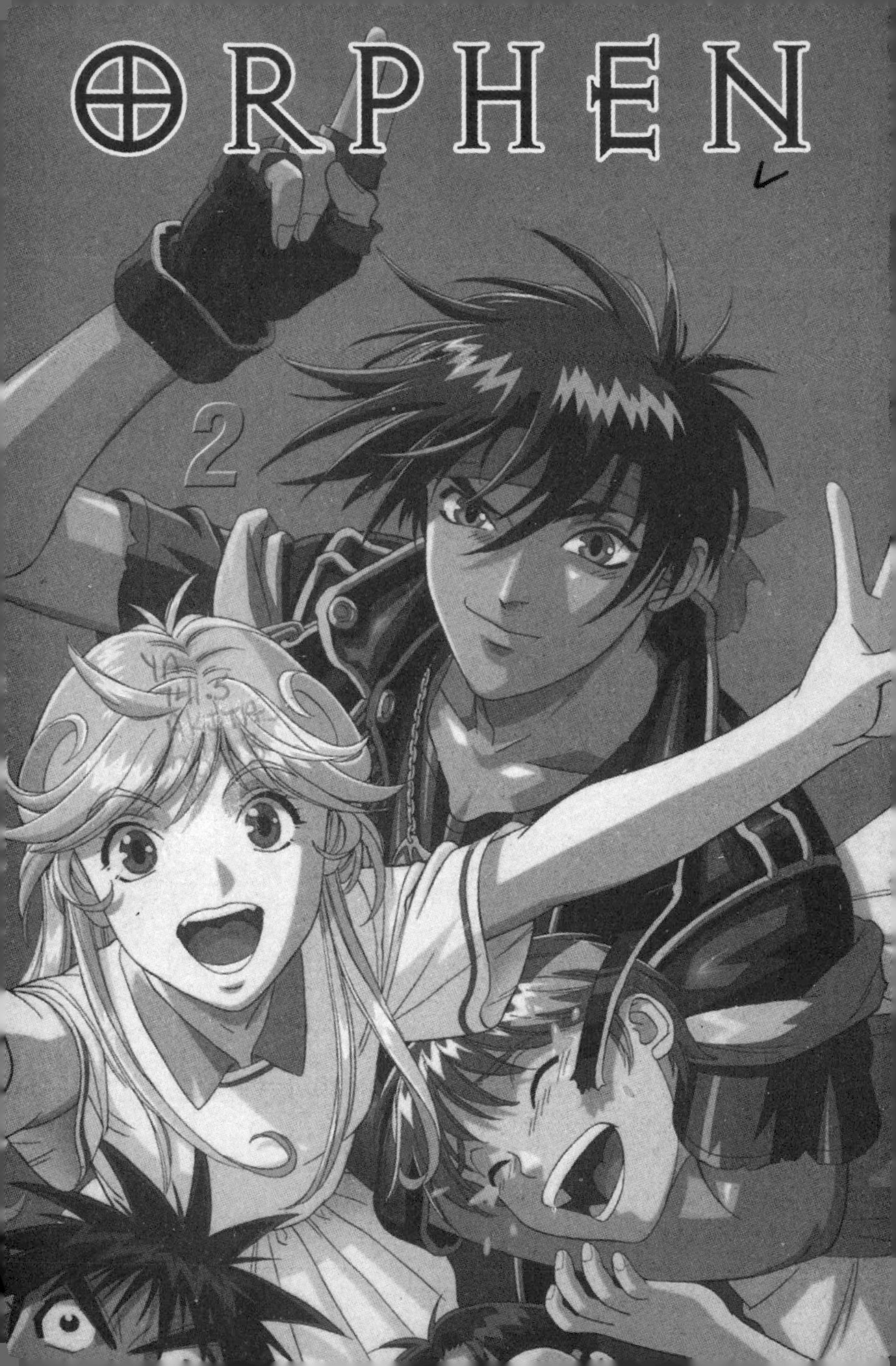
ORPHEN
2